by the
balls

by the balls

MEMOIR OF A FOOTBALL TRAGIC

LES MURRAY

RANDOM HOUSE AUSTRALIA

Random House Australia Pty Ltd
20 Alfred Street, Milsons Point, NSW 2061
http://www.randomhouse.com.au

Sydney   New York   Toronto
London   Auckland   Johannesburg

First published by Random House Australia 2006

National Library of Australia
Cataloguing-in-Publication Entry

   Murray, Les, 1945– .
   By the balls.

   ISBN 978 1 74051 355 5.
   ISBN 1 74051 355 X.

   1. Murray, Les, 1945– . 2. Sportscasters – Australia –
   Biography. 3. Immigrants – Australia – Biography.
   4. Soccer – Australia. I. Title.

   796.334092

Back cover photo by Patrick Jones
Cover design by Christabella Designs
Typeset in 12/15 pt Garamond 3 by Midland Typesetters, Australia
Printed and bound by Griffin Press, Netley, South Australia

10 9 8 7 6 5 4 3 2 1

To the ladies in my life: Tania, Natalie and Cida

Contents

Foreword

I met Les Murray for the first time in 1992. As FIFA's Secretary
General, I was in charge of the Youth World Cup in Sydney,
which took place a year later, and I was impressed by the organisation and dedication our Australian friends had put into preparing the tournament: they put on a truly magnificent event – and
Les was very much part of it. Already then one of Australia's
leading football experts and sports anchors, Les commented on the
game for SBS Television where he later became Head of Sport.
Rarely have I met a man with such a deep and vast knowledge of
our game and all of its facets. He never denied – nor should he
have – his Hungarian roots, and he always held high the values his
ancestors had taught him. And the very values football has on offer:
team spirit, individual excellence for the benefit of a like-minded
group of players, fairness, dedication, determination and – alas! –
hope. Like few other journalists, and no doubt because of his own
origins, Les always valued the aspect of hope inherent to our game.
Hope for a better life; hope to break out of an underprivileged
social background; quite generally: hope for a better life. Football
has always managed to give hope, to this very day. We need not go

to South America, Africa or Asia where the future of football is rapidly taking shape. We can look into our own backyards and find exceptional talent, even prodigies such as Rooney or Shevchenko, Zidane or Ballack. None of them was born with the proverbial silver spoon, but all of them had to fight and convince others of their talent. And football recognises talent, encourages it and helps it along.

Les, at first a media contact in far away Australia, rapidly became a voice we all had to listen to at FIFA. His expertise is unrivalled, his professionalism poignant and his integrity complete. All these are reasons why FIFA, and myself when I was re-elected President in 2002, invited him to serve on the FIFA Ethics and Fair Play Committee. Today, we know that this was a good choice and today, we know that Les Murray has many more facets to him than would meet the eye: he is a fair player, a sound expert and a good man. His instinct detects hidden flaws, recognises inaccuracies with lightning speed and his judgement is always fair, respectful and clear.

FIFA has won a critical and analytical mind which helps us run our affairs in decency and with transparency. And it in this spirit that I commend him for his autobiography, which is an exciting read and offers wisdom, knowledge and excitement alike. And above all: the love for our game.

Joseph S. Blatter
FIFA President
March 2006

Introduction

In the mid-1990s, the Australian cult band TISM released a song titled 'What Nationality is Les Murray?' It referred to my curious and indecipherable accent, something my own ears cannot detect because I genuinely believe that I speak just like any other Aussie.

But it did suggest that my moderate fame and semi-celebrity status in Australia poses some unanswered questions. Like, who exactly is this bloke? Where does he come from? Who is this silver haired git with his pronounced eyebrows, and strange melody to his vowels, intruding into our lounge rooms every day, prattling and pontificating about sport, most of it foreign, including that so-called 'world game'? Reason enough, probably, that the story be told and the skeletons in the closet be revealed.

Yet writing a book about my life was not something I contemplated with any kind of seriousness or enthusiasm. I was kind of pushed into it.

It was Andy Harper, a good friend and a collaborator on two previous football books, Johnny Warren's *Sheilas, Wogs and Poofters* and *Mr and Mrs Soccer*, who first raised the supposition that there might be a need for one. A good six years ago he started asking me impatiently, 'When is the book coming out?' Note the terminology: not 'your' book but 'the' book. I always waved him away. Autobiographies and memoirs, I would protest, are for people preparing for their graves.

Then came the publication of *Sheilas* and *Mr and Mrs Soccer*. Both made quite a splash among football readers and the die was cast. Random House made the approach and I guess I shouldn't have been surprised. There was a book about Johnny's life, then a book about the friendship between Johnny and me, so perhaps it was natural that a book about my life should round off the trilogy.

Of course, for a long time, I knew there would be a book one day, a story to be told of my life and its winding journey. But I didn't want to write a football book, and so this is not just another narrative about football adding to the many thousands that hug the shelves of bookstores and libraries around the world. What I wanted to tell was a story about how and why a young boy got smitten by the beautiful game, a bug from which he could never recover, and how that preoccupation went on to shape his life. So that is what you have in your hand – not a football book, but a story about a 'footballee', a victim of the game's seductive powers.

For the title I am indebted to another friend, Damien Lovelock, who came up with it. Trust him to do so. My original title was 'The Great Poison' but that, admittedly, was a bit gloomy and negative. Football, however poisonous and addictive, is after all a source of joy, pleasure and often laughter. Better to have a title that evokes all that.

I am indebted, of course, to many others, those who helped me write this book but more importantly those who made the personal sacrifices along the way that allowed me a life whose story became in the end worth telling. My late mother, Elizabeth, a towering source of encouragement, gave me the values that now allow me to sleep well at night. My brothers, Andrew and Joe, always went along as empathetic collaborators and have been my silent partners in a life given over to football and its narcotic juices. They always understood and still do.

Then there are the women, those who boldly gambled and shared their lives with me. I am indebted to Eva, the mother of my children, who brought them up to be great sources of joy and pride to me, all the while putting up with the silly football preoccupation that drove my career and my passions.

To Diana, my partner of seven years, whose sweet blue eyes drove me to despair and in whom I found a source of liberation and a mateship that gave me new hope, new purpose and a new life.

To Cida, who invigorated and fired me with her Brazilian spirit, who gave and gave – still does – and then stood aside, silently and willingly when the need arose, because I was busy, lost to her, writing and writing this book.

Most of all I thank my daughters, Tania and Natalie, sweet, decent, talented and beautiful, and sources of real reward for a life which, for all the football and the pleasures it brought, would have been empty without them.

All these people close to me suffered at some time and to some degree because of my football and other preoccupations and distractions. I stand accused and humbly plead guilty.

Then there are all those not so close but to whom I also owe a tremendous debt. These are the milling throng of nameless Australian football fans who, like me, believed and kept believing. Without their faith, empathy and unbridled love for the game my work, and that of other football tragics like me, would have counted for nought.

Finally I need to thank SBS, my professional lord and master for the past 25 years, but who did more than just make out the pay cheques and still does. All my senior management bosses could line up to admit that they were not congenital football fans and had no emotional link to the game, yet they were gallant enough to trust me with the emotional stuff, allowing me considerable editorial latitude to convey my often subjective views and priorities about football to the audience, believing that I was the expert and I should be left alone to do the work of building a football audience. More importantly, they maintained a steadfast support for football and its place on SBS. I do not believe there is another television station, in Australia or elsewhere, that can compare with the unswerving commitment to a single sport that SBS has given, and continues to give, to football.

As you will find out from the pages of this book I have made many friends but didn't avoid making enemies. This I regret, as unavoidable as that was, because most of the people I offended were football people, kindred spirits who were part of my faith and who, too, wanted their beloved game to be embraced by the larger Australian flock.

As a final point, I desisted from making this book simply another tool in my long quest to promote football. Goodness knows, I do enough of that day in and day out for a living. Though there is plenty here on my thoughts about football and why I revere it so, it is essentially a story, told as objectively and impassively as I could, about a man and his journey and about how football helped shape that journey and his values.

And I wanted to tell the story in my own words. There was the easier and less time-consuming option of having it written for me. But I felt it was best to narrate the journey in the first person, even if it was in my English as a second language.

Has it been a good life, rewarding and full or otherwise? You be the judge. But for me, in the words of Edith Piaf, *je ne regret rien.*

1

Blame it on Stalin

It was the spring of 1962, late in the evening. The swoons of Ben E. King wafted out of the small radio on my bedroom desk. I was swotting for my high school graduation exam, barely a month away. The song was the Latin classic Amor, or at least King's unique, early-Soul rendition of it. The soft soothing tones of the singer, the way he step-laddered his baritone up and down and around those notes, was a warm source of sideline relaxation, a narcotic to help me conquer the pressures of academia. A singer to study by. And relaxed I was; a happy and contented young man, with few cares in the world, as I approached my 17th birthday, bursting with confidence that the exams, and life, would be a breeze.

Then a knock came on the front door. My father, mother, my two brothers and I gathered to see who this late night visitor might be. It was an old family friend, Charlie, looking very serious. Closing the door behind him, Charlie took two steps forward and declined the invitation to sit. 'I have sad news', he began. 'Our young friend and team-mate, Imre, has died under tragic circumstances.'

I was new to the concept of death for, until then, no one close – family or friend – had ever died. I had never been to a funeral. But I knew what 'tragic circumstances' meant. It was suicide. Imre, a young footballer, a lover of life, a man I admired and wanted to emulate, had taken his own life.

It was a monumental shock to my soul, driving me into a spin of despair and doubt, of dark questioning and searching. What is the sense and meaning of it? Why are we here? What is the reason for existence, if life, and its journey, can be derailed so suddenly and so easily in this way? Why be born at all if the sheer pleasure of living can be so willingly surrendered? These were the questions I was asking as a bare-chested, post-pubescent teenager.

Yet out of the shock I emerged a survivor. And I managed it because of a fortunate blessing and a source of strength: my love for football, the drug that was to fuel and sustain the rest of my life.

Nowadays, Budakeszi is a thriving growth area on the far outskirts of Budapest, the capital of Hungary. When I last visited it, in 1997, I spotted regiments of tourists in buses driving through. An Italian in a red Ferrari, with a gorgeous blonde in the passenger seat, stopped to buy a bottle of Coke in a shop diagonally opposite the house where I spent the earliest years of my childhood. Around the town church, where as a kid I would go to mass on Sundays, and where I had my first communion at the age of eight, they were now digging to expose ancient Roman ruins.

But in my day, Budakeszi was a village, totally isolated from the rest of the world, which included the metropolis of Budapest barely 12 kilometres away. It was a place of small neat houses rendered in white with red tiled roofs, where carts driven by brown horses with large posteriors formed much of the road traffic and where the procuring of a litre of milk meant a stroll to the local cow owner who would oblige with a tin can full of the stuff, spurted straight from the udder. Most of the inhabitants were 'Svábs', ethnic Germans who had populated pockets of Hungary in the 19th century. Budakeszi, in the local parlance, was a 'Sváb' town.

I was born in late 1945, in the provincial Hungarian city of Pápa, 28 kilometres west of Budapest, where my parents had found refuge from the ravaging bombings of the capital by the Allies in 1944. When I was barely one, and the hostilities of World War II had died down, my father acquired a job at a factory near Budakeszi. It was here that my parents decided to settle.

Those were the days of social revolution and change in Hungary. The country, thanks to a Nazi-led coup, allied itself with Germany during the war, so was on the losing side. Hungary backed the wrong horse yet again. The same thing had happened three decades earlier when Hungary lost two-thirds of its territory after World War I: the price of defeat as decreed at the Treaty of Trianon. Now, following rigged elections in 1948, the victorious Soviets imposed their will. Hungary was to be a communist state, annexed as part of the Warsaw Pact. And that, among other things, meant that anyone of so-called 'bourgeois descent' – like my father – was to be bumped to the back of the queue. This was now a workers state and 'workers' came first.

My father, Joseph Ürge, was the son of a school teacher mother and a protestant priest father who vanished on the Russian front during World War I. My father was a graduate in horticulture and was once in charge of the opulent gardens of the Count of Almássy (the same aristocrat depicted in the movie, *The English Patient*). My mother, Elizabeth, was the daughter of the titled Ernö von Ihrig, once treasury advisor in the government of Admiral Miklós Horthy, ruler of Hungary for most of the years between the two world wars. Fancy stuff this, the point being that neither of the pedigrees exactly endeared my parents to the new regime and its agenda of promoting the cause of the proletariat. My father, at best, could join the ranks of the blue collar workers; hence, the factory job in Budakeszi.

I remember my early childhood, like most do, as enjoyable and fun. We lived in a two-bedroom apartment on a housing estate on the outskirts of town, my brothers Andrew and Joe, and I sleeping

in one room. We had a garden plot, where we grew essential vege-
tables and even fattened a pig whose demise guaranteed the family's
meat supply for an entire winter.

During down time from school we played in the garden with the
only play equipment we could afford – a bald tennis ball – which
became a community resource. Kids from the other apartments
would join in, teams would be picked, and we would play until
dark. We played *kiskapu*, or small goals, whereby a goal at each end
of the designated field would be made of two small objects, a metre
or so apart, and we had a game. It was only later I found out that
the great Hungarian exponents of football of the time, like Ferenc
Puskás, József Bozsik and Sándor Kocsis, grew up doing the same
thing. They played *grund foci* or street football.

This was Hungary in the early 1950s. There was no such thing
as organised football for kids; no under six or even under 12 competitions. We grabbed a ball when we could, found a plot to play
on – and play we did, until we dropped. There was no coaching, no
fancy instruction, no referee. It was all laissez-faire stuff. We played
only for the joy of scoring, winning and taking the mickey, and
went home to our homework happy or sad, depending on how we
had performed.

Hungary was poor; so poor that no one in the neighbourhood
owned a proper, leather football. I remember a rare event, when a
foreign kid – a German – joined our school. I think his name was
Hermann. On his first day, he brought along a size five leather
football. We were all in awe. It was the first time I had laid eyes on
such a thing. When he introduced the ball to the small throng of
eager, would-be footballers at a lunchtime game, it was pande-
monium. Every kid, including me, was obsessed by the need to get
a touch of the thing, to poke at it, kick it. The game was a moving
maul of infantile humanity, an incongruous mess, as participants
scurried to get a taste of the luxury. It was quite the ugliest game
of football I have ever seen or been a part of.

This was a time when my education in football was at its pre-
birth, for I had yet to see a proper game. My father spoke fleetingly

about the game and about his brief career in it. He was a left winger in his day, he claimed, and I can attest to the left bit, having seen him occasionally kick the ball with us down on the green. He claimed to have played for a modest Budapest club named Lampart and to have been with them during the one season the club spent in the Hungarian First Division (NB-I). No player records can be found to verify this haughty claim and thus establish my illustrious football heritage. But records show that a club called Lampart did indeed complete season 1941–42 in NB-I, winning just eight of its 30 matches, for a goal difference of 48:93, and finishing in third-last place, which sent them straight back to NB-II, thereupon they disappeared without trace.

My father was quite a handsome man, already prematurely grey when I first laid eyes on him, with a pair of bushy eyebrows that lined up well with the air of paternal authority he liked to convey towards his sons. We addressed him in the formal third person ('Could father help with my homework please?') and in his company we behaved, or else it was the stick. And we did get the stick on occasions, such as the time I was late home from school, arriving after dark, having been diverted by a game of infectious *grund foci* on the way. I was mercilessly belted by the old man. Though I was just a kid, football already had much to answer for in my life.

But I was yet to attain any kind of enlightenment about the wondrous beauties of this game and the reasons it had conquered billions around the world. In fact, at that time, I didn't have the faintest idea that it had conquered anyone except my two brothers, some neighbouring kids and me. I finally began to understand when my father took us – Andrew, Joe and me – to a game. It was no glamour fixture. We walked to the local town common, stood on the sidelines of a makeshift playing field and watched a game in the local, inter-village championship. Tall, sturdy, athletic young men lined up before kick-off at the edge of the field, the members of each team smartly clad in uniforms of distinctive colours. They jogged gently in a beeline to the centre, lined up laterally on either side of three older men dressed in black, each raised one arm and, facing the small crowd, shouted in unison: '*Éljen! Éljen! Éljen!*' – literally translated: 'Long Live! Long Live! Long Live!' They then turned to face the sparse gathering on the opposite side and repeated the ritual.

I was already impressed by the elegant, collective formality of it. But there was more to come. Immediately the lads began to play, I was driven by an instinct, uncultivated by anyone including my father, to support 'my team'. Budakeszi, as I recall, wore blue and white; within minutes, I adopted these colours as if they were those of the blood that ran through my veins. For no reason I could possibly fathom at that age, I wanted them to win. They were 'us' and I was 'them': I was part of the team. The tribal instinct, that which makes sport at once so beautiful and so ugly, had begun to take hold.

I was captive to the partisan impulse – but there was more to it as well. When the boys began to play my young eyes widened. I was gripped, mesmerised, by their ability to manipulate a bouncing sphere with their feet. Feet, I thought, were for standing and walking. Hands were made for grasping, grabbing, catching and throwing. But here, in this surreal defiance of nature, these boys were doing all that with their feet. Here, hands were redundant.

The sphere would roll from man to man, in an arrow-straight line, hugging the ground. Occasionally it would lift and fly in a sweet convex arc, propelled by a foot, and fall obediently at another foot, where it would stop dead and become prisoner to human command. The sphere, the ball – despite its unpredictability and lack of flat sides – would remain under control and do as it was told, would not bounce away, simply because it was being commanded by men who had feet for hands.

The impression was indelible. It was the essence of my induction to football and, later, of my realisation as to why the beautiful game was beautiful, and what set it apart from all other diversions.

Still, this was a village game and after it, we went home. I was, at the time, sheltered from the game's higher altitudes, the elite teams and the elite games, even though they were being played out scarcely further than my backyard.

At that time, Hungary, my Hungary, had the world's best football team – even though I didn't know it. It was a Wednesday, 25 November 1953. The weather was as bleak as the grey mist of lifelessness that pervaded the nation's spirit. Yet out of the mist burst an optimism, a new life – like the petals of violets in the late winter snow – all because of a game of football.

When I came home from school that afternoon my parents were already rejoicing. Their smiles were wider than I had ever seen. 'We won!' they exclaimed. 'Hammered them, 6-3.' 'Hammered whom?' I asked. As they laughed and talked, I came to realise that our Hungarian footballers had defeated the England team – which had not been beaten by a foreign team on home soil since football was invented – in London.

Such joy and laughter were rare events in Hungary in 1953. Conquest in the name of nationhood – when that nation is oppressed and stripped of its pride – can be a welcome thing. For me, a kid of eight years, it was also a discovery of identity. I knew who I was and where I belonged but, until this game, there was no source of joy in it. Now, my child mind pounced on a rare opening and suddenly I was gripped by a sweet sense of belonging. My chin lifted, I joined in the laughter and strutted on, content that my mob had done something unique. We mattered in the world.

The team that did the conquering is still referred to in Hungary as the *Aranycsapat*, the Golden Team. Even in historic context, the title is deserved.

Hungary was then a country of nine million people, tightly squeezed into central Europe's Danube Valley. To its north and east are the Carpathian mountains. Traversing its centre, north to south, is the Danube, Europe's greatest river, which flows from the Black Forest in Germany to the Black Sea via six countries, over 2850 kilometres. The river divides the capital, Budapest (formed in 1873 by the union of Buda and Pest) and the country. To its west are the green rolling hills of Transdanubia, the lower vestiges of the Austrian Alps. To its east are the sweeping flats of the Great Plain, which nudge the Romanian border.

This Hungary was, and still is, a fraction of the area it once commanded. Conquered by the nomadic Magyars (today's Hungarians) of central Asia in the 9th century, a tribe which saw many later conquests which took its authority as far west as Spain; during the heady days of the Austro-Hungarian Empire, it extended into vast expanses of Czechoslovakia, Romania and the Balkans. Today, more than one third of the world's Hungarian population of 15 million lives outside the country's borders.

The loss of territory came about as a result of Hungary's alliances in the two world wars. The Treaty of Trianon, following World War I, stripped the nation of much of its land. And because the Hitler quislings took Hungary to war against the Allies in World War II, and lost, the country remained small, truncated and demoralised.

In 1948, Joseph Stalin took control and Hungary came into the orbit of the Soviet empire. This meant complete authoritarianism and control. Soviet-style propaganda was the order of the day and sport was at its core. To help spread the word of Marxist utopia, as other communist governments did, Hungary's governors threw untold resources at sport and the plan worked a treat. By 1952, in the Helsinki Olympic Games, tiny Hungary finished third behind the United States and the Soviet Union in the gold medal tally. This shower of gold included football, for by then the Golden Team was formed.

During that period, Hungary was breeding a disproportionately high number of quality footballers in a country which already had a renowned tradition in football. In the 1920s and 1930s, Hungary was exporting player excellence to the richer leagues of Italy and France. It was runner-up to Vittorio Pozzo's Italy in the 1938 World Cup. It was a leader in the admired central European school of football, with a curriculum based on intricate short passing, sweet technique, crippling cunning, high mobility and awesome shooting power.

Nevertheless, the evolution of the Golden Team was largely state engineered. The dictatorship brought closed borders. No player could be exported. The new generation of virtuosos was kept at home in the domestic league, watched by throngs that burst the small stadiums at the seams. But it was the national team, according to the government, that had to be the focus of the mission, for only the national team could act as a messenger of the faith abroad: the grand vehicle of communist propaganda.

Someone in the upper echelons of power had a brilliant idea: to concentrate the best players into no more than two clubs. That way, familiarity and tactical cohesion among the best could be built, through the medium of games week in and week out. Elite players who became mates could develop a sixth sense for technical unity in a rarefied sporting laboratory. There has been nothing like it in football before or since.

Select players were forcibly transferred to join others already at two clubs: Honvéd and MTK. Of the 11 players who took England apart at Wembley in November of 1953, 10 hailed from Honvéd and MTK. The right back, Jenö Buzánszki, of provincial Dorog, was the only exception.

Though I didn't know it then, the Golden Team, by late 1953, was not only a focus for global sporting admiration but a team that would change football forever. It had invented a tactical approach which, though it stuck with the principle that attack is the best form of defence, checkmated all comers with previously unseen methods and took football to a new stratosphere. In essence, it relied on unity of thought among the players – telepathic understanding, liberal changing of pre-prescribed positions, mobility, and movement off the ball – pleated with glorious technique in passing and shooting, that wrong-footed static opponents.

When Hungary took on England on that November day at Wembley in 1953, it led 1-0 inside 60 seconds. Nándor

Hidegkúti, a tall, lithe player with a Franciscan bald spot, wore the number nine on his back, a message to his English marker that he would be the apex of the Magyar attack, the man to watch. But Hidegkúti retreated, leaving his marker puzzled as to whether to go with him, or stay and police his area in front of the goalkeeper. He chose to stay, leaving Hidegkúti the space in which to unleash a missile that sailed past the England goalkeeper and trigger one of the momentous triumphs of sporting history.

To this day, any Hungarian worth his salt who was around at the time, will rattle off the Hungarian line-up without taking a breath: Grosics; Buzánszki, Lóránt, Lantos; Bozsik, Zakariás; Budai, Kocsis, Hidegkúti, Puskás, Czibor. The figures 6-3 remain an historic landmark in the Hungarian mindset. Films have been made and books have been written with the simple title: '6-3'. These numbers represent the measure by which Hungary's sporting prowess will ultimately be defined, at least by Hungarians.

Yet that was just one episode in a golden period for the Golden Team. The *Aranycsapat* went four years and 31 games unbeaten. Moreover, it lost just one game between 1950 and 1955: in 51 games it scored 220 goals, an astonishing average of more than four goals a game. Nothing in the world game has surpassed that before or since.

That one loss, however – the team's solitary defeat in half a decade – was enough not only to unseat Hungary as the world's supreme football power but to help spark a political revolution that would change the world.

It came on 4 July 1954. I was in pain from a badly infected right foot, legacy of a thorn I had stepped on. My mother pleaded with my father to take me to the doctor but the old man would have none of it: I wouldn't die of septicaemia before the game was over; the foot and the doctor could wait.

It was the World Cup final against West Germany in Berne, the Swiss capital. Along with all of Hungary and most of the world, we listened to the commentary on radio. The nation was transfixed. Glancing out the window, I saw emptiness, and time frozen. There were no cars, no children at play, no pedestrians. A dog barking in the distance was the only sign of dissention from the social paralysis.

Hungary had begun its World Cup campaign that year with a 9-0 mauling of South Korea. Kocsis and Puskás both scored hat tricks but it was no big deal. The Koreans were Third World prey. Then came West Germany whom the Magyars hammered 8-3, an easy win in anyone's language. But there was a slight worry. Puskás, the Magyar captain and leader, hobbled off injured in the 60th minute, and didn't return to the team – under controversial circumstances – until the final: three games and 14 days later.

Even without Puskás, then hailed as the world's best player, Hungary romped on. It beat Brazil 4-2 in the quarter finals. In the semi finals the victim was the reigning world champion, Uruguay, again 4-2, though on this occasion after extra time. The quality and purity of football on view that day, 30 June 1954, in Lausanne, was to be nominated later by football historians as the finest game ever played.

But the tiring chore of having had to play the might of Brazil and Uruguay on the way to the final was to prove taxing for the Hungarians. Adding to their problems was the matter of Puskás' fitness. Was he ready? Could the team risk playing him if he wasn't? Conversely, could the team risk playing without him in such an important game? In the end, he was selected to play, a bold decision by coach Gusztáv Sebes for which he would later wear the blame for Hungary's defeat.

Come the final, György Szepesi, the eloquent radio commentator (later to be a vice-president of FIFA) wove his glorious prose as the Hungarians began their customary early raids.

Inside eight minutes the Magyars led 2-0; Puskás scored the first, and the scene appeared set for a repeat of the earlier 8-3 slaughter the Hungarians had bestowed on the Germans.

But it was not to be. The gritty and resolute Germans fought back. By half time it was 2-2. In the 84th minute, as the rain poured, the mud deepened, and the Hungarians struggled to retain the balance and footing that was a requirement for their kind of game, Helmut Rahn found space on the right flank and hammered in the third German goal – the winner – at once condemning Hungary to resignation and despair. Late in the game, Puskás' sweet left foot steered the ball into the net again but the linesman flagged for offside and it was disallowed. Film evidence would later prove that the goal had been legitimate – but that was just part of the injustice of it all. Having the hailed best team in the world and then having it beaten by a modest foe in a World Cup final was bad enough without seeing it lose by bad refereeing.

My father, in the darkest of moods, hauled me on his shoulder and carried me grudgingly to the doctor. On the way he grumbled repeatedly, 'Bloody Puskás, he sure fucked this up,' alleging that the captain played while carrying an injury, only so he could be the one to lift the trophy after a win that seemed inevitable.

An innocent and well-behaved eight-year-old, I stayed silent, only tightening the grip around my father's shoulders so that I wouldn't fall. In the circumstances, that was my only possible way of conveying to him the hug I felt he needed. I think he knew. And I think he also knew that, by now, I too had been smitten by the football bug and had been struck by grief. The good doctor cured my foot and his skilled procedure left no scars. But the emotional impact of that day left its mark on me, as it did on every Hungarian, for life.

The tragedy of that defeat needs to be put into broader context. Here was a small but proud country, oppressed by imperial might, its people poor, hungry, and stripped of their dignity, with a unique chance to regain its self respect via the opiate of sport and a global conquest. Doubly painful was the fact that Hungary's place in the World Cup final was well deserved. It was a roaring favourite. Its win would have been no upset, as was Uruguay's in 1950, or

Denmark's European crown in 1992 or that of Greece in Euro 2004. The Magyars had been unbeaten for four years and their futuristic football attracted the admiration of the world. Everyone, except perhaps the Germans, wanted and expected Hungary to win. But it was not to be. And Hungarians knew – we knew – that such a chance would never come again.

Following Berne the country descended into darkness. The suave boulevards of Budapest, which had been florally decorated and prepared for the victorious team's homecoming, were now frequented by angry groups of men fuming for retribution and suspecting that the corrupt regime had sold the country out. Not much of it made any sense. Was Puskás, the army major, selected for the final due to government pressure? Was Gusztáv Sebes, the team coach and a devout communist, being manipulated in his selections and tactics? What was it that mysteriously doped the modest Germans to perform such Herculean efforts? One popular rumour favoured the notion that the 2-3 in Berne had been a trade-off by the government for a fleet of German Mercedes-Benzes. Members of the Golden Team were sneaked back into the country via a variety of secret routes, at staggered times, to ensure there was no hostile welcoming party.

Hungary, which for all its material and political poverty had been so buoyant and upbeat before the World Cup, was now depressed and angry again, resigned to utter hopelessness. The drug of football, and the sweet highs it promised to deliver, had turned out to be a scam. Football, and the loss in Berne, laid the seeds for a people's uprising that would alter the course of history – for me, for Hungary, and for the world.

2

Revolution and escape

Two and a bit years later, on a cloudy, chilly October afternoon in Budakeszi, I was walking home from school past the tailor shop where my mother worked. When she saw me, she ran out of the shop, stood in front of me and crouched down so her eyes could meet mine. Grabbing and squeezing both my hands, she said: 'When you get home, tell your father that they are demonstrating in the streets of Budapest. Did you hear what I said? They are demonstrating in the streets of Budapest. Now go.'

I walked on with an increased stride, wondering what all the fuss was about. I had never heard the word 'demonstrate' and didn't have the faintest idea what it meant. I now know why. People's demonstrations were not exactly a common thing in a Stalinist state.

By the time I got home my father already knew, and was uninterruptible as he listened fixedly to the latest developments on the radio. Brothers Andrew and Joe and I sat in silence looking on, wondering. Our young minds gradually realised that something profound was happening; something that would change our lives forever.

On that day – 23 October 1956 – bands of idealistic students marched courageously down the major boulevards of Budapest making demands for change. They marched peacefully but resolutely, demanding state acquiescence to basic rights they felt the people were entitled to.

There were a variety of triggers for this unforeseen and – in a Stalinist state – unthinkable development. Deepening popular discontent fuelled the contempt in which the governors were held. And Joseph Stalin, who had died three years earlier, and whose tyranny had ruled the country since 1948, was now being openly exposed by the communists themselves as someone less than perfect. In February that year, at the Communist Party Congress in Moscow, the new Soviet leader, Nikita Khrushchev, made an historic speech that condemned Stalin and his methods. This implied an unprecedented admission that all was not utopian in the supposedly utopian world of Leninist revolution. For the first time since the dictatorship of the proletariat was declared in 1919, communism appeared vulnerable and the people pounced.

Added to all this, though the fact is not widely noted in formal history, I have no doubt that the failed promises of the state-manufactured Golden Team, and the dark disillusionment of the Berne loss in 1954, were major contributors to the anger and resentment that fuelled the Hungarian uprising. I believe that had Hungary won that game, the contentment may have lasted and there may not have been a mood for an uprising two years later.

The people were on the march, the genie had escaped, and the authorities were caught unprepared. The Ürge family, in our Budakeszi apartment, was monitoring the swift changes on state-run radio with fascination and optimism. Initially, the demonstrators were described as a counter-revolutionary rabble. Then, suddenly and without explanation, the same announcer switched, and hailed the marchers as legitimate claimants of democratic rights and freedoms. Finally, the voices turned dark again, announcing that the evil forces of counter-revolution had been defeated and the perfect dream world of communism had been returned.

The quake that shook the world to its political foundations, and altered the course of my life, took just 13 days. The uprising, begun on 23 October, won a brief victory before being crushed by Soviet tanks on 4 November – a day before my 11th birthday.

The activity in our neighbourhood in Budakeszi, during those brief 13 days of abrupt and divisive conflict, vividly reflected personal alliances. For example, the apartment above ours was occupied by an officer in the Hungarian Red Army, Lieutenant Petermann, a party man who, prior to the uprising, was always a visible and dominant figure, strutting about in his uniform, saluting to the neighbourhood. When the revolt broke out he disappeared, only re-emerging when it was all over and the Soviet tanks had done their business. Similarly, all others in the neighbourhood who were party members and had been verbose, card-carrying proponents of the Marxist dogma fell silent and went underground. Conversely, the majority – who had been disgusted by the oppression – suddenly became visible, active and round-chested.

Among the latter, my family was the most prominent. My parents were not shy in exhibiting their support for the cause célèbre and, of course, their kids followed suit. My father, though he took no active part in the fighting, was vocal and demonstrative in his support of the revolution, a keen organiser of community support for the brave young men who bore the fighting against the tyrants in the streets of Budapest.

For me, an impressionable 10-year-old, these were inspirational times which helped shape my values. Here were the people of our small country – a drop in the large pond of the vast Soviet empire – rising up to challenge power and might, giving hope to the hopeless and power to the weak. And they did it basically with sticks and stones. Not far from where we lived was a Red Army compound, a symbol and tool of the oppression under which we lived. Yet almost as soon as the revolt broke out, the soldiers and officers of the barracks, along with the rest of the Hungarian army, turned to side with the revolutionaries. Their act was a confirmation that good was on our side and that maybe, just maybe, the evils of tyranny could be conquered. The level of elation we felt at that time is difficult to describe.

I remember a gathering of the citizenry in the main square of Budakeszi, where defiant speeches were made by artists and intellectuals and where passionate young men, with new-found courage, shouted scorn on the authorities and pledged their determination to join the fighters. A middle-aged woman with a finely chiselled face and dishevelled hair stood on the podium and, staring defiantly into the sky, recited a poem that advocated freedom for all Hungarians. She was Márta Mezey, a resident of Budakeszi and a prominent actress. At the end the decibels and the temperature suddenly subsided as the mob, standing erect, broke into song and, eyes flooded with tears, sang the anthem.

One young man, sporting a tight shirt with sleeves rolled above the biceps, demanded from the by-standing police access to guns. What guns the police held, if they held any at all, was an unknown. But to us, the young man's defiant inquiry was evidence of how things had been turned upside down in a matter of days. People in that society were terrified of the police. To stand up to them was to invite arrest and jail or, at the very least, a good beating.

Among the various uniformed guardians of the dictatorship, the most hated was the AVH: the *Állam Védelmi Hatóság* (National Defence Authority). They were the secret police, as vicious and despised as the Stasi in East Germany or, later, Ceaucescu's Securitate in Romania. We heard many horror stories about them. One I remember, told by my father, was of an acquaintance who was asked a question by a friendly stranger in a bar: 'What do you think of our Prime Minister?' The acquaintance, lulled into honest confidence by drink, let fly with some sincere views, expletives included. The stranger produced his AVH badge and took the man away. My father never saw him again.

Once the demonstration and the speeches in the square ended we went home. But a more proactive section, led by the young man in the tight shirt, proceeded to the home of a local AVH officer, Colonel Fazekas, and demanded an audience. The colonel battened down all doors, refused the visitation and fired gun shots from a window, one of which hit and felled the mob's young chieftain. Enraged, the mob stormed the house and broke in only to find the colonel lying dead. He had shot himself in the mouth. They dragged his body onto the street, disembowelled it and left it there to be spat upon and rot.

Such was the hatred and anger in the populace. Such was the need of the people to exact retribution for years of repression, humiliation and indignity. Colonel Fazekas, in their eyes, had been a quisling and an instrument of popular misery. The unseemly way in which he, or at least his remains, had been disposed of was a demonstration that the people had regained their power; that tyranny was dead and should never return.

But the euphoria was to be short-lived. The young freedom fighter died from his wounds. And with him, symbolically, went all hope as things turned dark again. The revolution was crushed.

But for me and my family, a door opened onto a new life. And for the world at large, the events in Budapest of 1956 also set new horizons. Indeed, the uprising had a massive global impact, causing the then bipolar world of capitalism versus communism to wobble on its axis. It was a massive public relations blow against the image of Marxism – as it was ruled from Moscow – as a dogma and an ideal. In Hungary, the ideology based on equality and workers rights had to be enforced by tanks and guns, and was ultimately challenged and rejected by the poor and the workers themselves. In October 1956, communist governments from Berlin to Beijing shook in their jackboots in fear of the Budapest autumn growing into a global winter of demise for their dogma. The uprising was quelled, but the world was never the same again.

This crushing of the revolt was immediately followed by purges, jailings and executions. Imre Nagy, the recently installed Prime Minister, was taken away and executed somewhere in the provinces, the whereabouts and circumstances remaining unclear for decades.

The new, Moscow-sponsored regime learned from experience that if it wanted to avoid mutiny, it had to loosen the strings of tyranny, at least in the economic sense, and keep peoples' bellies full. Soon the regime began to liberalise the Marxist blueprint of central economic control and allowed a degree of private ownership and small-business profiteering. On the surface, the government continued to pay loud lip service to the spirit of Marx and Lenin but under the table it allowed capitalism to flourish. The new dogma, later dubbed 'goulash communism', made Hungary the most economically prosperous country in the communist bloc.

The Hungarian experience, both the violent revolt of 1956 and the liberalisation its lessons led to, began a slow tidal wave that would eventually drown the advancement of communism as a profound global threat to capitalism and set in train the process that would end the Cold War. Other communist regimes, including the Chinese in the 1970s, copied the Hungarian model of economic reform, with even more radical advances towards liberalism evident in Mikhail Gorbachev's perestroika during the 1980s.

When it was all over, the voice on the radio was again talking of counter-revolution. It told us how a man called János Kádár had formed a new government and asked the Soviet Union for 'help' to crush the dark rebellion and oust the rabble and scum that threatened the utopia of a socialist Hungary. My parents knew this was the end. It meant that Nikita Khrushchev, the Soviet leader, had sent in the Red Army and brought the dream of revolution to a premature end.

Within hours, Soviet tanks had surrounded Budapest. My brothers and I walked to Budaörsi Út, one of the highways that skirted the greater city near our home. The road was a traffic jam of stationary Soviet tanks, bumper to bumper, with soldiers sitting around smoking, chatting, waiting. Their orders were to wait and give the freedom fighters a chance to surrender. And if they didn't, go in and blow them to hell.

We knew there would be no surrender. We went back home, sat in silence for a few hours and went to bed. In the coming days the mood of the neighbourhood reverted to that which existed prior to the revolution. Those who had supported the uprising fell silent again and sank into a state of resignation. The party hacks re-emerged from hiding, re-pinned their red stars and pranced about with cocky assuredness. Their children stared, and pointed fingers at us.

One afternoon, with my parents out of the house and only Andrew, Joe and me at home, a group of a dozen or so boys gathered ominously in the yard under our balcony. These were some of the children of the socialist revolution, brainwashed clean by their parents and masters. They hurled profanities in our direction and pelted the apartment with snowballs, many of which landed inside our home. By the end, our small but neat and tidy apartment resembled a pigsty. We realised then that this was just the beginning. For the Ürge family, as for all those who had been openly sympathetic to the revolt, there would be heavy retribution.

A few days later, on 9 December 1956, a cold winter's morning, we were shaken awake by my mother. 'Wake up. We're going,' she said. 'Going where?' I asked. It was 2 am. Much too early for school. 'Never mind. Just get dressed. Quick.' Obediently, we moved swiftly in the dead of night. We were hauled, all five of us, onto the back of a truck. It was bitterly cold and uncomfortable. But we sat in silence. The truck took us to one of Budapest's three major railway stations: the one that services the west, the route to the Austrian border.

Once we were on the train the penny dropped: we were defecting. We were about to become dissidents. Refugees. For years, I had been listening to my parents talking about getting out, escaping: finding a way to a new life of freedom and some kind of bliss. This was no desperate run for the border. It was a meticulously planned conspiracy, devised in collusion with our neighbours, the Keresztes family, a young couple with two small

children, who took the same journey. The Keresztes couple and my
parents were the only people who knew the plan: with the secret
police hovering, they told no one. My parents, bless their souls,
were a lot smarter than I knew at the time.

The Keresztes couple had contacts near the border and my
parents also had contacts: people who could help facilitate the
escape. The plan was to head to a small village near the Austrian
border under the pretence of attending a country wedding. We
were to take the train west to Szombathely, the country's western-
most large city. There we were to change trains and head south to
Körmend where we would spend a night with a long-forgotten
acquaintance of my mother. From Körmend, we would be taken to
the nearby village of Pinkamindszent, a kilometre or so from the
border, where a farming family was teed up to walk us to freedom.
All along the way, our contacts, who would be paid for their
trouble, had been prepared for our arrival. Our papers had to be in
order and our stories had to be synchronised. There could be no
foul-ups, for that would spell arrest and demise.

As the train rattled west, the signs of police presence were everywhere. Uniformed men would board at each stop, check IDs and
ask questions. The authorities were not stupid. At one point, the
train passed through the station of Székesfehérvár, a major city
between Budapest and the Austrian border. From a train heading
in the other direction, people leaned out of their windows and
screamed to us: 'Forget it. There are too many police. Too many
Russians. You will be turned back!'

But we made it to Szombathely, where we spent the night at the
railway station, sleeping on wooden benches. It was, as I recall, the
most uncomfortable night I have ever had. My mother grew up in
that city and had close friends and relatives living a few hundred
metres away. It must have been harrowing for her not to be able to
contact them. But she didn't. She hung in. This was a top secret
mission. No one was to know.

In the morning, we took the train to Körmend and along the way
we struck our first obstacle, a most frightening experience which

could well have been our undoing. As we neared Körmend, the train screeched to a halt. Uniformed AVH officers came on board. The papers, and the story, of my parents were apparently not beyond suspicion, as one officer introduced himself to my father by smacking him square across the face. We were all hauled off the train and taken to a nearby army barracks. There, we were separated from my father, and locked in a small room with four walls and not much else. My father was somewhere else – we did not know where. We were there for six hours. All the while, my father was being interrogated. For all we knew, he had been arrested, tortured or killed. But he must have been convincing, for he was released and allowed to reunite with his family.

In retrospect, I am grateful for the political incorrectness of those times. My father, as the head of the family, was the only one to be questioned. The authorities could have questioned any of us: his wife or his three young, vulnerable children. Under that kind of pressure, I am sure any of us might have wilted and blurted out the truth.

Released and greatly relieved, we walked the rest of the way to Körmend. As we entered the outskirts of the town we noticed the uneasy presence of a mysterious man dressed in black, and with a decided limp, who appeared to be tailing us. 'Speed up. Run!' my father yelled. 'This lame duck is after us. He's probably secret police.' As it turned out the man, far from being AVH, was on our side: an intermediary in the grand plan. He was to guide us to our next destination.

That destination was a neat, suburban house, the home of a quietly spoken, neatly groomed elderly woman. She was an important knot on the string of conspiracy, a vague connection recruited by my mother, although they had never previously met. Indeed, she had no investment in helping us and every reason, given the dubious nature of the vague connection, to be dismissive or even hostile. To this day I do not know if she was paid. If she was, it would have been meagre for my parents had next to nothing. If she wasn't, then she helped us purely out of a sense of decency, an urge to assume a small role in defying the evils of the day.

She was reserved, even cold, but welcomed us out of the snow into her warm house. She gave us food, hot coffee and beds for the night. Her house was our one-night stopover before proceeding to a small village on the border the next day. As my parents sipped their coffee and engaged in idle conversation before retiring, we were joined by some locals, all of whom were trusted co-conspirators, one of them an old peasant woman, complete with black scarf and a craggy face but jocular and loud. The Keresztes family also arrived.

There was a bang on the front door. We froze. The old peasant woman peered out the window through a gap in the curtains. 'Russian soldiers. Stay cool,' she said. She let them in. They were drunk. The old woman spoke to them in broken Russian, gave them a nip of whisky each and the soldiers, after a couple of hearty laughs, left. We were deeply relieved, but frightened out of our wits.

Minutes later, there was another knock on the door and two men entered from the dark. They were young and swarthily handsome, each half-shaven with a shock of black hair, one of them with a thick, dark moustache. They were dressed in dark grey, in long leather boots, machine guns in hands and sashes of bullets across their chests. They were freedom fighters, sympathetic to our cause. One of them asked my father for a cigarette. As my father timidly raised his hand to give him a light, the young man grabbed my father's wrist. 'You are shaking, you are frightened,' the young man said. 'Don't be. Fear is the enemy. You will be fine, you will be free. Stay calm. Right is on your side.' My father inquired: 'Why don't you come with us? You are just a few kilometres from freedom. You are young, your life is ahead of you.' The young man drew a deep breath of nicotine. 'Not yet,' he said. 'We still have a little work to do.' Some days later, we learned that both young men were dead, cut down in their exuberant young fight for right.

The next day, a bright, freezing morning, we assembled for instructions. We were to be taken to a small village by horse and cart, disguised as a peasant family going to a peasant wedding. The Keresztes family would follow the next day. We were to look like peasants and act the part. My mother, then an attractive city woman of 44, but looking 30, was asked to assume a new role. No make-up, black scarf and drab clothes. The old peasant woman was to drive the cart. Subdued, scared, crumpled humbly under blankets in the back of the cart, we set off for our last stop before negotiating our final leap to the promised land.

As we neared the outskirts of the village, another major scare loomed: a checkpoint manned by two Russian soldiers in uniform. They were there to filter out would-be defectors. The old woman turned her head and said: 'Stay calm. I will handle it. Don't say a word.' As the soldiers waved down the cart the old woman engaged with them in her meagre Russian, humouring them and managing to persuade them that we were indeed part of a wedding party. The soldiers waved us on. The old woman was beside herself with delight at how well she handled the crisis, laughing and rollicking, mocking the soldiers. For a short while, she was the queen of people-trafficking; she had found a vocation for which she had a decided gift. But her confidence, as things would later prove, was premature.

The cart wheeled into the village of Pinkamindszent, little more than a hamlet, population probably under a thousand, with houses of precise, rectangular symmetry, rendered in pristine white with dark red tiled roofs. A dirt road, cleared of snow and wet with slosh, took us to a large house with two floors and an expansive yard, at the back of which stood a high wooden building with no windows. We were welcomed by a tall, thin young man called Louis who spoke with a thick provincial accent, wore a small, dark green, narrow-brimmed hat and exuded a warmth and humility we knew to expect from country folk. The old woman turned the cart and headed back to Körmend.

Inside the house we were greeted less warmly. There was, to be sure, cosy relief as the potbelly stove radiated its throbbing respite from the bitter temperatures outside. But there was no such comfort from Louis' family who sat wordlessly, staring with cold, inquisitive regard at such rarely seen city folk and their assumed claim to a higher standing. My parents felt uneasy and threatened. But they had to accommodate and conform. This was the family that would guide us across the border and guarantee our future.

After small talk and coffee, the negotiations began. What could we pay for this service? What did my parents have, if anything, that might represent the right price? Years later, I realised that, however unkind our hosts might have seemed at the time, this was the way of things when one decides to be a refugee. One sets forth in the darkness on a precarious adventure over roads full of potholes, where dangers lurk at every corner, where lives of children are at stake, where no stranger can be trusted, where there is an essential need to rely on help from those who know the potholes and the dangers and who are experts at negotiating them. These people, in more scornful, modern parlance, are known as people traffickers. But the expression, in my view, is unkind, given that it reflects far too disparagingly on people who are an essential part of the refugee process: people without whom successful quests for freedom would be impossible. They expect to be paid for their service, a fact that is neither unusual nor particularly relevant in the big scheme of things.

My parents began to peel off whatever they had: cash, jewellery, valuable clothing. My mother, given the bitterly cold winter, was wearing a *bunda* (Hungarian for fur coat), a thing which in the culture of Hungary, a country which regularly experienced sub-zero winter temperatures, was neither unusual nor any kind of status symbol. Almost every citizen of Hungary owned a *bunda*. The old man of the Pinkamindszent family, the head of the clan, looked at the *bunda* and asked my mother acerbically: 'What about that coat?' At that moment Louis, the young son of the clan, intervened and gave his father a halting glance: 'That's enough. Forget the coat. We have enough.' The negotiations were over.

We could all begin to relax and settle. There were just a few more hours to kill. At precisely midnight Louis would walk us across the border, freedom would be ours, and all this would be over. But there was one more major crisis lurking.

My younger brother Joe, then just eight, saw something odd as he looked out the window and raised the alarm. We all turned and looked. To our horror, we saw the Keresztes family and the old peasant woman walking on the main road leading into town, escorted by two Russian soldiers. They had been arrested. The old woman, obviously cocky with confidence, had gone back to Körmend and persuaded the Keresztes family that the coast was clear and decided to bring them to Pinkamindszent a day ahead of schedule. The soldiers who had been told a similar tale about a country wedding only a few hours earlier, must have become suspicious and nabbed them. Now we were in danger and our hosts knew it. The soldiers would surely scour the town looking for the 'other' family which had told the same cock and bull story. The old woman would be questioned and she would surely tell where she delivered that other family.

We had to be hidden. Louis immediately summoned us to gather quickly and proceed to the big wooden building at the back of the yard. The building had two levels. The lower level was the stables. The upper level was reserved for the stacking of hay. Louis instructed us to climb to the upper level, bury ourselves under the hay and not make a sound. We were to wait in silence until there was a knock on the gate of the building accompanied by the word 'Louis'.

We did as we were told and stayed under the hay for a solid four hours without so much as a peep from any of us. It was eerily quiet and we were so scared we barely breathed. But the danger passed and finally, out of the still night, came the knock on the gate and the voice of Louis. We climbed down from under the hay, shook ourselves off and got ready, placing our future into Louis' hands.

The clock showed midnight as we set off for the border: our family of five, and Louis. It was a dangerous walk for all of us, but Louis took the greatest risk. If we were caught he would surely go to jail, as assisting defectors was a serious crime, much greater than attempting to defect. The night was still and cold, the terrain pancake flat. A cover of shallow snow illuminated the sky. Visibility was good, a mixed blessing, given that it made us more vulnerable to being spotted by the frontier guards, perched high in their lookout towers a few hundred metres apart.

Louis allowed my parents to lead and walked at the back of the group, holding the hands of the two youngest boys: Joe and me. Nobody spoke. The rhythmic crackling of snow under our feet was the only noise to interrupt the stillness. We saw the vague, intimidating outlines of the towers in the distance. But they were far away. Louis knew the terrain well, and the best and safest way to slip between the guards. We heard shots in the distance. Louis told us not to be alarmed, for they were only shooting in the air. The towers were manned by Hungarian soldiers who were, in the main, sympathetic to the cause; their sporadic shooting was aimed less at refugees than at impressing their commanders.

We walked for what seemed an eternity but was probably no more than half an hour, until Louis commanded us to stop. He told us we had already crossed the Hungarian border and we were now in no man's land, a buffer of a few hundred metres between frontiers. Louis said this was as far as he could go. He gave us instructions to keep walking in the same direction, saying that after a kilometre or so we would encounter an Austrian village. He embraced and kissed each of us, said goodbye, turned around and headed back to Pinkamindszent, his figure, as we stood and stared, slowly disappearing into the night.

Louis was an agent of conspiracy, a 'people trafficker', helping the captive and the helpless negotiate a precarious avenue to freedom. He was, I believe, genuinely on our side and, to this day, remains a hero for me. I have not seen him since but would give anything to do so, to parley about that adventure, and to thank him.

As we began our walk into Austria we knew not what awaited us. Falsehoods about country weddings, the assortment of lies my father told his interrogators in the barracks, whatever funny papers my parents were carrying were of no use to us now. From this point, we had to tell the truth and surrender ourselves to whatever fate our new hosts would decide for us. But that is the way of the political refugee. He runs for his life, with only the clothes on his back, lying and cheating his way past those who would stop him, taking enormous risks, endangering himself and his children, carrying no passport, no visa nor any identification. He carries only his dreams, and his hopes that he will be believed and that the receiving hosts will sympathise and not turn him back to a fate worse than the one he has left.

My parents had tried defecting before. Before I was born, as the savage hostilities of the war threatened, they headed west to Austria. It was there, in a squalid refugee camp, that my sister Katalin – my parents' first child – died of pneumonia at the age of five in my mother's arms. Despair and agonising homesickness drove them back to Hungary. Attempting defection again was not a decision my parents took lightly.

As we walked on, still with the crackling snow under our feet, we began to hear human noises in the distance. They were singing. Finally, we got close enough to approach the source of the noise, for noise rather than music is mostly what it was. It was a pair of Austrian drunks, happily staggering home from a long night at the local keller. My father began to speak to them in fluent German; the sound of it will live forever in my memory. While he had told us that he spoke German (a requirement of his earlier life in the Austro-Hungarian Empire), I had never heard him speak it. Now that I did, it rang sweet. I finally realised we were in foreign land and that maybe – just maybe – we had made it.

My father told the two men who we were, what journey we were on and why we were trudging through the snow in the dead of night. One of the drunks broke out into loud laughter, slapped my father on the back and slurred: 'Well, welcome. You are free.'

Moisture filled our eyes, and it was not because of the bracing cold, nor the whistling wind that was brushing against our skins. We cried because, on this most uncomfortable of nights, church-mouse poor and with nothing to our names, with our future as uncertain as the weather, with all that we had risked and left behind, we were being told that we were welcome and that we were free.

From that point our adventure took a smoother turn, though it remained difficult, eventful and full of uncertainty for quite some time. This should be put in historical context. Being Hungarian refugees in 1956 was a lot easier than the experiences that face would-be escapees from a host of war-ravaged and despotic regimes today. The revolution was the biggest news story of the decade (the Hungarian Freedom Fighter was *Time* magazine's man of the year that year), generating a massive global humanitarian response and sympathy to the plight of its victims. Anyone who chose to flee the crushing advances of the Soviet tanks was not only welcomed in the West but seen as a hero.

The two drunks directed us to the village church where we dutifully reported and discovered that we were not alone: the church was already a makeshift refugee camp, a one-night stopover point. Beds with white sheets were lined up as in a hospital ward, where refugees would spend the night before being transported to one of hundreds of more permanent camps that dotted the country. We were taken the next day to a place called Pack, a ski resort high in the hills above the city of Graz, where a resort hotel, now an abode for dozens of Magyars, became our next home.

After a couple of weeks there we were bussed to Salzburg, a city of incomparable beauty and Mozart, where we would stay until a decision was made, either by us or by someone else, as to where our family would go to settle and rebuild its life.

In the refugee camp – an army barracks called Kampröder, emptied and converted for the task – life was not easy, but for us boys it was not hard either. Kids, by and large, are accepting of whatever fate befalls them and get on with life. Besides, we didn't have to go to school so we weren't complaining. We were communally housed in a large dormitory room with three other families and no demarcations for privacy. Domestic fights within the families – and there were plenty of them – were great sources of entertainment as they wafted to and fro in the room. The families were given shelter and food and a small amount of cash. Our staple diet was spam: processed meat stuffed into a can and tasting like preserved plastic. Eating this stuff, for those brought up on flavour-some and spicy Magyar cuisine, was no easy thing.

Kampröder, where we spent five months, was in a glorious location and, as refugee camps go, it must have been as good as it gets. The snow-covered Alps hovered majestically and dominated the view. The River Salzach, which divides Austria and Germany, was a short distance away. We would take walking trips to its banks and occasionally stop for a coffee at one of the riverside villages, sit back and wonder what the future would hold.

We were in processing mode. The many hundreds of thousands of Hungarian refugees who were gathered in various camps around Austria were now being processed. Where we were to go from here was not entirely up to us. While most refugees nominated their preferred destination – the majority wanted to go to the United States – it was not that simple. Indeed, a few weeks after we arrived in Salzburg, a pocket of refugees, frustrated by the delays in processing by the Americans, staged a hunger strike. The incident made global headlines. The US government, trying to diffuse the PR damage, despatched Eleanor Roosevelt to the scene. It worked. The belligerents calmed down and processing of immigration to the US speeded up.

We had relatives in both the US and Australia. My mother had a cousin living in upstate New York, while my father had a brother who lived in Wollongong, south of Sydney. Both had been post-war refugees. So my parents put their application in for both countries.

It would have seemed easy to go just about anywhere. Most countries warmly opened their doors to Hungarian refugees, some more enthusiastically than others. Many set up temporary diplo-matic offices in Austria for the sheer purpose of processing appli-cants and some of them actively campaigned amongst the refugees themselves. One man, an agent for South Africa, actually persuaded my father that that's where we should go. The rest of the family was totally against the notion but my father stood firm. The South African invitation had a definite competitive edge over the others: my father was to be given a job, a family house, a maid and a gun (presumably to be used for self-defence). So we packed our meagre belongings and boarded the bus destined for the nearest port, from where we would sail to Africa. On the way out of the compound the bus stopped at the gate, a routine checkpoint for the screening of ID documents. As the driver got off, my father turned to us and said: 'Come on. We're getting off the bus. If you are all against us going to South Africa, then I guess so am I.' That's how desperately close we came to ending up South Africans rather than Australians!

Still, the chance remained that we would become Americans. I might have ended up an ideological redneck and a follower of baseball rather than football, speaking English with a Texas drawl.

But divine providence intervened. In early May of 1957, almost precisely six months after we had crossed the border, the word came that we had been accepted by Australia. Joy filled the family. Even if we knew little about the country, we knew that it was democratic, free and safe. We thought of the Keresztes family, which was back in Budakeszi; of the many relatives and friends we had left behind; and of the huge, irreversible step we had taken. We were embarking on a journey of no return, to a land far far away, about whose language and culture we knew nothing and where our future was full of uncertainty and mystery.

3

Poisoned forever

Travelling to Australia from Europe in the 1950s was arduous, particularly for a family of refugees. For a start, I am unsure who paid for our trip, although I suspect it was mostly the Australian government. Those were the days of 'assisted migration', whereby the government paid a large portion of the migrants' airfare and helped them settle into the country. Australia's population was under 10 million and the country needed people, especially working men who could boost its industries and provide labour on huge infrastructure projects such as the Snowy Mountains power scheme. They were also the days of the dreaded White Australia Policy, whereby migrants from the UK had to pay a paltry £10 (the Australian government paid the rest), those from Italy had to pay half their airfare and non-whites couldn't come in at all. I guess we were considered white.

From Salzburg we were taken by bus to Linz, on the Danube, in Austria's north. In Linz we boarded a plane for the long leg to Australia. The four-engined former troop carrier, a turbo-prop monster, needed five refuelling stops to reach its destination. The last of these stops – our first chance to plant our feet on Australian soil – was in Darwin. Though the stop was for barely an hour, and forming real impressions was impossible, one incident left its mark. At the door of the terminal stood our first Australian. He wore a starched white shirt, a tie, an Akubra hat, Bermuda shorts and long socks with sandals and was so laid back he nearly fell over. More significantly, he was rolling a cigarette. This stunned me. In Hungary, ready-made cigarettes were a minor luxury. My father, who also rolled his own, would occasionally send me – when he felt rich – down to the corner store to buy him five, 10 or perhaps 15 cigarettes. So here we were, taking our first steps in the land of milk and honey where money grew on trees and, in the Magyar parlance, fences were built of sausages – and the first Aussie we see is rolling his own.

Flying over the Australian land mass provides a captivating first lesson on the country: how far and different it is from every other place on earth. Vast flat deserts and arid lands spread out in a kaleidoscope of three colours: reds, browns and purples. As you edge nearer to the coastlines, lush trees begin to dot the landscape and interrupt the monotony, eventually gathering to become forests where the uniformity is interrupted only by gently rising puffs of smoke, as isolated bushfires rage unbeknown to and undisturbed by humanity. These were now real impressions as our plane rattled south from Darwin to Wagga Wagga. Why Wagga Wagga, a small inland city, and not Sydney or Melbourne? Because it had the nearest airport to Bonegilla, the migrant hostel which was to be our first home in Australia.

By the time we landed and took the bus journey from the town to the hostel it was already dark. It was late May 1957, a public holiday – Empire Day – celebrated in those days with a 'cracker night'. Later to be outlawed and erased from Australian culture, these were annual occasions when it was tradition for the populace to light bonfires, let off rockets and firecrackers and generally frighten cats and delight children. As the bus cruised through the small towns on the way to Bonegilla, the scenery seemed to glow, with huge bonfires burning and fireworks lighting up the sky. My father leaned over and said to me: 'Aren't these Australians nice, the way they have gone to all this trouble to welcome us?'

Bonegilla is not a name that flatters Australia's historic sensibilities. It became defunct in 1971, which was just as well, given its record as a migrant hostel not famous for five-star hospitality. Since turned into a Migrant Experience Heritage Park, it was a standard-issue compound of modest, thin-walled huts, offering no protection from the elements. Each hut was equipped with the barest furniture and a single-bar electric heater. That spelt a Spartan existence by day and sheer, shivering misery by night if you happened to be stuck there during the colder months, as we were. And here was the first irony of our immigration. Given that Australia's warm climate was among the country's first attractions as a destination, we were astonished to discover how cold it was. It was May – still technically autumn – but we froze in the inland chill. Nobody warned us of this and we wondered what had happened as the family gathered each night around that bar heater, shivering and rubbing palms. To paraphrase Mark Twain, who muttered something similar about San Francisco, the coldest winter I ever had was an autumn I spent in Bonegilla.

Still, I don't remember any of us complaining. Such discomforts were in the context of where we were as refugees: in a country that had taken us in, where we wanted to be, and where we had to cop what was coming and make the best of our opportunities.

Our first deep impressions of Australia were all about the country's sweet innocence in terms of how far and different it was from where we had come. One episode I recall epitomised it well. Our enthusiastic hosts put on a show at a local hall, designed to be hospitable to the camp's inhabitants and show them a good time. The place was packed with immigrants and refugees, raucous and buoyant, eager to enjoy a good show, the like of which they had not had a chance to sample for many months.

A short man with red hair and a huge nose came on stage and, in a high tenor voice, exploded into the Italian popular classic *Funiculi Funicula*. But the plan – to impress a horde of immigrants – fell

flat. Or should have fallen flat. The problem was that the singer
was bad, very bad: off key all the way. And the crowd responded
with a deafening concert of whistles. Whistling at a public show in
Hungary and elsewhere in Europe is a form of jeering or showing
disapproval. What the audience didn't know was that in Australia
it is the opposite: the little man with the big nose came back for
three encores.

Wollongong, on the South Coast of NSW, was, and still is, a classic
Australian catchment area for migrants. Supported by the sea on
one side and the lush green mountains of the Great Dividing Range
on the other, it is a string of modest low- to middle-class suburbs,
quiet and safe, distant from and generally untouched by the world's
disturbances. It was, in 1957, a sweet venue for economic opportunity and social contentment. Dreadfully dull for a European, to
be sure, but agreeable none the less.

Its centrepiece for migrants was the Port Kembla steelworks, a
magnet for newcomers seeking jobs. And it was in Wollongong
that we settled: the place chosen for us by my uncle who arranged
a job in the steelworks for my father. At last we could begin to
sample the country and the culture we had adopted.

This period represented the beginning of the great migrant
boom in Australia. Australia needed people, especially people of
working age, to build the industries that would fuel the economy
of the 'lucky country' to the full throttle of its potential. Migrants
worked in factories, in the mines, on the roads and on the sugar
cane fields. They were ambitious, industrious and untiring. Far
from today's norm, when border protectionism and xenophobia are
running rife, the government then went out of its way to attract
migrants and the people generally welcomed them. They called us
'new Australians', a cute label which, for me, smacked of warmth
and hospitality, a kind of *mi casa, su casa* message to reinforce the
notion that we should feel at home.

We tried to make the best of the opportunity and I don't remember my parents ever complaining about the cards they had been dealt. But there were plenty of culture shocks. When migrants arrive in a country, before the forces of assimilation begin to grip, they act as they did back home, expressing surprise and even disgust if the natives appear to fall short of their expectations of 'civilised' behaviour. I remember going to the movies — a Saturday afternoon matinee — with the family all dressed formally in our Sunday best. As we settled in our seats we noted the locals who filed in wearing shorts and thongs, accompanied by the aroma of fish and chips wrapped in used newspapers. The question arose: 'What kind of country had we come to?'

These impressions extended to every aspect of the new culture we had plunged into. The place was eternally dull and colourless. Nightlife was non-existent. There were no restaurants or cafes. And the cuisine was the worst of it: my father described the taste of a good old Aussie steak as something akin to eating the sole of a shoe. He had warned me about that. On the way over, when I asked him about Australian cuisine and what Australians ate, he said: 'They are barbarians. They eat lamb.' In Hungary the consumption of lamb, or at least mutton, is just about unheard of. I have been to Sydney dinner parties where lamb was served and the Hungarian guests simply refused to eat it, rose from their chairs and went home.

All of this, strangely, proved to be most beneficial to my survival instincts as a migrant. Our deduction was that Australia was a philistine country, a colonial outpost where some ground needed to be made up before the local culture could measure up to that of we Europeans. Rightly or wrongly, it bred a superiority complex. I was, after all, a European. Far from being desperate to be accepted by the locals, and far from feeling inferior to them, I considered that I was here to make a positive contribution to the local culture and they were lucky to have me. Pompous and wrong? Maybe. But it helped me overcome the migrant inclination towards so desperately wanting to be one of the locals that one sheds one's heritage and sacrifices one's past in order to blend into the new world. This,

I believe, was a powerful element in ensuring that I not only kept my identity but managed to survive the shaky journey of migration and assimilation.

Of all the things that stunned me about Australia as a young migrant, the most disappointing was the diminutive role played by football (they called it soccer) in the lives of the people. When I arrived, I found the Australian sporting landscape astonishing. I had come from a country and a part of the world where football was the major – if not the only – sporting preoccupation. If their interests ever strayed beyond football, the natives of my former world paid attention only to a handful of other global sports like athletics, swimming, volleyball, gymnastics and boxing.

In Australia, I couldn't find any of that. Instead, I saw a society absorbed on weekends by horse racing and cricket – the strangest of sports where men, all clad in long white pants with no colour distinction between opposing teams, would play a game for five days. Or rugby league and union, and a strange game called Aussie Rules, where burly men ran around shoving each other in dispute over a ball shaped like an egg. I found it beyond belief that a country could actually exist in which football was not the predominant sporting driver of society. Sure, football was played in the schools (although not in private ones, a primary reason my brothers and I were not enrolled in a Catholic school) and at an amateur level around the suburbs. But it held no presence in the minds of the populace. Alfredo di Stefano, who was the greatest footballer of the day, and according to some the greatest of all time, may have been the neighbourhood Italian fruiterer to the average Australian.

This observation had a deep and lasting impact on my mindset as an immigrant. To be sure, and despite the culture shocks, I liked Australia, felt relaxed and free here. Having taken a deep breath of its fresh air of innocence, I looked forward to a sweet life in the lucky country. But this football thing and its relegated place in Australia's social priorities bothered me deeply even then. It struck an urgent instinctive chord in my mind, spurring me to sway those nearest to me to the beauties of the game and to shake others in my adopted country into discovering the world's one true sporting faith. It began with schoolyard squabbles with pimply mates over what was the best and the world's most important sport and ended with me becoming a kind of professional zealot, an unordained high priest of the universal religion.

Yet football's deepest impact on me – the episode that would infect my soul forever with what I call 'the great poison' – was not one that I imported from my European world. It happened in Australia, the philistine cricket country, in the Wollongong suburb of Warrawong. It was mid-1960. I was 14. Real Madrid had just won the European Cup for the fifth time in a row, beating Eintracht Frankfurt 7-3 in the final in Glasgow. This was the time of black and white TV, some years before satellite signals made it possible to access events live from far-flung corners of the planet. So we could only read about the game in the newspapers and be alerted that it had been something special. Special was hardly the word.

There was still no television set in the Ürge household, a garage converted into a two-bedroom flat in the backyard of a house owned by an Italian landlord. After three years in Australia, we were still poor. My father's shift work in the steelworks and my mother's odd shift as a cleaner were the only sources of income to support a family that included three growing and gluttonous boys. We boys slept in one room, my parents in another and the small square which posed as a lounge room was converted into another bedroom and sub-let to a boarder. A small kitchen with a small laminated table and five chairs acted as the abode's living quarters.

We, the boys, spent most of our non-homework time in the nearby streets, riding the one bike we shared or playing football with a cheap rubber ball. When you're a child, poverty is neither debilitating nor demoralising. Children accept these things as their lot. We knew we were poor but never complained, even when the mandatory school uniform was out of my parents' economic reach.

My mother once took me to a department store to fit me out with the splendidly coloured bottle green and grey uniform of Berkeley High. I tried on the gear and stood smiling proudly in front of the mirror, a contented little citizen. But the store manager checked our credit rating and rejected the purchase. I had to undress and retreat, minus one more little dream. The incident left no deep scar on me but my mother was heartbroken.

I recall having a crush (not my first) on a girl from school. Her name was Carol Love, an apt name for a pretty girl – the prettiest in the school – with almond eyes, honey blonde hair and curves as soft as the morning clouds. She sat next to me on the bus one morning and started talking to me. As I slumped forward in a fidget of discomfort I noticed that I was wearing cheap plastic shoes which were already fraying on the edges. I don't know if she noticed, and there's a good chance she didn't, but that was where my relationship with Carol Love began and ended. Still, I survived the trauma and went on unbruised. Being poor for a kid of 14 is no big deal.

But back to that European Cup final. A Hungarian friend of the family, Charlie Varga, lived a couple of blocks away with his plump Swiss wife (who spoke a kind of broken Hungarian) and a hairy Alsatian dog given to intermittent bursts of flatulence. Charlie had a television set and invited us to come over and watch the replay.

The prime attraction for this late-night exodus by the Ürge family (the telecast was slotted at 10 pm) was Ferenc Puskás, the Magyar idol, who had quite some part to play in the game. Puskás, by now a resurrected icon and his role in the 1954 World Cup finals shelved as a thing of history, was a gun striker with Real Madrid who had signed him after he defected following the turmoil of the 1956 up-rising. I spent my earliest years admiring Puskás from afar, knowing him from radio commentaries, newspaper articles and anecdotal accounts by family, friends and neighbours, but I had never seen him play, either live or on film. Puskás, more than any other Hungarian at that time, fuelled our sense of identity and communal pride. Even settled in Australia, we Hungarians still burned with the desire to see our Ferenc counted among the football masters of the world.

What followed was a mesmerising exhibition, not only of football but of sport and all its spiritual ideals. Most of that was down to Real Madrid which won the game 7-3, but that was not all of it. It was the way they did it. Clad in all white, Madrid – at least technically – embodied the angelic, virginal innocence of sport at its purest. The victory was achieved with elegance, style, cocky arrogance and bravado, in a sporting spirit the like of which we have never seen since. It left an imprint on me that would shape my future, my ideals about sport and about life itself.

Puskás, a squat figure who had turned 33 by then, will be remembered as a dominant force in the match alongside the even older, taller and more regal leader of the team, the Argentine master Alfredo di Stefano. The two shared all of Madrid's seven goals, Puskás scoring four and Di Stefano three, but to credit only them with the exhibition would be an injustice to the broad spirit and purity of the football. This was a spectacle that required the co-opt of 22 players of equal will, spirit and sporting values. Frankfurt made a game of it, played it in admirable spirit – in fact, led early – but was eventually overrun by the sheer class of Madrid's gloriously assembled technicians.

The sweet baritone of the BBC's Kenneth Wolstenholme calling the play stays in my memory, as he followed the route of the ball through endless streams of perfect passing by the Madrid collective: Santamaria, Pachin, Zarraga, Del Sol, Canario, Di Stefano, Gento and Puskás. It was such technical perfection, such a sample of sporting romance that, folklore claims, most of the 130,000 neutral fans who were on hand at Glasgow's Hampden Park stood and applauded for a full hour after the final whistle, so beguiled were they by what they had just seen.

At the end of it all, as the whistle blew, Puskás – being nearest to the ball – commandeered it as a souvenir. The now well-worn television footage shows one of the Frankfurt players rushing to the Madrid number 10, pleading with him, beseeching him to give up the ball. After a few seconds, Puskás loosened his hold and surrendered the ball to the humble German. That Puskás should have done this, knowing he was giving up the ball with which, many say, the greatest game of all time was played, was not untypical of him nor of truly great players generally. He knew that his own name would be engraved forever not just on this game but on the sport of football, given his historic contribution to both. But for the modest Frankfurt foot soldier, name long forgotten, souveniring that Hampden match-ball would be his abiding link to the classic game. Most of all, that brief episode was a sweet salute to the glorious spirit in which that game was played.

For its technical artistry, its romantic utopianism, its capacity to embrace all that is ideal in football, the 1960 European Cup final has never been surpassed and probably never will. After that, football began to change. It became more expedient, more cynical, more defensive and more coach-bench driven. Ultimately, at its elite level, football was swept into an irreversible spiral of winning at any cost and naked greed. For many, the 1960 European Cup final was 'the last game'.

As we strolled home from Charlie Varga's place, all was quiet and contemplative apart from the odd murmuring of 'what a game'. We all knew that we had seen something special, and not just because Ferenc, our compatriot, had done so well. For me, then 14, the impact was enduring. I was already a well-formed football fan and my deep sense of European-ness would never allow me to deviate from that. But this game and its bewitching spectacle put paid to any hope that I would ever be anything other than a believer in football the true faith, and treat all others who didn't so believeth as anything other than poor infidels. More than ever before, I now understood why football was the game that had conquered the world. Though I didn't realise it at the time, that night spawned the germination of a missionary zeal – a determination to alter the sporting mindset of Australians; a zeal that would spur me on for the rest of my life.

When we got home I slumped straight into bed and swayed

myself to sleep, imagining that I was lining up for Real Madrid, at inside right to Di Stefano's centre forward and Puskás' inside left. That was to be my pre-sleep ritual every night for years to come. (Later in life, I played next to Puskás in an actual game, a kind of belated dream-come-true that so consumed my emotions I surrendered to nerves, a hopeless mess.)

From that point, football became a passion and an obsession. I grabbed every opportunity to watch, study and read about the game, though opportunities were scarce indeed in 1960s Australia. The newspapers covered the local leagues but there was nothing on football at large. This was the era of the great Real Madrid, the Benfica of Eusebio and the great Santos of Pelé. But Australia scarcely knew it. Thankfully, its ABC network did transmit the English FA Cup finals: a diminutive annual window to the big world of the world game; a source of oxygen to keep alive the notion that we were not totally isolated from the rest of the world.

I loved those FA Cup finals, even though I wondered why we were not getting to see the equivalents from other countries like, say, Belgium. In 1961 Tottenham Hotspur, under the management of the great Bill Nicholson, beat Leicester City. I was awestruck by the football. A speedy little winger called Riley kept marauding down the right for Leicester, a chap of profound sporting integrity and a true trier whose honest endeavours were found wanting against the crunching left flank of the Tottenham defence.

The following year, we saw Tottenham play Burnley in the final, Spurs winning handsomely with one of the greatest teams in the annals of English football: Brown-Hopkins, Norman, Baker-Blanchflower, McKay-Medwin, White, Smith, Greaves, Jones.

For the best part of 20 years, the annual FA Cup final and a weekly BBC half-hour called *Saturday Sport*, in which we saw a few minutes of highlights of English first division games, were the only television exposure football received in Australia. The agony of the drought seemed never-ending until SBS, an Australian television network with a strategic bent for football, came along in 1980.

Finding things to read about football was almost as difficult. There was a weekly newspaper called *Soccer World*, started by another Hungarian post-1956 émigré, Marcell Nagy, a former president of the Hungarian football association. Its chief editor was Paul Dean, alias for Andrew Dettre, another Hungarian. Its editor was a Frenchman, Lou Gautier, who later became a lifelong friend. Because it was printed on green newsprint, we called it 'the green paper'. Though it dealt mostly with Australian football it did carry a page of news from abroad. I was the first in line at the local newsagent every Thursday morning when the green paper appeared.

But the most welcome source of reading was a monthly magazine called *World Soccer* which began publication in 1961. It was (and still is) a brilliant journal for those who needed to keep up to date with what was happening in the world game. It dealt with football at large and reading it once a month gave one a broad knowledge of the game's happenings. It was from this magazine that I learned about the great players of the day, the great teams, the great games and the modern tactical trends. I learned about Eusebio, and Coluna, and Sivori, and Garrincha, and Facchetti, and Helmut Haller; about the flying Eagles of Benfica and the dreadfully defensive Helenio Herrera and his Inter Milan. I learned foreign words and phrases like *catenaccio* and *jogo bonito* and *libero* and *hors de combat* and *wundermanschaft*. It was here that I learned about the 'sweeper system' or the 'Swiss bolt' of Karl Rappan, the 'overlapping fullback' and tactical formations like 4-4-4 and 4-3-3.

Many years later, I would be labelled a 'soccer expert', which I have never claimed to be. But if the claim has any validation, my formative 'academia' of such 'expertise' was *World Soccer*. The magazine arrived in Australia by ship and would hit the Australian news-stands some three months after publication. No matter. Reading football news three months late was the only alternative to not reading it at all. I would read the magazine from cover to cover and then read it again, two or three times more. I would bury my head in it on the school bus, or in a hidden corner of the school yard during lunch, rudely brushing away all comers.

Berkeley High was maybe the most multicultural school in all of Australia. Sixty per cent of its 1500 students were of non-English speaking background. The dux of the school in the year that I entered, was Anna Milicic, a petite girl of Serbian parentage with big round eyes and a mop of shiny black hair. From what I heard, she graduated fluent in Latin. The European migrant kids of those days, especially from Central Europe and the Balkans, were the Asian students of today: the hardest working, the most dedicated, the most ambitious, and therefore the best.

Berkeley was one of only two high schools on the south side of Wollongong, a city whose vocational focus was the Port Kembla steelworks, staffed by many thousands of migrants: Italians, Yugoslavs, Maltese, Polish, Germans, Hungarians and, of course, a good quota of English, Scottish, Irish and Welsh.

Berkeley High was my baptism in the challenges that face a migrant child. I entered high school with a less than flattering academic assessment from the teachers at my primary school where I had spent less than six months after arriving in the new country. Because my English was still mediocre and perhaps because I was some kind of social underdog (a non-English speaking migrant), I was thrown into a high school class of low achievers and also-rans. When my father queried this with the school principal, he was told the best I could become, if I stayed in that class, would be a bricklayer or a carpenter (decent trades — but my father wanted me to become a doctor). He was told that there was, however, a way out: if I achieved high enough marks, I could jump to a higher level at the end of each year and graduate into a class that would allow me to gain matriculation to university. So I buckled down to hard work and swotted like there was no tomorrow. At the end of each school year I leapt up a level, ending up in a class, five years later, from where I could gain matriculation and enter the workforce an educated young man, ready to make a success of my fledgling life in this new land.

Amidst all these challenges and the hard sweat, there had to be a diversion and – you guessed it – football was it. Of course there were other distractions, as there tend to be in a co-ed high school. But they were distractions not diversions. And distractions, mostly, tended to land me in trouble. The girls were beautiful and I fell in love with most of them. One, Anna Maria, stole my heart and, had I been a drop less sane, I would never have recovered from it.

In retrospect, it is difficult to fathom how I would ever have got through that difficult period without football and the splendid, serene refuge it provided. Thankfully, and not surprisingly given its ethnic mix, Berkeley High was strong on football. I was immediately picked for the school rep football team although I was not that good a footballer. We newly arrived Europeans were seen as natural soccer players and that automatically qualified me as a selectee. The school physical education (PE) teacher, Mr Wood, doubled as our instructor in woodwork. He knew as much about football as I did about dovetail joints and, thanks to that, I was sufficiently impressive to be selected regularly.

This became the ultimate thrill of my life, my raison d'être. I died for each Thursday, sports day, when I could run out in the colours of Berkeley and be the inside right to Di Stefano and Puskás for an hour and a half. There were no Di Stefanos in our team and I was certainly no Luis Del Sol (the actual inside right to Di Stefano and Puskás). But we did win the regional school championship in my 16th year in 1962, thanks largely to our centre forward, Salvatore Barnaba. We called him Sav. He was, despite his Neapolitan heritage, as white as marble, freckly and red haired, a hereditary throwback to a Gaelic interference with the genetic history of southern Italy. Sav could juggle a cigarette butt for hours and I once saw him in the schoolyard mesmerise several dozen would-be challengers by dribbling and owning a tennis ball, his medium for deceit and laughter, then retiring and walking away when he had had enough. Sav scored the decider in our 1-0 win in the final and became a significant party to my one and only role in a recordable victory of a 'major' tournament.

Sav went on to play for South Coast United, an elite club in what was then Australia's most elite league. But his coach, ex-Blackpool Jimmy Kelly, insisted on 'one touch football' and no dribbling, and Sav succumbed and died as a player of immense potential. His career as a footballer was stunted at 19 and he later became a successful restaurateur. Nowadays I am often asked to be witness to arising young talents who may become World Cup stars for Australia. Alas, I have not seen one as good as Salvatore Barnaba.

Berkeley High is situated on the banks of Lake Illawarra, a huge body of water then encircled by wee suburbs of fibro and weatherboard cottages, mostly inhabited by hard-slogging migrants living out their dreams. Berkeley was a Housing Commission suburb, a community of families whose means did not allow them to buy their own homes at market value. Government assistance meant these people could own their own modest abode in a modest suburb, basically at the same cost as paying rent. It was classically Australian, at least in those days, a way of ensuring that 'new Australians' who were not clever or entrepreneurial enough to compete didn't end up on the streets. We became, in the vernacular, 'housos', moving into our Housing Commission home when I was 13.

Our street ran alongside the expansive school sportsground: two football fields complete with goalposts; 200 metres of grasslands stretching from the school building to the edge of the lake. As we looked out from our front door, the lake was on our right, the school away to our left and opposite, vast flat greenery taunting us to jump the fence and play. All we needed was a ball. So each day we succumbed to the temptation. At the school bell we – my brothers and I – hurried home, dropped our books, donned the boots, grabbed the ball, hurdled the fence and played until it was dark. Andrew was a natural goalkeeper, tall and lean with long arms, decked out splendidly in black. Joe and I were outfield players. We would warm up by tapping the ball to each other, gentle passes to gain accuracy and feel. Then Andrew would take his place between the posts as Joe and I fired in the shots, bullets of stinging venom that would either test Andrew's agility and reflexes or see the ball sail wildly wide into the distance, requiring laborious retrieval. The antidote was better shooting. Practice made perfect and we hammered on until it got better. We would conclude with a miniature game of two against one which, lopsided though it was, satisfied the natural hunger for competition and victory. When it got too dark, we went home to our homework.

This went on every day for years. On weekends the process started in the morning and carried on all day. On occasion other boys joined in, at times many of them, and we had epic games of struggle and fire and shouting.

This was the way of things then. Football was our only diversion and there was no need for any other. In any case, we were too poor to afford other diversions. While other kids engaged in competitive tennis, golf, fishing, water skiing or even sailing on Lake Illawarra, we had our ball and our one-against-two games. It kept us off the streets: we were not part of any gangs, nor did we have the chance to be swayed by temptations of youth like crime, alcohol or drugs. We even missed out on enrolment into organised junior football, which was not a good thing. It meant that our football education was limited and, though we grew up well honed on individual technique because of all that incessant practice with the ball, we knew nothing about team play. Later, when I tried to break into professional football, I realised that this limitation would play a governing role in my failure to become another Puskás.

Overall, though, I can only be thankful for those days, for they guaranteed me an innocent youth and built in me a harmless addiction for football and the purity of sport.

I must have been around 16 when an opportunity did come for me to play real football, with a real team, in real competition. And it was not forced by my talent for the game either, but by my heritage. The Ürge family was basically football mad and, led by my father, it hit upon the idea of forming a football club for the local Hungarian community of Wollongong: a kind of sporting refuge for young Magyar migrants of the area, a healthy weekend outlet – especially for single men – away from the pub and the beer. So, with like-minded others within the community, we formed a club. It was named Pannonia, the Latin name for the Roman province where part of modern Hungary now sits. And I was among the first players to be recruited. We played in all-white except for a thin strip of red and green hooped across the chest, representing the colours of the Hungarian flag. It replicated the outfit in which the Hungarian Olympic team played, the team that won gold at the Helsinki Games of 1952.

It all took off like a grass fire. The community was galvanised. There was a sense of unity among the local Magyars, a new purpose to living life away from the long night shifts at the steelworks. We played and won games. Hundreds gathered around the suburban grounds, cheering and shouting.

As a teenager bubbling with enthusiasm, exuberance and joy, I was having the time of my life. I was playing in uniform with a number on my back, wearing colours not dissimilar to those of Real Madrid, stroking a white ball in front of a noisy crowd. But I knew, even then, that my Hungarian-ness, and not my skills, had most to do with that.

Pannonia died as a club within a couple of years. But by then it had served its purpose: to provide a source of recreational comfort for a small community otherwise stressed by its need to work and struggle while in transition from an old life into a new. Meanwhile football, as a medium of success within that struggle, continued to play a large role in shaping my thinking and my future.

4

The football ghetto

It was around mid-1959 that I first tasted football's real magic and awesome power as a live spectator sport. I was 13. My parents took us to a game at Memorial Park in Corrimal, just north of Wollongong, and we soon realised the significance: one of the teams was Budapest SC (Budapest Sports Club) – a Hungarian team.

The small suburban ground was packed with around 5000 fans, at least half of whom must have been Hungarian. As we joined the milling throng, I was struck by the sound of familiar tones. I knew the game was between the local Corrimal team and Budapest SC, which obviously represented the Hungarian community, but I scarcely expected this many of my kinfolk to be there. It was awesome. I had not seen so many Hungarians in one place since the refugee camps of Austria. Suddenly, and for the first time since arriving in Australia, I felt at home. I was among my mob.

That feeling got even stronger once the game got going. Budapest played in red shirts, white shorts and green socks, the colours of the Magyar national team. From the moment the team emerged from the dressing room, I was an obsessed Budapest fan,

49

an emotional wreck whose very being was governed by whether that team won or lost. They were my boys. Budapest, which later became one of the great clubs in the annals of football in Australia, was vastly outclassed that afternoon by the robust, hard running Corrimal, then a club of immense local tradition and strength. But I didn't see it that way at the time. I thought the referee was a blind clot and a cheat to boot, and Budapest was dreadfully unlucky. Corrimal won 9-2. I had been initiated into the myopic world of the partisan football fan.

The experience of that Sunday afternoon was, on later and more mature reflection, extremely important to me and my family in the process of our assimilation into our new society. This sounds para-doxical, given that what Budapest SC gave me that day, and for many years later as I followed that team, was a sense of belonging not to my new country but to my old. Yet it actually eased and even quickened the assimilation process.

Those who have been immigrants to a new land will understand this. With immigration there is a wide variety of dire difficulties and hostilities. A new migrant is a day-to-day stranger in his chosen land: cold, naked and lonely. He has trouble with the language. He is likely to be in a job with lower status and less dignity than that for which he is qualified (for example, a certified physician or architect might be driving a taxi or working a conveyor belt). He is treated by a pin-head, dumb-ass foreman like an inferior. He is probably discriminated against and spoken down to, and may even be the subject of racism.

It is from these things that migrants need an escape and a refuge, at least momentarily. It is why migrants band together and seek their own friends, their own grocers, butchers, dentists and doctors. It is why so-called ghettos are formed.

Yet, contrary to the myth, such ghettos are generally temporary and are rarely forces of permanent social division. They are merely agents of transition, easing the pains of migration and facilitating assimilation. Once the migrant gains confidence, masters the language and the local customs, and gains acceptance, which might be through a second generation, he moves on. He leaves the ghetto and enters his new society as an equal.

It is in this context that I became a prisoner of Budapest SC. That day in Corrimal I entered the football ghetto. I found warmth and momentary refuge, albeit for a couple of hours a week, away from the cold of the hostilities and challenges I was facing as a spirited immigrant, eager to make the best of the cards I had been dealt. Later, I was accepted and even respected as an Australian of some worth. The boys in red, white and green that day at Memorial Park were a big help and I doubt if it would have happened without them.

But all that was unknown to us then. Budapest SC was just a football team we followed and, boy, did we follow it. By 'we' I mean the entire family, which was very close-knit: We were from a European culture where the sanctity of family unity was everything. We went everywhere and did everything together. Dinner invitations to my parents were a rarity because they would always go with the kids in tow. Potential hosts shied away from welcoming such an intimidating throng, which included three adolescent boys who'd eat the tiles off their roofs.

Budapest SC became the centre of our social world. My mother was the only one who wasn't a congenital football fan. She would have preferred that we stay home for a family lunch on Sunday afternoons. But, adopting the mantra: 'If you can't beat 'em, join 'em', she came to the games instead of staying home to do the ironing. She adopted the fanaticism and became a football expert like the rest of us. Many years later, when I was covering the 1990 World Cup and she was 78, she rang me in Rome and said: 'Tell Azeglio Vicini [the Italy coach] that he's a complete idiot for not selecting Baggio for the semi final.' She was right: Italy lost and Baggio's absence was deemed by the world's pundits to be the cause.

Meanwhile, I lived for the thrill of following Budapest SC. Because the team played in Sydney and we lived in Wollongong, a light year of 70 kilometres away, we couldn't see them every week.

Occasionally, for the big games, we would pack into our tiny car, a Baby Austin, and drive up. Hauling the weight of the family, the engine would invariably overheat on the infamous Bulli Pass, causing an interlude of angry frustration and fraying tempers. The nominal two-hour trip blew out to four hours every time and we would just make it, seconds before kick-off.

The players were my idols. While my school mates got off on Elvis Presley and Bobby Darin, I followed my dreams through Johnny Galambos, Les Schaumann and Frank Lang, young Hungarian boys – part-time footballers – who chased a leather sphere around on weekends as a diversion from laying bricks and concreting kerbs.

They were young refugees, like me, to whom I could relate. And they were good players, or at least better than I could be. Galambos was a running target man, as swift as the wind, who scored goals at will, provided the timing of the last pass was right. Schaumann, a left footer, was a smooth and audacious trickster with impeccable control and a yen for turning opponents into instant fools. Lang was a tall, lithe piece of majesty, strutting about with regal elegance, head up, facing the sky, spraying about passes of slide-rule accuracy and weight.

And despite the naïve times in which we lived, we were subjected to some clever and futuristic marketing. When Budapest SC took the field, each player entered with a football in one hand and a bunch of red and white carnations in the other. Before kick-off they would kick the footballs into the crowd and throw the flowers to the nearest and luckiest onlookers. To a wide-eyed and pimply teenager, this was conquering stuff. I was won over forever. I wonder if today's clever $200,000-a-year marketing brains would ever think of it.

Budapest SC played pretty football, with a bias for supple creativity and art: the kind of football on which I was brought up, the kind which reflected my culture. They were no Real Madrid but they played to the same philosophy. Budapest SC was not just a source of comfort due to its ethnic identity. It was also a mirror of my own chosen football ideology whereby skill and guile, and the style of winning, mattered more than winning itself. The experience of following Budapest SC, like Real vs Eintracht, helped fashion my thinking as to how the beautiful game should be played.

Each migrant group that came to Australia during that mass influx of newcomers made its rich contribution to altering, and in my view bettering, what was before it. In the case of the Hungarians, it was their football, their ambitious business acumen and their sense of bohemia. Note that Hungarians were political – not economic – migrants. The economic migrants that poured in from places like Italy and Greece, and – earlier – Germany and Holland, were mostly from poor regions and country villages, where living standards were meagre and emigration was the only escape route. Political migrants were different, and made a different impact on their new society.

Many Hungarians who took their first jobs on the factory floor or at the wheel of a taxi, soon became practising doctors, engineers and merchants. Recreating their ways of old, they would rendezvous at a cafe over an espresso and debate the ills of the world. But there were no cafes. So they created them. It was the Hungarians, as much if not more than any other migrant community, who triggered the cafe and restaurant culture of Australia's big cities in the late 1950s. As soon as they could muster enough money, they would rent a place on the busy streets of Kings Cross or St Kilda, install an espresso machine and open a cafe. The husband would continue driving his taxi while the wife ran the cafe. The steaming espressos were soon augmented by delicious home-made cakes, then varieties of snacks and, presto, the cafe became a restaurant. Budapest-style bohemia began to arrive in Australia. Their legacies remain. The Gelato Bar on Bondi Beach, admired for its mouth-watering cakes and Hungarian fare, is still one of the strip's most famous spots. The Cosmopolitan in Sydney's Double Bay, probably Australia's first outdoor cafe, is still part-owned by Hungarians: the waiting staff is mostly of Magyar tongue and well-heeled

Hungarians frequent it daily, chatting away in the old language over a short black and a walnut tart. The Twenty One across the street, still Hungarian owned, serves the best wiener schnitzel in Sydney and a glorious matzo dumpling soup.

One such Hungarian noshery was the Oasis restaurant on Sydney's Elizabeth Street, whose excellent chef and proprietor, Gyula *bàcsi* (Uncle Julius), was a football tragic and a mad Budapest SC fan. This was the headquarters of the Magyar football family, where fans of Budapest SC would lunch pre-game and talk feverishly about the team, the selection and whether the coach deserved a knighthood or the immediate sack. The Budapest SC team itself lunched there before each Sunday game. Way back then in the early 1960s, Budapest SC would check its players into a hotel on Fridays and cultivate the brotherhood in preparation for the Sunday afternoon game, culminating with their relaxing pre-game lunch at the Oasis. Such strategic team bonding only became the norm in professional sport in Australia 20 years later. Football, as usual, was ahead of its time.

When we found out about this, we would drive up from Wollongong in time for the lunch, sitting within breathing distance of the players at the Oasis. We were literally stalking them. As we tucked into our veal goulash and nockerls, we snuck gleeful sideways looks at spritely Johnny Warren, and muscular, square-jawed Manfred Schafer, bewildered at how short he was when he appeared so tall on the field. Then we went off to the game to shout ourselves hoarse in support of our boys. Neither Warren nor Schafer were Hungarians. But they may as well have been, for they played and fought for Budapest SC and that meant they were one of us.

Being central European migrants and living in Wollongong in the early 1960s was not easy – as football fans, that is. The local football culture was old, deeply set and long on tradition. The area's district soccer association, the Illawarra SA, was founded in the 1880s. The early games played in the Illawarra were among the first in Australia. Those who played football there were hardy men, mostly coal miners and steel workers. And they played the game according to their own image: rugged and abrasive, fiercely unafraid, with the strength of lions and the smoothness of a horse blanket. This was very different from the dainty, stylish version of the game I had already come to idolise. I remember Bobby Bignell, the captain of Australia's Olympic team in 1956, playing for Corrimal. He was a short, bony man, a warrior with shoulder blades protruding like shark's fins and knees pointed like poisoned arrows. When he tackled you, you ran the risk of being sliced in half.

In retrospect, I recognise the richness of those qualities. But it was not my kind of football. The football of the craggy coal miners and that of my pretty-football culture were ideological opposites. So to support the local team in the then most elite competition in the country ran against my instincts. When professionalism came to the Illawarra, that team was South Coast United, an outfit made up of robust locals and imports of a similar ilk from the lower divisions of England and Scotland. They had good players, like their captain-coach, ex-Blackpool Jimmy Kelly, a sharp-shooting inside left who hailed from Halifax called Graham Barnett, and a young firebrand Aussie striker called Maxie Tolson – who became famous for nearly crippling a goalkeeper but went on to wear Australia's colours in the 1974 World Cup. But they were known as the 'hard runners' of the league and I couldn't support them. Generally, I went for their opponents, most often teams who came down from Sydney playing much more the style of game I admired. The kingpins of that ilk were Budapest SC.

South Coast played at Woonona Oval which was not oval at all. It was rectangular and small, with spectators packed hard against an iron bar fence no more than two metres from the touchlines. Behind one goal was a steep, grassy hill with a building on top sporting a large hoarding advertising a brand of beer. My father, who liked his drink, once climbed up to it thinking it was a pub, only to find that the building housed the dressing rooms; the only liquid available was a bucket-full of water with ice.

On a good day, which was mostly every home game, eight or nine thousand fans would pack the venue and create an electric, buoyant atmosphere. It was one of those grounds where the fans seemed to play a tangible role in the outcome. We attended every one of South Coast's home games but would invariably cheer for the visitors, especially when Budapest SC came to town. One game I recall thrilled us to the bones. Budapest SC came as the underdog, up for the taking and ready to be over-run by the physical torture of the big men of 'the coast'. After a thrilling see-saw battle, rampant with agro, fine goals and incident, Budapest SC won 4-3. One Hungarian fan, who had made the journey in spite of the urge to stay home and sip coffee in Double Bay, muttered: 'Now I have to face the drive back to Sydney. But to hell with it: we won!'

Winning was everything to these people, even though style was at the core of the cause. The experience taught me that in sport, style and nobility alone were not everything. You also had to win. Later, I also learned that winning, on its own, was not everything either.

Following Budapest SC was now engulfing our lives. In late 1963, after I had graduated from high school and turned 18, the family moved to Sydney. My mother, a chic city woman all her life, was thrilled. We boys were too. The big smoke was where it was all happening: night lights, girls and football. There was some resistance from the old man, but in the end he weakened.

What eventually pacified him was a freak opportunity to become a wheel in the inner sanctum of Budapest SC. At the time, there was a vacancy at the club for a gear steward: he who washed the team apparel, making sure the boys were properly outfitted for training and looked their sparkling best for the weekend game. Some bright spark – I don't remember who – pointed his finger at this grey-haired enthusiast, my father, and suddenly we were gear stewards of Budapest SC. By 'we' I mean that my father did little of the work. He supervised and stood back, puffing on a cigarette, and enjoying the 'status'. Most of the work was done by the rest of the family: my mother did the washing and ironing and my younger brother, Joe, ensured that the gear was there, spick and span, in the dressing room at the behest of the players.

There was no remuneration for this, of course. The work was done on the fuel of love for the cause. We, the family, went to extraordinary lengths to ensure that Budapest SC, more than any other team, represented the height of fashion and appearance. The Ürge family would occasionally even pay for the procurement of a complete strip. These were the days when outfitting a team was a major expense for the clubs, long before kit sponsorships. In 1967, when our beloved Budapest won the Grand Final and enjoyed the greatest day in its history, it did so in a splendid all-white outfit, *a la* Real Madrid, totally paid for and donated by the Ürge family.

The equipment, whether for training or the showpiece games, had to look right. In those days teams trained at night, under low, cheap lights with worn leather balls. 'We are working out in candle light with a black ball. How do you expect us to perform in a game?' complained one player more used to professional European conditions. So, to ease the task for the players, we would get out the can of Dulux and the brushes, and paint the balls white. This went on every week, training after training, game after game. This was not the era of Adidas or Nike balls being thrown at the team as promotional trappings. Clubs bought their own balls, and making them look like fresh, genuinely new match-balls was a way of making the team look professional and classy. And it worked. Budapest SC was seen then as the class act of the football establishment.

My brothers and I, despite the wonderful gear steward opportunity and the chance to sniff first-hand the armpit aroma of our idols, joined Budapest SC primarily with the intention of becoming professional players (more about that later). But the club management didn't see us that way. What they saw was a family of wide-eyed Hungarian enthusiasts whose remarkable passions for the team could be harnessed to the team's advantage. Already the Budapest SC management was beginning to age, and agendas were put in place for replenishment. Andrew and I were invited to become committee members. I was to be assistant secretary and Andrew was to be the taker of minutes. I was 18, Andrew was 20. The 'positions' were of nil authority. Andrew and I, shy boys, would go to the meetings on Monday evenings, stay quiet, listen and observe. We were of no consequence and our views mattered not at all.

But it gave us a good early education in football club management. They rabbited on about finances and bottom lines for hours, boring us to tears. But inevitably they would eventually turn to team affairs: whether the coach was a genius or a loser and who should play centre back as opposed to another. This was more exciting stuff. One night there was a full-blown revolt in the committee room. One faction wanted the coach sacked while another felt he was a genius. Expletives were exchanged and ancestries were brought into question before the grey-haired gentlemen settled and came to some sort of compromise agreement.

But the arrangement did not last. Before long, both Andrew and I were out. The reason was my own first flirtation with a vocation that was to shape my professional life many years later: football journalism. My career then, though, was in the medical field, a choice emanating from the results of a high school 'vocational guidance' test which concluded that I had been pre-ordained to be a doctor. Not having parents who could afford to fund a six-year full-time slog in medical school, I chose the cheaper option of a cadetship in medical technology. This meant working by day in pathology labs, gazing down microscopes, counting white cells and examining specimens of faeces, and by night attending classes where we dissected rats and rabbits.

But my dreams had more to do with football and my envy of those who made a living out of it — like players, coaches and football writers. Not being much of a success as a player or a coach, I hit upon the idea of publishing a football magazine. I would be the chief writer. Andrew, who was artistically inclined, would be the designer. A journalist friend, George Kennedy, would be the editor. We got to work and the magazine, *Soccer Illustrated*, was on the streets within weeks. In it, I had a number of articles, including an interview with Lev Yashin, the legendary Russian goalkeeper, the first international football celebrity of many I was to meet. Also in the magazine was an article, written by me, that was mildly critical of Budapest SC. Following the journal's publication, Andrew and I attended our regular Monday night club committee meeting and were pilloried by the members for having the gall, as club management members, to be involved in a magazine that criticised the club. For the first time, the notion of 'conflict of interest' dawned on me. Andrew and I immediately resigned.

The magazine lasted one issue. We knew little about journalism and absolutely nothing about business. *Soccer Illustrated*, like so many other such publications launched by naïve men of football passion, died and left only debts. But it was a good lesson: I never tried such a venture again. Moreover, the Budapest SC conflict and the resignation taught me much about one noble principle of journalism: to have the courage to tell the truth as one sees it and not to have it compromised by personal interest. It would have been easy to retract the article, apologise, abandon a stillborn publication and retain the lofty status of club committee men. But we chose the alternative and to this day I have not regretted the decision.

For all that, our affection for Budapest SC remained. That is the nature of the football beast. We can pick our friends but we have no choice when it comes to our parents, brothers, sisters and our football club. Budapest SC was the greatest source of my youthful joys. Later the Hungarian label, so dear to the club's history, was willingly shed in the name of progress, but to this day, I follow the team through thick and thin, drawing equal measures of pain and laughter every time they play.

The team made the 1967 Grand Final against arch enemy Apia, whose efficient brilliance had twice before steamrolled the Budapest SC ambitions, in 1964 and 1965. And it was going to happen again. By midway through the first half, Apia led 2-0. The game was awash with hate and aggro. Victor Fernandez, a deftly skilful Argentinean, playing for my boys, was floored in a nasty tackle by Cliff Van Blerk, Apia's bony and utterly discomforting right back, the father of the later-to-be-Socceroo, Jason Van Blerk. Johnny Warren, a personal mate of Fernandez, galloped 40 metres across the field to mete out retribution to Van Blerk and decked him with the sweetest of right hooks. The referee, confused, sent off both Van Blerk and Fernandez. Warren survived. With 20 men now on the park, the game opened. Seconds before the half-time break Herbert Stegbauer, an elegant fullback who had no business being where he was, rose to head home a goal and the teams turned with 2-1 to Apia.

The second half was an antithesis of the first. Budapest SC, clad in its regal all-white, not only looked like Real Madrid but played like it. There was the gear, the élan and the style – but there was also hunger and ambition and mongrel. That game again taught me that in football, style and technique – while essential – were naked qualities without the inner drive to compete and fight: that urge to clench the fist and assure a sweet awakening the next day in the knowledge that one has given it his best shot and that there has been no loafing on the job. The boys in white were on fire and, angry at the thought of being done over again, grabbed their chance and galloped into their place as the best team in the land. They scored 4 in the second half to win 5-2. My own hero of the match was David Cliss, a small, boyishly handsome, wavy-haired mid-fielder, once of Chelsea, who conducted the second half reprisal with commanding magnanimity, sweet passes, deft dribbles and lethal finishing. It is with sadness that I write this, given that Cliss is now dead: he died a helpless alcoholic, his body discovered amid squalor in a country caravan park. Vicious is fate when one considers that I am now writing books – and being commissioned to do so – while then I was Cliss' admirer, willing to do anything to swap his place with mine.

After the game my mum and dad, my brothers and I all shed tears of joy. It was 1967, 10 years since our arrival in Australia.

I was 21, but still harbouring a need to prove that my heritage had something to contribute to my new country. Now my team, our team – Budapest SC – had become king and that need was satisfied. I was content.

The ultimate victory went way beyond that 1967 triumph. As events were to prove, the contribution Budapest SC, and my little Magyar community, made to the advancement of football and to its appreciation in Australia was profound.

As one of many migrant community clubs, Budapest SC was the first to recognise a need to blend into the Australian mainstream, to assimilate. So Budapest SC became Budapest-St George and then St George-Budapest and finally just St George. It adopted a Sydney geographic locality that gave it an identity beyond its ethnic heritage. The St George district is probably the most renowned sporting hub in Australia: the conquering home turf of Don Bradman, of Ken Rosewall, and the fabulous rugby league team that won 11 titles on the trot in the 1960s and 1970s. The Hungarian label, so dear to the club's history, was willingly shed in the name of progress.

The leader of this crusade was club president Alex Pongrass, a millionaire Hungarian migrant, who coaxed members into accepting that there was no investment in clinging to ethnic roots, marginalisation and eventual death. In 1967, St George set up liquor-licensed club premises, the first of the migrant-centred football clubs to do so. Till then, it had run its meetings and administration in private homes and the backrooms of restaurants. Now, the 1967 Grand Final win could be celebrated in the team's own home – its citadel of achievement – amongst the poker machines and the tall glasses of beer. The place, in the southern Sydney suburb of Mortdale, was jammed to its ceilings as fans sang and danced. A crusty old gentleman, the St George president before it became 'ethnicised' by the Hungarians, shuffled up to me in the throng and said: 'We have tried for 80 years to achieve this and thanks to you lot we have now done it.' My backbone straightened and I felt immensely proud. I will never forget that moment.

St George continued to pioneer the path of football's future. It imported a coach called Frank Arok from Yugoslavia, the first ever full-time coach in Australia. He was to assemble and build a team that became the most successful in Australia's history. In 1972 the St George team, by then coached by Rale Rasic (who was to coach Australia to the 1974 World Cup finals), went to Tokyo and won a prestigious international tournament. This remains football's best ever international achievement by an Australian club team. That team formed the bulk of the Socceroos team that swept Australia into the World Cup finals of 1974. At various times, as many as nine or 10 St George players were in the Australian squad and when Australia took the field against East Germany in its opening game of the 1974 World Cup finals, five of the 11 were St George players.

Later, St George was the first club to even own, and build, its own stadium. This was another Pongrass vision which sparked the community into action. Hundreds of passionate Magyar football aficionados dug deep into their physical and economic resources to collect bricks and mortar and fashion an arena that was at once modern and comfortable, one owned by football and not borrowed or rented from others.

And then – in 1977 – there was the coup de grâce, the creation of the National Soccer League, the NSL: the first national league of any sport in Australia, thanks once again to St George and even more to the Hungarian influence. It was Alex Pongrass who co-opted his friend Frank Lowy (or was it the other way around?), an even more successful businessman but an equal football nut, into the secret plan that led to the establishment of the league. Lowy was the president of Hakoah, a Jewish-backed club. Pongrass and

Lowy were both of Hungarian Jewish heritage: they spoke and thought in a common language. In 1975, a private meeting took place at the St George club, grandly named Soccer House. Representatives from all of Australia's strongest football clubs were among the invitees. Sir Arthur George, president of the Australian Soccer Federation, knew about the meeting and the plans, but he was a passive player. The enthusiasm for the project was broad, and the political hurdles small and easily overcome by operators as smart and crafty as Pongrass and Lowy. In March 1977, the national league got underway.

Frank Lowy was the NSL's first president. Its chief executive was John Frank, an agile young manager, perhaps not coincidentally also of Hungarian background. Little wonder that the era is recalled as one in which football was being run by the 'Hungarian mafia'. (Even I was a small player, as a budding young commentator on Channel Ten's coverage of the league's inaugural season.)

In its early years, the NSL was buoyant, vibrant and full of promise. But the love affair between the Pongrass/Lowy tandem and the NSL was not to last. The dread of inter-club power politics became too repulsive for both men. Lowy soon resigned, Pongrass severed all ties (though he remained loyal to St George) and even John Frank was soon gone. From there, it was mostly downhill for the much heralded league. Those who took over, it appeared, were more interested in power than football and eventually, though it took 20 years, the league died under its own weight.

It sounds presumptuous, even indecent, to suggest that the league crumbled because it wasn't run by a Magyar clique. What is true, however, is that Pongrass and Lowy were successful men in their own right and didn't need high profile roles in sport. They were immensely pragmatic businessmen but they also had passion. Pongrass continued to channel his passion through his beloved St George while Lowy spent many more years protecting the Jewish cause with his presidency of Hakoah. They were passionate football men of vision. Way back in 1977, they realised that the NSL had to operate under a non-ethnic guise. In an effort to gain marketability and facilitate acceptance by the broad sporting community, they got rid of ethnic sounding club names: Hakoah became Sydney City, Juventus became Adelaide City, Hellas became South Melbourne and so on. The notion was 20 years before its time and probably premature but the vision, none the less, was right. After their departure, the league regressed into football's old ways, the ethnic names reappeared and the game was again rezoned as the exclusive domain of the 'wogs' and their insularism and infighting.

Only St George battled on with its inventiveness. It was a small club with dwindling attendances, but still won two league championships in its 15-year life as part of the NSL, largely thanks to the dynamism and skill of Frank Arok. It embraced enthusiastically the cause of developing players and became an established identity in one of Australia's strongest, and most populous, sporting districts. It was prolific in producing talent and its legacy went on for over a decade after its demise as a prominent club in the early 1990s. It was the first club in Australia to have a legitimate player apprenticeship scheme, modelled on Europe's most developed, and it still has no peer for its vision.

But it all came to a sad end for Australia's pioneering and futuristic club. In 1992, a political manoeuvre saw St George banished from the NSL. The club languished in the lower echelons of regional football and continues to exist as a district community entity with neither resources nor tangible right to return as the predominant football force it once was. The Hungarian ties are now gone. Alex Pongrass is dead, and most of the many thousands of Magyar expats who built the club and the stadium are either in cemeteries or have left football in disillusionment. Soccer House has been sold and redeveloped as apartments. The stadium still stands as a tottering, broken down monument to the dreams of the migrants who got their hands dirty to build it.

Its legacies live, but with painful ironies. As Australian football, again under the leadership of Frank Lowy, begins to live out a bright new life, St George languishes, unremembered, in a regional league. More to the point, it has voluntarily severed itself from its own history. The St George emblem was once composed of a shield split down the middle, with the Australian flag on one side and the Hungarian red, white and green on the other, symbolising the marriage between the host country and the heritage of one of its many migrant groups. The redesigned emblem, a stick man with a halo depicting a saint, crudely dispenses with the memory of the club's Hungarian roots. The club colours are purely red and white – the colours of the district of St George – with not a patch of green anywhere to be seen. This is neither right, necessary nor fair.

Each morning the stadium groundsman, Mishi, awakes, feeds his two Alsatian guard dogs and goes about his business of mowing the grass, tending to the sprinklers and maintaining what is left of the once admired arena. An old Hungarian immigrant who lives in a small apartment within the stadium compound, Mishi has been doing this for 25 years. He and his dogs remain as the solitary link between St George and its roots.

5

Di Stefano, Puskás and me

Let's face it: most of us who have the remotest affectionate association with football are frustrated players. We may be officials, coaches, referees, commentators, football writers or just fans, and be pretty good at what we do. But we would willingly swap places with those who kick the leather regularly and who do it well. For as long as we breathe, we envy those young men – and women, nowadays – who have the gift to be good players. My heroes are not football writers or broadcasters – however brilliant – but people like Di Stefano, Puskás, Pelé, Maradona and Ronaldinho. Even now, to be able to just once execute a Cruyff dribble like the great Johann did, I would trade in my house, my career and even my Eagles DVD.

So we all start off as players, or would-be players; dreamers in love with emulating our playing idols. I was never any great shakes as a player, though I am happy to brag with a smile and a clear conscience that I did play and even got paid for it. The high point of my 'career' was to play for the reserves of my beloved St George. I was the team-mate of people like Joe Pompor, Salvador Isaac, Frank Lang and Joe Vasváry, all of whom I admired as a child but all of whom, from time to time, got left out of the first team and were discarded to 'play with the kids'. I recall one such game – I was 18 – in which I darted into the opposing penalty area, shielded the ball and got floored with a tackle from behind, gaining a penalty. I was swamped by my team-mates. Isaac, a burly Argentinean with muscles on his shoes, gave me an appreciative bear hug that stopped me breathing. From that penalty, we won the game. I was, for many days, as high as a kite.

I literally dreamed of being a player. I was 14 and firmly believed that to be great in this world and in this life one had to be a good footballer. And then I saw Real Madrid beat Eintracht Frankfurt in that European Cup final of 1960, in which Alfredo di Stefano scored three and Ferenc Puskás hit four. That did it. For months afterwards, I went to sleep each night imagining that I was number eight to Di Stefano's number nine and Puskás' number 10. I never considered what had happened to Luis Del Sol, an excellent schemer who played number eight that day in Glasgow. Who cared? I replaced him.

Until I came to Australia at age 11, I had no experience of playing in a proper team. In Europe, certainly in those days, there was no organised junior football at that age level. The talented kids, discovered and hauled off the streets where they had been playing since toddlers, joined elite clubs at 13 and 14 and were coached and fashioned as future stars. That was it: the only avenue for under-age boys to play in an institutionalised way. This stuff of 'under six' tots playing in suburban leagues, complete with Nike gear, a leather ball, goals with nets and a referee with a whistle, was unheard of in Europe then.

The first chance I got to dip into the realm of real playing, where my uniform was distinct from that of the opposing players, was at age 12 with my school, Berkeley High, where, immediately on induction, I was selected in the school rep side. To be honest, I was in and out of the team. It would break my heart when some lazy sod who never came to training would turn up for the game, complete with polished boots, and get selected ahead of me. The option of homicide lingered in my brain. But still, playing as a striker, I managed 22 goals in one particular season, making me top scorer. I don't know how I did it, for this apparently immense potential was never fulfilled.

One of the problems may have been that my parents, protective in their European ways and probably unaware that such things as junior suburban teams existed, never enlisted me or my brothers to play for a Saturday afternoon junior club. Andrew, Joe and I played in the park across the road all through weekends and after school, practising shooting, passing, juggling, dribbling and so on. That was the extent of my pre-pubescent playing education. I never properly got a chance to play in a real team, or have a real coach, before I made my grand attempt to break into the big time at age 16.

That came when Andrew and I were signed up by a local lower-division club team called Wollongong Hellas. It was fun and we both did well. It was a Greek community team and we played in front of large, noisy, passionate crowds who would cramp the touchlines of the tiny suburban grounds on which we played. Andrew was a splendid goalkeeper and saved the team from humiliation a number of times. I played on the left wing and scored a variety of goals. It was a joyous time until, suddenly, it all turned nasty. In a game of particularly high stakes, the referee made a series of mistakes and decisions all of which went against Hellas. The backside fell out of our world. The fans invaded the pitch, we ran for our lives and my last vision of the episode is of the referee being beaten about the posterior with a corner flag.

In the wake of that Hellas collapse, however, there was a chance of reprieve for Andrew and me: Pannonia, then another small ethnic club in the district's lower divisions for whom we had played before, wanted both of us back. We confronted the Hellas president, a young small-business magnate who must have been all of 23, and told him we wanted out. At first, he rejected the notion outright. 'You're not going anywhere,' he said. But we dug in. The scandal of the pitch invasion and the bad headlines threatened our future credibility as players.

To try and sort things out, the Hellas president summoned us for a meeting at a local cafe he owned. He coaxed and massaged us to change our decision as the fried calamari was piled on and the metaxa got poured. But Andrew and I stood our ground. When it became clear that things were non-negotiable, the president looked us in the eye, thumped his fist on the table, and said: 'OK, I will release you. But the transfer fee is £25 for each of you'.

The fee was paid and brother Andrew and I can forever claim that we were once players with prices on our heads. At Pannonia we were coached by the great Rudolf Deményi, a one-time Hungarian international left half, who had settled in Wollongong. It was he who taught me that in heading the ball the power comes from the waist, not the neck. But it was a short stint.

A year later, in late 1963, our family moved to Sydney, settling first in Burwood, then later in Ashfield, and finally in Bondi. Now there might be an opportunity, in the cosmopolitan big smoke, for my talents to be recognised and to blossom. I had trialled earlier for South Coast United, the local big club in Wollongong, but was overlooked. I dismissed that as a case of provincial heathens not knowing a good thing when they saw it. 'The Coast' were not much more than a bunch of hard-running bruisers anyway, I reassured myself, and I was a 'touch' player. I would wait and see what Sydney had to offer.

We made the move in December, off-season and down time for most of the clubs. In those days, the football season began in March and preparation work didn't begin until early January. But one club, Sydney FC Prague, was already in training. This was no surprise. Prague then was the pioneer club on the Australian football landscape. It boasted having the best players, playing the best football and was winning most things.

By way of a family contact, I was invited to take part in their pre-season training. They trained at the ES Marks Field, the headquarters of Sydney football at the time, and one of only a handful of floodlit grounds in the metropolis. My dream was to play for Budapest SC; an opportunity to play for Prague was one I could take or leave. But the chance was there to train with a top team and

I thought I might as well go along.

The Prague coach was Stefan Cambal, who had just been brought in from Czechoslovakia: the first celebrity import coach in Australia's football history. A tall, elegant, multilingual intellectual with receding grey hair and a regal presence, Cambal had impressive history. He had played centre back for the Czechoslovakia team that lost the World Cup final to Italy in 1934. He was educated in the classic central European football school. And he hailed from Bratislava, once an important metropolis in the Austro-Hungarian Empire, and spoke fluent Hungarian.

We had an immediate rapport. And so far as my trial as a player went he appeared to like what he saw. Two weeks after my debut at the Prague training sessions, Cambal pulled me aside in the dressing room and told me he fancied me as a player. He said I was a 'technical player', a Hungarian term for a footballer whose core strengths lay in his skill and ball technique, adding that Prague had to look to young local players of this type as a way of investing in the future, abandoning and replacing the club's historical bent for importing talent.

As I towelled myself off post-shower, he flashed before me a blue contract form. This was a significant thing. In those days there were two ways in which clubs could sign up young players: on a blue form or a white form. The white form meant you were signed as an amateur, registered by the club but allowed to leave whenever you wanted. The blue form was a professional bond which, once signed, tied you to the club forever. An offer on a blue form demonstrated commitment and belief by the club in your abilities and was to be taken seriously.

What flashed before me in that instant was the very real possibility that I could make it as a professional footballer. A seriously qualified third party, Stefan Cambal – an eminent coach – was saying so. This was Prague, the most noble club in the land at the time, and it wanted me: my childhood dream fulfilled. I should have signed there and then and gone off to get seriously drunk on the most expensive champagne.

But I rejected the offer. It would be easy to say now that it was the biggest mistake I ever made. That would imply, however, that I might have made it as another Di Stefano – and I suspect that would be a deceptive retrospective evaluation of my football talents. I had other opportunities later to prove myself – though none as good as the Prague offer – and I failed. Indeed, who is to say that, even if I had signed the blue form for Prague, I would not have been found out later, perhaps by Stefan Cambal himself?

The reason I knocked back Prague was my romantic, adolescent love for Budapest SC: my club. It was always my dream to play for them and I figured that if a club as elite and as well versed in talent-spotting as Prague wanted me, surely I would be a walk-in at the more modest Budapest. I couldn't have been more wrong.

I waited a few more days until Budapest began its pre-season and fronted up for a trial, as did both my brothers. By then, my father had been hired as the club gear steward so we had an in with the club committee, all of whom were Hungarians and, I thought, sympathetic. Brothers Andrew and Joe both trialled as goalkeepers but both missed the cut. The club had an abundance of incumbent keepers in the youth grades and though both my brothers were gifted they never got a look-in. Andrew, in particular, deserved better. He was tall and lean, of a classic goalkeeper's build, with superb reflexes and a tremendous work ethic. But he wore glasses and this was a time before contact lenses. The fear was that his eyesight made him a dangerous choice as a goalkeeper.

I was now the family's only hope of yielding a successful player. I was hired and on a blue form. I was given training gear and, to my even greater astonishment, after my first training session I was handed an envelope with cash in it (as were all the players). I felt on top of the world. I was being paid to play football even before I had played a proper match. Though I wasn't in the first team frame, I trained and mingled with some of my idols: Johnny Warren, Frank Lang, Manfred Schafer and the Argentineans, Victor Fernandez, Hugo Rodriguez and Salvador Isaac.

Isaac, who now lives in Buenos Aires, is still a friend and I visit him every time I get a chance. He was a terrific inspiration. A burly fighter of a player, he saw the raw passion and ambition in this skinny kid and encouraged me at every turn. He told me, 'Be a footballer. Look at me. I made over a thousand pounds this year from playing alone. With this money I'll go back to Argentina, buy a business and make a success of my life.' Which is what he did. Of all the top flight players that I mixed with then, Isaac is the only one who remembers me as a player. It may be a commentary on the memorable spectacle that I must have been, but I am grateful to him anyway.

Sadly, my rags to riches story pretty well ended there. The first problem was that there were no Stefan Cambals at Budapest SC. I soon suspected that I had been contracted out of deference to my father rather than for my exhibited qualities as a new Puskás. The head coach at the club was the late Laurie Hegyes, a Hungarian expat who once had a short spell at Ferencváros, Hungary's greatest and most popular club. But Hegyes had been a hard-running winger with a penchant for arse-up hard work in his playing days and he liked players built in his own image.

I was not one of those. Growing up as an admirer of technically gifted orchestrators, or 'brain players' as the Magyars called them, I naturally tried to mould my style of play in the likeness of the crafty and skilful playmakers. Not for me the stuff of getting stuck in, rolling up the sleeves, working like a coalminer and running like a Zatopek. I was no Pelé, but my ball technique was good and my passes were accurate. In the more modern vernacular, I was not a 'water carrier'. But with Laurie Hegyes, this did not work in my favour. Worse, the youth coach at Budapest at the time – my coach – was Nick Sokoloff, an ex-goalkeeper, a Newcastle-bred Aussie, who built shrines to muscle, naked grit and the type of football that was diametrically opposite to my cultural beliefs.

Even my Hungarian-ness didn't help. After I missed out on selection before one game, an official whispered in my ear: 'Sorry, but we have to be careful about picking you. We don't want to be accused of favouring you because you are Hungarian.'

After two seasons in and out of the Budapest SC reserves, with my morale low and with plenty of other distractions like wine, women and song compensating for my disappointments, I decided that this Budapest thing was leading nowhere. At 21, I abandoned all hope of making it as a successful professional player and began to look for an alternative place where at least I could play, was guaranteed a game and could enjoy my young years as a footballer.

I asked for a clearance from Budapest and was not surprised when my request met with little resistance. I joined Yugal, then a club with a fabulous first team, full of gloriously accomplished players who had migrated from the top echelons of Yugoslav football, but which relied only on imports, made no investment in youth football and fielded utter mediocrity in its lower ranks. Its second and third grade teams perennially finished last. Surely, I thought, I would get a run there. I was right.

For the next two years I had the time of my life. Yugal espoused all the football philosophies and ideologies I believed in. Its head coach was Ferdo Dunaj, an elegant playmaker in his time, classically moulded in the central European academy of the game and who insisted that his ideology permeated down through the ranks of the club. Such as I was, I was welcomed at the club. This was no Prague, there was no Stefan Cambal, the club was poor and it didn't pay players other than its ex-Red Star Belgrade celebrities. But every week I got a game and that is all I was after.

Even at Yugal, though, the door was closed to local youngsters of ambition. If you were not an ex-Yugoslav professional, or a protected friend of a committee man, you had to be satisfied with a run in the reserves and accept your lot as someone there to make up the numbers, a party to the club's requirement to field at least three teams.

In late 1969, as I was turning 24, I made a conscious divorce from my long-held ambition to be a successful footballer. By then I understood that the dream was at an end, that I was getting too long in the tooth to keep on trying and that, while still young, it was wiser for me to try other things. I went on to fashion a life of alternative successes, mostly by accident, but without the slightest regret for having tried to live out my childhood fantasies. My love for football, as a driver of the things that I wanted to do, persisted. I was, obviously, no great shakes as a player but that was a small thing and did little to discourage and dampen my urge to spread the word. There would be other players, better than me, encouraging the Australian populace to embrace the beautiful game.

Many years later, when I was already a recognised television man, someone came up to me in a bar and said: 'I know you. I recognise you.' I stood back, expecting him to prattle on about having seen me on the box. To my surprise, he said: 'I remember you. I saw you playing for St George.'

Of all the comments, positive or negative, over the years from 'people in the street', that exchange stands out.

Playing football, as the millions who do so daily will testify, is one of the great joys of life. It is a simple game that draws no distinction between the short and the tall, the fat and the thin, the young and the old, the male and the female, the rich and the poor. Recently, on a Brazilian beach, I marvelled at two locals tapping a ball to each other, with feet, head and occasionally the shoulders, without the ball touching the ground for 50 minutes. That in itself was perhaps not so remarkable – except that one of them was a woman. You can play football virtually anywhere. When we were kids and there was a storm outside, we would play in our bedrooms. People have played it in deserts, in jungles, on oil rigs and on snow-capped peaks.

Football, for those who have ever dabbled in playing it, has a poisonous magnetism. You see a round ball in a park somewhere and you are charmed immediately by a spell which compels you to abandon all intentions other than to play with it, to caress it, to roll it onto your instep, lift it, juggle it and then, in an act of the ultimate bravura, fire it like a missile at the nearest tree. It is the sweetest of sensations and you don't lose the taste until you die.

Partly, this is because the ball is round. On my daily walks in Sydney's Centennial Park I weave through a maze of football activity. There are football games everywhere, to the right and to the left of me. Occasionally, when I am spotted, someone stops the game and shouts: 'G'day Les!' I wave back and the game resumes. Then I see a muscle-bound tall man with his young son carrying an oval shaped ball. They pass it to each other hand to hand. Then they engage in kicking it. The big guy kicks it to the little guy. The boy mistimes his catch and the ball bounces on, acutely changing direction as it does, bobbling wildly and unpredictably as the boy chases frantically to retrieve it, before the obdurate ball settles dead in the grass. I smile and feel pity. If only that ball was round. Then the kid could have stopped it on his chest and, as it fell, kicked it back to the old man with a sweet half volley. Now that would have been fun. If only they knew.

I still play a bit and, in fact, have never stopped playing. The only difference between how much I played in my 20s and do now is that now I have less time to play. My age and vastly reduced fitness has nothing to do with it. Football, unless you are a professional or play in a competitive environment, has little to do with fitness or age. The skill you learned by playing as a kid never leaves you.

That is why technique – the ability to command the ball with your feet – is so essential in football. If you have that you will play, and partake of the fun of playing, until you can no longer walk.

Despite my dreams, I did not become a Di Stefano or Puskás, nor even a footballing mortal of a much lesser ilk. But I dare to say that I enjoyed playing just as much as they ever did because, insofar as the joy of playing this game is concerned, football poses no discrimination.

6

The meaning of life

The urge to search comes to different people at different times. To some people, it never comes at all. By 'search', I mean a need to find answers to deep questions one has not previously bothered to ask. Early life for humans is usually none too troublesome, so the questions rarely arise. It was certainly carefree for me, despite the potential turmoils presented by poverty, political oppression, being a refugee and the challenges of settling into a new land and a new culture. Children don't worry about that stuff: my two brothers and I had totally happy childhoods. We accepted what we had, never sought any more and enjoyed life with the cards dealt to us. I don't remember any of us ever asking our parents to buy us a bicycle because the kid next door had one. As long as we had a pair of feet and a ball we were happy.

So I have not questioned the wherefores of my existence, asked where my life will lead me and whether it has been worth it all. They are the sorts of questions one asks during a midlife crisis: I never had a midlife crisis. I don't even remember turning 40; that's how insignificant the occasion was to me. My theory is that the reason I was so free of those emotional commotions in my mid years was because my crisis came early, before I turned 18, with the death of Imre Kiss.

Not that everything in the household of my childhood was perfect. My father was an alcoholic and a pretty hopeless one. Not a day went by when he didn't drink and it was rare that he went to bed sober. A common routine was for him to stop off at a pub after work, tipple on for hours with one of his equally beer-soaked Hungarian mates, and bring that mate home in the late hours to continue the merriment. My mother was an excellent self-taught piano player and could play a thousand Hungarian folk songs. So when my father arrived home, with his unexpected guest, the command went out for her to play. My mother, dead tired from having put in a shift as a cleaner in addition to the day's housework, obediently took the stool and played as the two men slurred through their nostalgic dirges until they got tired and we could all go to sleep.

My mother was a classic European wife, vintage early 20th century. As contemptuous as she was of my father's addiction to liquor, and as much as she suffered because of it, she lived with it, accepted it and, for the sake of the children, never contemplated leaving him. She hailed from a time and a culture when the word of the husband was law. She referred to my father as *uram*, Hungarian for 'my lord', an old-fashioned expression even then rarely used in Hungary. She was a dedicated mother, utterly unselfish where the needs of her children were concerned, strong and resolute in her mission to raise her boys happy, healthy and content with life. She was a beautiful woman who dressed and walked with the elegance of Grace Kelly and oozed class from every facet of her being. Yet, in her lot as a migrant trying to make good, she worked as a cleaner by day and cooked, scrubbed and ironed at night in order to fulfil what she saw as her natural responsibility.

Neither of my parents was good with money. Arriving in a country where debt was a way of life, they took full advantage of the opportunities of 'hire purchase', whereby one could buy a house-ful of furniture, a lawn mower and even a car without parting with a penny up front. Within a short time they were so hopelessly buried in debt they may as well have grabbed a rope and hung themselves in order to escape the calamity with a bit of dignity. What saved them was a terrible car accident which nearly killed my mother. Out of the compensation case they received £4000, a mighty sum in the early 1960s, just about enough to buy a house. That paid off the debts and my parents could look ahead again, this time being a little more careful with the sharks who attempted to woo them into the luxury trap of buying on credit. Ironically, that accident saved their lives, as well as teaching their sons a lot about the dangers of financial debt.

It was a turbulent relationship between my parents, and my father was to blame for most of the turbulence. He drank, spent an enormous amount on his habit despite the poverty of his family, and was brutal, even violent, when challenged by my mother. Yet for all that, I had a perverse respect for him. My European upbringing taught me to always respect my elders no matter what their faults. And some of the respect was deserved. I found my father profoundly astute in many things, especially football and politics. He was a brilliant chess player and taught his sons how to play almost before they could walk. He could almost invariably foretell the result of a football match while I, as a naïve dreamer, was hoping for the opposite. As soon as the Vietnam War broke out he condemned it, saying the Americans were stupid, the war was stupid and it would end in calamity. I argued with him then because, after all, we had escaped from communism and surely what the Americans were doing in fighting the red devil was correct. But he was, of course, right. The war went on for another dozen years and it ended in a disastrous defeat for the anti-communist cause. If he were alive today he would have slammed as dumb the invasion of Iraq and, again, he would have been right.

Observing all the family turbulence from the sidelines, but largely unaffected by it, I was a happy teenager. I was in my final year of high school, a good student, strolling along nicely on target for top marks in my matriculation exams. I wanted to be a doctor and, knowing that my parents couldn't afford to put me through medical school, I was shooting for a university scholarship, not an unrealistic goal given my academic record until then. More importantly, I was playing for Pannonia, one of two ethnic Hungarian clubs in the lower divisions of the Illawarra, where I was seen as some kind of promising talent and admired by the few hundred Magyars who encircled the suburban greens where we played each Sunday afternoon.

One of the team-mates I looked up to was a young man called Imre Kiss (pronounced 'kish'). He was tall, splendidly built and handsome, in his late 20s, a good 10 years or so older than me, but experienced and wise. In one training session, he jogged with me as we lapped the field and just chatted to me, showering me with all sorts of advice about what I needed to fix about my game and how I needed to fashion my avenue to greatness. He was always clean, smelled good, and was well dressed: the eyes of the older, attached ladies of the community were always on him. Imre, a right winger and, ironically, a rival for my position in the team, became my role model and my friend.

But he was a lonely man, an immigrant bachelor who lived with his own demons. In this he was not alone. Australia's massive migrant intake of that time had a high proportion of young men, adventurers most of them, who didn't exactly find their paradise in the land of milk and honey. They were foreigners, working in menial jobs, short of family and friends and even shorter of women. The government-sponsored migrant scheme asked for male workers who could lift things and carry Australia forward with their brawn, muscle and ambition. It left to chance their other personal needs, like social companionship and love. Local women shunned them: they were wogs. They worked in the steelworks and went home each day to their empty solitude, wondering whether all the money they were earning through many hours of overtime had been worth it. Maybe it would have been smarter to stay at home in Europe and enjoy the cosy comforts of family, friends and ladies who looked up to them rather than down.

Imre Kiss was one of those. He lived in a lonely flat in Cringila, a hillside suburb hugging the Port Kembla steelworks; so close, in fact, that you almost needed a jackhammer to cut through the choking pollution. One lonely and terrible night he took a rope, made his way up the hill to an abandoned tin shack and hanged himself.

The news hit me like a bomb. How, I asked, could a young man with so much going for him take his own life? How, indeed, could anyone take his own life and surrender the infinite joy of living? These were the questions I began asking and others followed, as query upon query about life and its meaning mounted in my young head. As I searched I gazed into the future, wondering if it was possible that such a dark end was to be my own fate. Was it possible that even someone like me, who got a thrill out of the experience of waking each morning, could be driven by a sense of failure to such depths of despair as to contemplate such utter surrender? Suicide was new to me and, till then, I had thought it was the reserve of the hopeless and the crazy. But as far as I could see, Imre Kiss was neither hopeless nor crazy.

The event, as my mind spiralled into permanent preoccupation, had a profound effect on me and on the rest of my life. It dominated and haunted my soul to the point where I could barely think of anything else. My capacity to concentrate on normal daily activities slumped. My schoolwork suffered and I began to fear that my looming exams would be a catastrophe. My mother, as mothers do, began to see the behavioural changes and knew there was a problem. When I was a small boy she would often catch me gazing out the window deep in thought and say, 'Stop thinking. You think too much. It will get you into trouble.' Now she knew I had been thinking too much again.

We had a talk and I explained to her that the death of Imre had shocked me deeply. Far from my having got over it, it was now growing like a tumour in my brain. She took me to the family GP and explained to the doctor that I had spiritual problems. Spiritual is a soft Hungarian synonym for psychological. The doctor tried his best to cheer me up and gave me a book to read, telling me to come back and see him a week later. Much to my disappointment, the book was a Christian evangelical work which preached that the glory of God was life's real source of joy. Though I was brought up a Catholic, I was never religious and wasn't much of a believer. So I found no solace or conviction in the argument that loving Jesus defined the meaning of life: the book idea didn't work, and I went back to the doctor and told him so. He understood and said, sympathetically: 'Either you have faith or you don't.'

Taking an alternative tack, he explained to me that posing the question, 'What is the meaning of life?' was the stuff of philosophy, and even philosophers did not seem to agree on the answer anyway. He gently admonished me for even pondering such things when life, especially at my age, was so full of joy and promise. He opened the curtains and said, 'Take a look out there.' It was a glorious Australian late spring day, with the sky a vibrant blue, and a big grinning afternoon sun. Birds twittered in the trees, children played and happy people walked the street tending to their daily chores. 'Isn't that beautiful?' he asked. 'What is the meaning of life? Who knows? The answer probably lies somewhere in the subjective for we get out of life mostly what we enjoy in it.'

I went home to think long and hard about what the doctor had said. There was a lot of reflection and consulting of books and wise third parties. In the end, I concluded that life was a gift and it was folly to ask why one had been chosen for the privilege of receiving it. To do so was the impolite act of looking a gift horse in the mouth. Life had been good to me thus far and the future looked even more fun. How silly, then, to allow dark thoughts, driven by not much more than youthful curiosity and self-indulgence, to enter my head and entertain derailment from such a joyride. So I turned my face to the wind, raised a smile and decided that I had to get on with it. Meaning of life? What's it all about? It beat me, and I doubted whether Schiller, Nietzsche, Camus or Sartre had much of an idea either. So I abandoned my search and turned to what I had: my capacity to enjoy living and life. Imre Kiss was dead and, though he was my friend, it was not my place to be preoccupied with the reasons why.

I was lucky, in that I had a buoyant and healthy capacity for curiosity and for enjoying things. I loved nature. I would spend hours following trails of ants in the backyard until I found their nest and would go searching for the queen. I majored in biology in my university entrance exams. I loved history and never read novels; only biographies and accounts of the great and significant turning points in the annals which led to where we are today. I loved music, especially rock and roll which was another major influence on my persona and values in later life.

But above all, I loved football. Of all the things I loved, this was the one to which I could offer the least resistance. If I was to turn this new page, and refuel my soul in the name of moving on, it was, I figured, through football that I had the best chance.

So I surrendered myself totally to it. I had already been a thorough aficionado of the game for many years but now it became a calculated and deliberate obsession. I read, watched and listened to everything that had the barest link to the game and remembered all that I had observed, down to the finest fact and detail. Before long I was a heaving encyclopaedia of football, unchallenged by anyone around me, and I became a kind of community nutter, an eccentric minor celebrity, untouchable and best left alone when it came to arguments on football.

I surmounted the deep trauma – the 'spiritual' upheaval Imre's suicide had plunged me into – and found a new beginning. The brief but troubling eruption of teenage melancholy was over. It was too late to save my exams, which I did pass but only barely. But I gained from the experience. It was there that I learned, for example, that failure is acceptable, at times even beneficial, provided one learns from it. I became more of a thinking young man, now more prone to wanting to find the reasons why and, above all, to be satisfied with nothing less than the truth.

I suppose one could question the sanity of giving oneself totally to something as inconsequential as football. But, as I was later to learn, football is hardly inconsequential. Besides, football turned out to be good to me. Like some divine spiritual guardian, it has protected and rewarded me ever since I chose it: not as a diversion, but as a faith.

7

Flower power and football

I would have loved to pursue a career in football immediately. But that opportunity was not readily forthcoming in early 1960s Australia. Indeed, it is not so readily forthcoming even now. Much like anywhere else, football career openings in those days required one to be a player, a coach or a football reporter. But in Australia, such jobs were desperately rare and low paying and in any case, I had no notable credentials.

So I was resigned to pursuing alternatives. Out of high school, I chose medical technology as my vocation. Why medical technology? Well, this is interesting, even in retrospect. At high school, I was required to undergo one of those vocational guidance tests where you are asked all sorts of mind-paralysing questions related to logic, and have to associate triangles with circles and vice versa. The results showed that I was most suited to a career in medicine. Bottom of the long list of suitabilities, which included carpentry, was journalism. Obviously, the tests were not brilliantly designed, given that my career in the medical game ended up being a short-lived flop and I was later to make a successful living, over decades, as a journalist.

My parents were too poor to fund the six full-time years of university for medicine, so I went into the cheaper option of medical technology. For some years this was my work: wearing a white gown, gazing down microscopes counting monocytes and neutrophils, cross-matching blood for transfusions and preparing bacterial cultures from specimens of urine and stool. In fairness to the profession, it was a most interesting vocation. Perhaps at a different age and with a more fully grown brain I would have appreciated the opportunity and persevered. But this was the mid-1960s and I was still in my teens: young, curious, restless and wild.

More to the point, this was the era of the Beatles and the beginnings of the Vietnam War. John F. Kennedy had not long been assassinated and Martin Luther King was stirring things up in Alabama, preparing to embark on his march on Washington. Cassius Clay had just become world champion and was mouthing all kinds of stuff about black rights. There was a sweet, fresh breeze of awakening blowing through the impressionable minds of the young. Rock and roll was the music of the time but it began to drum to a new beat. The hair on the heads of young men was growing longer.

I knew even then that these things may be generational and the mere by-products of youth. But as the trend hit, it felt somehow different, as though these dramatic changes indicated something beyond mere fashion statement. Nowadays, David Beckham will sport a Mohawk one day, a nude nut the next and by the following week an untidy, spiky mini-mane. But for what? What is he saying, other than that he wants to be different, unique?

In 1964 things were not so shallow. Then, growing your hair was associated with something deeper, deeper even than the accepted adolescent defiance of the norms of the mum-and-dad generation.

Initially, I wasn't conscious of the substance of it all. Indeed, given the circumstances of my upbringing and the political ideologies I had been touched by, I was a conservative and leaned politically to the right. As a refugee from a communist country, I supported America's entry into Vietnam, which I saw as a righteous attempt to erect a wall against the red menace whose tyranny I had seen and experienced. Blow them to hell, I thought. We in the free West could not afford to allow the expansion of the dark Soviet empire.

But my views soon changed, and thank God they did; I could have been one of those dreary, chinless, shallow Tories I now so detest. The change came as a result of my youthful capacity to be receptive to the arguments of others as well as a natural teenage yearning for credibility among my peers.

The defining moment – you guessed it – was football related. It was a small thing, but it changed my mindset about what is right, what is truth and what it means to behave with integrity. I was your standard issue teenage know-all, especially when it came to football. Because I read and observed everything possible in football, and retained most of it, I thought I knew more about the game than anyone, including its well trained coaches, its ex-players and its academics.

After training with St George-Budapest on the outer paddock of Sydney's Wentworth Park, it was routine for some of us to adjourn to a local pub for a cold ale or two. On one such night I got into a wild and irrational pub argument with the club's senior coach, Laurie Hegyes, and a splendid ex-player, Gyuri Kovács. Hegyes had once played for the elite Hungarian club Ferencváros, and St George-Budapest under his coaching was performing well: at that point in upper mid-table, a few points from the lead. Kovács had been an excellent centre half with the club and had recently retired. He hailed from the superb and envied Hungarian football school of the 1950s. Both knew pretty well what they were talking about when it came to football. But I thought I knew more and launched into both men, almost lecturing them about the modern tactical strategies the team should deploy. They argued back for a while before the older Hegyes ran out of patience, put his beer down and calmly reminded me that the egg shells were still on my arse and that I should think about going home to learn to tie my shoe laces before it was past my bedtime. The egg shell reference was an old

Magyar expression deriding youngsters who had barely hatched. Not stopping there, Hegyes went on to counter every argument I made, punching large holes in my foolproof convictions about modern tactics. When he had finished, he turned to Kovács and continued the football discourse as though I wasn't there.

I had been utterly humiliated; shown up as an arrogant young prat, too big for his boots, hell-bent on arguing for the sake of arguing and interested only in big-noting myself. That night I lay awake for hours, flushed, sweaty and embarrassed by it all. Perhaps it was my vanity and pride – but this could not go on. Here I was, engaging in the one subject I loved and knew something about, and I had been taken to the cleaners by two wiser men, having left myself open and naked for the counter-punch by a silly, shallow, adolescent, macho need for recognition.

At some point that night, I decided it was time for a change. If I had stood back and listened to the arguments of Laurie Hegyes, and had chosen to learn from them rather than defy them, maybe I would have been richer for it. Instead, I ended up a humiliated dick with a demonstrably empty agenda.

It was a most liberating experience, a kind of doorway into intellectual nirvana. All things suddenly became crystal clear: in any argument, truth is everything and, unless you have indisputable ownership of it, do not debate – back off, or you run the risk of falling flat on your arse. I slept sweetly for the rest of that night. And every day since then, I have tried to live by those principles. My old values were discarded and replaced by new ones. It was as though I became a new man.

The resonance of the mid-1960s was conducive to a new mindset among the impressionable young and many of us were willingly infected. This period saw the beginnings of 'flower power': a novel suggestion that peace and love were good things; a fashionable dogma that flew in the face of what the big wigs, sitting in their seats of power, thought should shape the world. Humanity was tottering on the brink of oblivion as the nuclear superpowers arm wrestled, threatening to kill us all. The Vietnam War was throttling up a notch. And kids were starting to question why.

Lucio, an old schoolmate from Berkeley, tracked me down and asked me to a party in some basement in Paddington, then still a poor Sydney suburb increasingly attractive to the scruffy and the long-haired. I went along. We drank sweet, fizzy wine and, in the dim light, listened to the melancholy dirge of Leonard Cohen and his signature tune, 'Suzanne'. Lucio had been my best mate at high school: a rosy cheeked, handsome stereotype of the northern Italian with whom I had regularly exchanged ideological convictions at lunchtimes. We didn't always agree, but we liked each other. He was a searcher too, and though his level of idealism had been ahead of mine, now – with the world infected by a sense of questioning and a need for change, coupled with my own new-found urge to find clarity and truth – I was catching up. The night was enlightening. Lucio and I, and a small gathering of young like minds, spent the hours probing, discussing and roundly condemning what the world had become and the political fiends who had taken it there. Violence, racism, inequality, greed, dishonesty, hypocrisy, expediency – all of humanity's sources of stench were identified as symptoms of our world's decadence. We, the young, had to resist and fight; do something about it. This was the music of the 1960s, the new vibration. Almost overnight, I became a willing dancer to its sweet, smiling tune. Lucio and I lost track of each other after that night but its impact stayed with me.

Rage at the Vietnam War was growing louder. The conflict was also coming closer and closer to Australians. A Hungarian friend received a letter from his worried mother, asking if we in Sydney could actually hear the sounds of explosions and gunfire in Indochina. The Prime Minister, Harold Holt, greeted American President Lyndon Baines Johnson in Canberra with the words, 'All the way with LBJ'. Young men and women were being enthusiastically sent to Nam at an accelerating rate, to be sacrificed as expressions of a kowtow to the United States. When demonstrators threw themselves in front of a limo containing Johnson and the New South Wales premier, Robert Askin, Askin instructed the driver to 'Run over the bastards!'

Conscription was introduced whereby men at age 20 – my age – were thrown into a lottery of doom. Luckily for me, my birth date wasn't drawn. I wonder now what I would have done had I been called up. I hope I would have gallantly defied the call and stood my ground as a conscientious objector, risking jail. But I don't know. All I know is that the idea of bearing arms for a cause I didn't believe in ran against my instincts and I am grateful that I didn't have to make the choice.

By 1968 the war was truly on the nose and was dividing the nation between the old and the young. The generation gap was not a new phenomenon and exists today as much as it ever did. But I believe it was never as wide as in the late 1960s, due largely to the obscenity of the escalating conflict. People began to march. I marched, too, down Sydney's George Street, in moratorium marches: silent and peaceful demonstrations inspired by the example of Martin Luther King but even more by the steadfast conviction of the young that peace and harmony could only be achieved by peaceful means.

I proudly sported a moratorium badge and, after one lunchtime march, returned to the office smiling, content that I had done my day's duty for humanity and maybe hammered a nail in the coffin of the pigs who were sending my mates to their gruesome deaths in Vietnam. I can only asume that my boss saw the badge as proof of being a traitor to the national cause because I was transferred the next day.

The spirit of the '60s, for all its caricatured fashions, its dope smoking and its unwashed scruffiness, shaped my values and my ideologies. Today's X-Generation largely treats the era with flippant disdain but it was the '60s generation that spawned the legislated social justice we now enjoy: human rights, racial equality, gender equality, the rights of the handicapped and so on. It also led to obtuse political correctness, which I regret, for I find Orwellian oppression of thought objectionable and offensive. But overall, the children of the '60s changed the world for the better and I consider myself extremely fortunate to have lived through that era of enlightenment. Just before beginning to write this book I went to see a revival of the '60s rock musical *Hair* and choked at the commanding truth of it. My two daughters were with me and I felt doubly touched that, without much coaxing from me, they understood.

The ultimate companion to the young in those times was rock and roll. I loved it; still do. Nothing substitutes for rock and roll as an oxygen for freedom and pounding defiance. My youth spanned the eras of Little Richard to The Eagles. There has, surely, been no other epoch in music that had such a bearing on human development and social consciousness. Why else would mega rock concerts, devised by Bob Geldof and others, remain as rallying forces for giving the world a wake-up call about its responsibilities on poverty, misery and injustice?

As an active rock and roller, I fell into show business by accident: the thought of a stage career, though mostly covert, was never far from my mind. Applause and public acknowledgment are intoxicating drugs. Whatever talent I had I inherited from my mother, a gifted performer in her youth. But she saw me as an actor, maybe a future John Barrymore or Laurence Olivier. Music was not in the picture.

It was the age of Elvis Presley and pretty-boy pop idols like Jimmy Darren, Fabian, Paul Anka, Bobby Darin, Dion, Frankie Avalon and Bobby Rydell. There was a movie titled *Sing Boy Sing*, starring a James Dean-like hunk called Tommy Sands. I went to see it over and over again. It told a sad story of a teenage superstar, idolised and rich but miserable, caught in the trappings of being a pop celebrity, unable to escape the grip of commercial exploitation, devoid of a private life, love and essential civilian freedoms. The film remained with me as an education; a warning against the temptations of the 'star trap' and how such blessings can be destructive, dark and debilitating. Later, when I became a public figure, I drew from the experience to temper my instincts to operate on the fuel of ego and vanity and run the risk of suffocating the real joys I was seeking in life.

At the time, though, it didn't stop me from wanting to taste the sweet smell of stage success. At Berkeley High, at an-end-of-year 'social', a classmate took to the stage and sang 'Venus', a hit song by Frankie Avalon, then in vogue. I was in awe. The girls, all so dollied and pretty, looked on wide-eyed and screamed. Quietly and enviously, I wished it was me on stage. It occurred to me then that the pursuit of a career in pop music might be fun and a good thing.

In my teens, someone told me I had a good singing voice. So in my early 20s, I took some singing lessons with a view to trying my hand at a career in cabaret, singing not rock and roll but the material of Sinatra, Al Martino and Matt Munro. Later, someone else said he knew of a working rock band that needed a singer and suggested I audition. I did, got the gig, and began a career – not of stardom or any kind of fame – but of utter personal exhilaration and joy. Nothing else, including the labour of love I now enjoy, has been such a source of sheer fun.

The band was called The Rubber Band, a six-piece with the classic line-up of lead and rhythm guitars, bass, drums and two singers, one male and one female. People still laugh at the name but I thought it clever. Its virtues were explained to me by the band's manager, Richard Debenham, who told me the best choice of name for a band is one that is easiest to remember.

The band members were all ex-high school classmates from Sydney's western suburbs. It was a part-time 'commercial rock band' doing 'covers': nothing original; only known hits replicated as faithfully as possible on stage – a healthy medium for having fun and making decent money on the side. It played Beatles, Stones, Motown, Atlantic Soul and anything the audience could dance to and hum along with. 'Gloria' by Van Morrison's Them and 'Running Bear', a poppy piece of 60s pap with a solid, driving beat, were huge with the semi-inebriated audiences. But, to be fair, we did some better stuff than that. The Beatles' 'Get Back' and 'Hey Jude', 'Proud Mary' by Creedence and McLean's 'American Pie' were other favourites in a repertoire of around 80 songs.

At the time, I lived at Bondi Beach and had to trek 25 kilometres west every Saturday afternoon to Rooty Hill where, in the rural isolation of a corrugated iron shed, we could practise to our heart's content and as loudly as we liked. The first song I rehearsed with the band was a hit called 'Soul Deep' by the Box Tops. Then there was 'Natural Born Woman' by Humble Pie and, upping the ante, 'Aquarius' from the musical *Hair*. With those three songs I made my debut with the band in Camperdown, in Sydney's inner west. The gig was attended by a horde of cute nurses from the nearby Royal Prince Alfred Hospital where, ironically, I had spent some years as a trainee medical technologist.

I spent four years as lead singer of The Rubber Band and another two with a similar band called Portrait: six years a musician – the most enjoyable period of my life.

For all the time I spent in hippiedom and rock and roll at a very impressionable age, I am relieved that I never succumbed to the temptation of drugs. There was plenty of it around, of course – mostly marijuana – and I did dabble in the weed. Late-night parties in 1969 would not have been parties if not held in crowded apartments or terrace houses dimly lit in red, with the haze of pot distorting the clarity of vision and mind. I had the odd drag from the odd joint, inhaling with gusto, and even got high. But I found pot's mind-altering effects, and the silly giggles it provoked, childish and undignifying. So I stopped dabbling. As a cigarette smoker and one with a taste for alcohol, not to mention women and football, I figure I had enough vices.

Indeed, the preponderance of drug taking by rockers was a huge mystery to me even then. Rock was such a sweet source of joy – so exciting, such a natural high – that I have never understood the need for and vulnerability to drugs by rock musicians.

But for the drug of rock and roll I will forever be grateful. I was a professional rocker from 1968 to 1974, and got addicted to its awesome energy, its numbing rhythms, its sweet melancholy and its penetrating messages. I loved its humble, working class mini-malism and its capacity to touch the hearts of all people. Just as football is the game of the people, rock is the music of the people – which might explain why I fell in love with both at first contact.

Moreover, in the era in which I began to truly engage with music, rock matured from being music sung by teenagers for teenagers to something more serious, complex and provocative. Propelled by the intense political concerns of the 1960s – the threat of a nuclear holocaust and the Vietnam War – rock became the language of protest and rebellion. It became youth-speak for in-your-face defiance and the impatient seeking of wisdom and truth. Music was off the leash, elusive to authority and the forces of social control. I found myself on stage not just a bopper, but a mouth-piece for change and the protection of ideals. To paraphrase Bob Dylan, something was happening and we didn't know what it was.

I was never a true political animal: the thought of engaging actively in politics – being part of its expedient lies – was, and still is, repugnant to me. But I am pleased that I lived through an era of profound political change, and was part of what I would call a 'good generation'. Its education left an indelible imprint on my values and persona: even at 60, I have not retreated from them. And rock and roll, as the fuel of the spirit of my youth, is responsible.

In the mid-1970s, just as I was stepping away from being a bum singer, football remained a strong influence on me. And football was an adequate opium alternative to what I was giving up. The period was certainly a zenith for the game in Australia, although its promise turned out to be empty. In late 1969 I watched on the edge of my seat at the old Sydney Sports Ground as Australia played Israel in its final World Cup qualifier. The prize was being part of

Mexico '70 which became, according to many, the greatest World Cup of all time.

Four years earlier Australia, yet to be baptised the Socceroos, had been annihilated by North Korea in neutral Cambodia 6-1 and 3-1 over two matches. It had been Australia's first-ever tilt at the World Cup which, by then, was a tournament already 35 years old. The score lines were a commentary on how late Australia had left its run as a country of any ambition in football. North Korea went on to become one of the great romantic stories in the annals of the World Cup, eliminating Italy and leading Portugal 3-0 before succumbing 5-3 to the powers of Eusebio in the quarter finals.

But lessons were learned by Australia and the level of ambition was ratcheted up. Now there was some serious preparation and even planning. Joe Vlasits, 'Uncle Joe' to the players, was appointed national coach. Vlasits, a sweet and affable man, was part of the 'Hungarian mafia'. He, along with another Magyar, Denis Adrigan, were among the leading lights in Australian coaching at the time. They led the formation of the Australian Soccer Coaches Federation, a means of giving coaches a voice and a role in lifting Australia's technical development. This was still an era when Hungary and the football of central Europe had eminent standing in the world, and the knowledge of men like Adrigan and Vlasits was respected.

Yet the opportunity of seeing Australia play was rare. Of the 26 matches Australia played between 1967 and 1969, only seven were played at home. In the chase for a place in the 1970 World Cup the team played eight games, all away from home, before the final cruncher against Israel came in Sydney. In those days there was zero television coverage of Australia's away matches. No wonder we were ravenous, by 1969, for a glimpse of the team and a chance to barrack them on. Australia lost the first leg in Tel Aviv 1-0, courtesy of an own goal. Now it was, in the first of a long series of similar World Cup experiences for the Socceroos, down to the last home qualifier. George Keith, in the past an utterly reliable fullback, gifted a clearance to Mordechai Shpigler, Israel's demi god of a player – its own Johnny Warren, who pounced and scored with ease. The towering Aussie talent, Johnny Watkiss, pulled one back for Australia, but it was too late. We were out.

I use the word 'we' deliberately. After 12 years in Australia, immersed in what the locals considered the 'foreigners' game' or 'wogball', this was the first time my heart truly thumped for my new country. And I daresay it would have been much the same for everybody in the stadium, packed to its capacity of 33,000. Scanning the stands and the milling throng, you could have played a game of 'spot the Aussie'. Apart from a small handful, the crowd was exclusively migrant, or 'wog' – like me. It was multiculturalism a decade before the word became fashionable: all the colours of the rainbow, personified and gathered in one place. Yet we all cheered passionately for Australia and went into pathological distress after the final whistle.

Many do not realise this: the migrant community, through the 1960s, '70s and even '80s, worked passionately and tirelessly at football, all the time dreaming that – one day – the natives would take to it, see its beauties and embrace it like they and their fore-fathers had been doing for a century. But dreaming wasn't enough. The people who ran the game in the mid-60s hit upon the idea that the way to realise the dream was to woo native-born Australians and unify them under the national flag. The way to achieve this was to field a successful national team and steer it into the World Cup finals. Those who came up with this thesis – football's governors at the time – were all first generation immigrants: Greeks, Hungarians, Czechs, Dutch, Italians. In the high levels of football governance, none was Australian born. People forget this. They forget that the seeds of bringing glory to Australia in the world's most important sport were sewn by 'wogs'.

There were lessons to be learned from 1969, too. And we who streamed out of the Sydney Sports Ground that day, our chins brushing the gravel, knew that the effort would be upped for the next attempt. And it was. The simpatico Uncle Joe Vlasits was jetti-soned as national coach. A largely unknown young man, still in his early 30s, called Zvonimir Rasic – or Rale Rasic to his mates – was appointed to take over. I remember being surprised. For a start, Rasic was from Melbourne. In those days, in all sports and in all senses, the distance between Sydney and Melbourne was vast. Sydney people were suspicious of Melbournites and vice versa. There was no exchange of sporting cultures between the two centres: we may as well have been on different planets. To those of us in Sydney, Rasic was an unknown.

We found out that Rasic, a player imported from Yugoslavia, had been a rugged and expedient right fullback, a Balkan who took no prisoners but knew how to pass the ball once his defensive chores had been completed. On retirement as a player he had some success as a coach in the Victorian State league; he was ambitious and a man of promise. His selection as national coach proved to be a master stroke.

Rasic was tall and regal, handsome, smooth and intelligent. For such a young man, he had an uncanny gift for words of wisdom. His English was not perfect but he had mastered enough of it to be able to impress and sway those who listened. Soon he was seen as a man fluent in the language of modern football, a new age European who was going to bring a telling change to our game and, in parti-cular, the fortunes of our national team. He kicked off his term with a bang, winning his first five games in charge, which included beating Iran, Israel and Greece away from home. That game against Greece had its own place in history: it was the first time Australia had ever beaten a European nation on its own soil.

Though we didn't see Rasic's team play too often at home, it was clear that he was fashioning a formidable outfit. Of course, he had some advantages, among them the opportunity to test his team. In the first two years of his tenure, the Socceroos played no less than 18 games, in vast contrast to what national coaches are afforded these days, when an entire year can pass (as it did in 1999) with-out the national team playing a single game. Rasic's second big advantage, in comparison with his successors, is that all his chosen players played and lived in Australia; he could call on any of them whenever he wished, whether it was for a qualifier against South Korea or a friendly against New Caledonia. In the early '70s, the club versus country annoyance was very much a thing of the future. And his third advantage – perhaps his biggest – was that the World Cup path was, with the exception of New Zealand, entirely through Asia. Some of the games were undoubtedly tough and dangerous, such as those against the Koreans and Iran. But there was no Scotland, Argentina or Uruguay standing in the way of the Socceroos achieving their dream, and Rale Rasic becoming a superstar in the annals of Australian sport.

As Rasic's fortunes were rising around 1971, I was in my mid-20s, a rock singer and a nobody in football. But I did get to know him. As a former committee man and player on the books of St George-Budapest, I still hovered around the team a lot. I did the club's PA announcements at its home games at Hurstville Oval. My father was still the club gear steward, my mother still washed the players' gear and my brother Joe – doing my father's work – was ever present in the dressing rooms. I found Rasic a man to be respected, maybe because of my European background, where just about anyone older than oneself is a man to be respected. I called him 'mester', the Hungarian for 'master': the label by which all players in Hungary call the coach. He, also a European, appreciated that.

Rasic was coaching St George, a superb squad he inherited from Frank Arok who had returned to Yugoslavia after two years revital-ising and rebuilding the club from its disastrous 1968 season, when it finished second last in the league. Under Rasic, the team won its domestic title and went on, in 1971, to bag the trophy in an international four-team tournament in Tokyo that included the Japanese national team and the champion club of Denmark. It was the finest achievement ever by an Australian club team in the inter-national arena to this day. When Rale Rasic picked his Socceroos squad to take to the 1974 World Cup finals in Germany, seven of the players were from St George.

It was under those circumstances that I first made the acquaintance of Rale Rasic in 1973. He was a high-flying, champion club coach, and at the same time was leading the Socceroos in what was to be a momentous conquest in the World Cup; I was an ardent young football fan and sometime club player.

Today, the Australian public responds more readily to football names like Kewell and Viduka, but there is no denying that until those two came along the two biggest names in the Australian game's history were Johnny Warren and Rale Rasic. And that in itself has its ironies.

When Rasic took over the national team, Johnny Warren, just 26, was the most revered figure in Australian football. He was the youthful captain of the Socceroos, a personable, boyish, handsome warrior for the national cause and the underdog game. The diminutive label 'Johnny', with which he was stuck until his death at the age of 60, was emblematic of the era in which he emerged as a teenager. His family – his mum and dad and his two brothers – never referred to him as Johnny. To them, he was just John. He first came to prominence in the late 1950s, the age of surging pop culture and teenage empowerment. Almost every teenage pop star of that era had a first name ending with 'y' or 'ie'. Johnny, Jimmy, Eddie, Frankie, Bobby: the pop world was a gallery of pubescent boys who we thought would never grow up, and at the sight of whom pubescent girls screamed hysterically. Johnny Warren somehow permeated this set, or at least became vulnerable to the notion that he was one of them: a pop star. And in the confines of the football demographic of the time, that's exactly what he was.

He emerged as a gem of a talent while playing for Canterbury as a 16-year-old in 1959. These were the so-called 'Canterbury Babes', a label that should be explained in the context of the times. It was just two years since the game's immigrant missionaries had wrestled control of the sport from the short-back-and-siders who ran it before them, and formed the breakaway Australian Soccer Federation. What they brought in was dominance and ownership of the game by first generation immigrants. According to the incumbent bystanders and gruff natives, who resented the takeover, the 'wogs had hijacked the game'. What they forgot was that the game was going nowhere as things were, and the 'takeover' was in fact a rescue of a sport doomed to take fifth place in the ranks of our sporting culture. The game was now booming but dominated by the migrant factor: migrant community clubs, migrant officials and, above all, migrant players of considerable technical excellence.

In 1961, clubs like Prague and Hakoah dominated, thanks largely to well-paid imports funded by runaway rich new immigrant backers. It was against this trend that Canterbury emerged as a successful district club, with Aussie-bred young players, mostly teenagers and defiantly able to challenge the forces of imported proficiency: hence the name, 'Canterbury Babes'. Canterbury won the 1961 NSW Grand Final, the most elite football accomplishment in the land.

Warren was a refreshing and convenient focus for home pride: he was Australian, a true blue of several generations. His iconic status was unchallengeable and grew over the next ten years. And then he got injured. In an accidental clash in a club game with FC Prague's Argentine import, Raúl Blanco, Warren tore a cruciate ligament in his knee. That he was out of the game for only two years was a testament to the skills of his surgeon and Warren's own indomitable courage. In those days, such an injury would have spelt career's end for any other man. While still in recuperation, Warren accepted an invitation to Malaysia to attend a FIFA coaching course conducted by Dettmar Cramer, then probably the world's most acknowledged football educator (and later to win the European Cup with Bayern Munich). Warren became dux of the course and remained till his death Australia's most highly credentialed coach.

As Warren continued to grapple with the pains of recovery and the pressures of doubt that hovered over his future as a player, Frank Arok was back at the helm of St George. It was he who was most instrumental in swaying Warren not to give up and to continue chasing his dream. Warren duly recovered, regained

dazzling form at club level and, back to his best, was re-selected by
Rasic for the national team.

But he did not regain the captaincy of his beloved Socceroos. In
Warren's absence, Rasic gave the arm band to Peter Wilson, a
splendid, rugged centre half with a commanding presence, long
blond hair and an Emilio Zapata moustache. No one could have
been more different from Johnny Warren. Wilson hailed from York-
shire and his main gig was working the pits of the coal mines in
south coast New South Wales. To me he was dour and unexciting,
and spoke with a thick 'ee by goom, mah boom's noomb' accent,
offering one-word answers at press conferences. With Wilson, the
role of the Socceroo captain as a powerful public spokesman for
football and the team – once so brilliantly performed by Warren –
had been made redundant.

In my view, not reappointing Warren as captain – whether deliberate and conspiratorial or just a case of misjudgment – was a huge
mistake. Rasic got it wrong. In the short but euphoric period of the
team's involvement in the World Cup, having Johnny Warren as
the much-loved and media savvy captain of the team would have
been a godsend for football; a major marketing plus for the game.
With Wilson as captain, that opportunity was lost. Later events
emphasised and confirmed the vast difference between the two men
in terms of their dedication to football. For the ensuing 31 years
until his death, Johnny Warren remained a tireless, selfless and
articulate missionary for football, maintaining both his rage and
his status as an icon of Australian sport. By contrast, in the late '70s
Wilson retired from playing and disappeared back to the mine
pits, a Harley-Davidson-riding recluse. He never re-emerged, even
to participate in the odd nostalgic celebration of 1974 with his
adoring team-mates.

There are those who believe that Rale Rasic declined to reappoint Johnny Warren as captain because he feared Warren's elite
profile as a threat to his own. Rasic then was a celebrity and a hero.
The media hung on his every word. He was courted by politicians
and showbiz celebrities. He was working the celebrity speaker

circuit. As he puts it, even today he could have a coffee and a sandwich anywhere free of charge, so much was he revered as a hero of the nation. Why would he, as the theory goes, reappoint Johnny Warren, an incumbent superhero, as captain when he – Rasic – was already perceived as the singular champion of the national cause?

For all that, Rasic was an excellent coach and drove Australia's campaign to make it into the World Cup finals with aplomb and cunning wisdom. He was the ethnic Balkan with an adopted but engrossing passion for his new country and a deep, instinctive understanding of what made his native charges tick. Ray Baartz, in one particular game, had an off first half. Rasic eyeballed him at half time and said: 'I am a Yugoslav, just a hired hand with an accent trying to help out this country. I don't matter much. But you are a dinky-di Australian, a true blue, a local hero from whom your country expects. So are you going to respond and do the right thing by your country or are you going to capitulate like a wimp?' Baartz went on to play the second half of his life.

Rasic understood the one weakness of the Australian players: their macho yen to be strong and tough, to rise, suffer and overcome, not to be weak. And he played on it. He packed his teams with a dynamic mixture of imported skill, tempered by the grunge and mongrel of the Anglo-Australian spirit. Players of sublime ability, sharpness and cunning like Atti Abonyi, Doug Utjesenovic, Branko Buljevic, Noddy Alston and the wee Scotsman, Jimmy Rooney, were married with the muscle and grit of Manfred Schafer, Peter Wilson and Col Curran, and bonded with the leadership qualities of Johnny Warren and Ray Richards. The greatest of Rasic's gifts, in my view, was his ability to read the mentalities of these players and stir such a multicultural mix of part-timers into a winning team unit.

This was 1973. Not long before, Gough Whitlam had been elected Australia's first Labor prime minister in more than two decades. With the soccer electorate, most of them working class migrants who saw themselves as underdogs, he was immensely popular. The president of the Australian Soccer Federation (ASF),

Sir Arthur George, was ambitious and shot high. He invited
Whitlam to the World Cup qualifier against Iraq in April of that
year. Never before had an incumbent Australian prime minister
attended a football match in an official capacity. To Sir Arthur's
shock Whitlam accepted, with the one proviso: that before kick-
off, the Australian 'anthem' would be not 'God Save the Queen' but
'Advance Australia Fair'. It was intended as a statement by the
forward looking and fiercely independent Whitlam who had an
agenda to wrest Australia away from its meek, colonial mentality:
'Advance Australia Fair' did not become Australia's official national
anthem until a decade later. Sir Arthur obliged and it proved a
most popular decision. When Whitlam was introduced at the
game, the crowd – most of whom were non-British immigrants –
roared its approval.

   Gough Whitlam, an instinctive revolutionary who seemingly
could do no wrong in that early, euphoric phase of his prime minis-
tership, extended his spell to football. In his period in office,
Australia qualified for the World Cup for the first time. This was
historically fitting, for it was during the Whitlam years that
Australians began to truly and unashamedly believe that it was cool
to be Australian. After Whitlam was ousted in 1975 by Governor-
General Sir John Kerr, revisionist conservatism returned to
Australian politics. And the Socceroos succumbed to a state of
colonial mediocrity; they lost their way as a team with the capabil-
ity and self-belief to make it again to the world's top stage.

   In 1973, qualification for the World Cup was a wondrous thing.
At the time, we football fans thought it would be some kind of
pathway to tangible and broad appreciation of our game by
Australian sporting society. But that was not to be: though we got
there, we did bugger all once we did. I watched the 1974 World
Cup on television and it was then that I formed my greatest criticism of Rasic: that he was conservative and seemed to lack courage.
When it came to facing highly reputed, classy opposition, I
thought he exuded fear: the kind of fear that, in sport, was decidedly un-Australian. In that World Cup Australia lost 2-0 to East

Germany, 3-0 to West Germany and drew 0-0 with Chile in a game ruined by torrential rain. Who knows what might have been had the heavens not opened in Berlin that day. In any case, it was too late: Australia was already out.

The Australians came home with their reputations superficially intact. After all, this was a team of semi-amateur players and, having conceded just five goals in three matches against some of the best in the world, as the king of Australian soccer clichés went: we were not disgraced. True, we weren't. The 16-team 1974 World Cup finals paraded just three countries from football's Third World: Haiti, Zaire and Australia. Both Haiti and Zaire, silly and tactically naïve, were walloped and humiliated; Australia was not. But my healthy sense of youthful idealism at the time told me we should have done more. I felt the team had been sent out with a mission only to contain the likely damage, rather than with a determination to win. The numbers stacked up to back this. True: Australia only conceded five goals. But also true: it scored none. This, to me as an Australian, was not good enough. I remain convinced that the Socceroos of 1974, had they been sent out to have a go, may have done more to leave a legacy of substance for the enhancement of football in our culture. In my view, the grand opportunity of the 1974 World Cup – to qualify for it and play in it – was probably squandered because it left no tangible mark on the game's broader advancement.

I realise that Rale Rasic felt he had valid reasons for choosing tactics of safety. After all, who could blame him for wanting to ensure that Australia's part-timers weren't humiliated in such an elite, worldly contest? But Australians hate to lose and, more than that, they hate to lose by not having a go. I am unsure if Rale Rasic, a European with a European approach to what is seen as a 'good result', understood that at the time. Perhaps this is what Johnny Warren meant when, 30 years on – just before his death – he passionately espoused the notion that we should not be so obsessed with qualifying for the World Cup as we should be with winning it. Surely that, Warren implied, is what Australia expects, as it does in every other sport. Put into that context, 1974 was not a success.

But to say that it was a failure would be harsh: the 1970s were a different era to the 2000s. Australia now has millionaire players who play for millionaire clubs: for whom to go well beyond just qualifying for a World Cup is a reasonable expectation. Unfortunately, because qualifying in 1974 has been Australia's highest ever achievement in football, we are still content with trying to duplicate it, whereas in any other sport we would demand and expect more.

Long before 1974, I had begun to formulate doubts and worries about the beauties of football. The sweet game of attack, creativity, bravado and tender innocence I had been poisoned by was already changing in the mid-60s. The purity of Hampden and the 1960 European Cup final was gone. It was the age of *Catenaccio*, a tactical philosophy of defensive expediency, whereby – more than ever before – the result meant more than the manner of achieving it. Inter Milan won the European Cup in 1963 and 1964 by such methods. Then came the worst of it: the World Cup of 1966. It was the first World Cup that was covered to any degree on Australian television. Courtesy of the ABC, we saw the two semi finals and the final. In one semi Germany beat the USSR, a game in which muscle and manhood triumphed over technique and creative substance. Then, in the other semi, England beat Portugal by similar means. The man who, for me, was the player of the tournament – Portugal's Eusebio – was intimidated out of the game by a bony, toothless executioner called Nobby Styles, and England advanced to the final. This, to me, was bad news, not because England made it but because Portugal, and especially Eusebio, did not. It was 'anti-football'. Romance, as an essence of football, was beginning to die.

England and Germany threw up a superb and thrilling final which went into extra time, England winning 4-2 after 120 minutes of unparalleled theatre. But it was not my kind of football. After the tournament, Eric Batty, an Englishman and my favourite columnist at the time, wrote in *World Soccer* a four-page post mortem titled: 'It was such a crying shame'. In it, he lamented the brutal and expedient football that dominated the tournament and especially the way England had won it. To him it was not 'real football', and he added that 'if the world is to now follow England, the game will surely die'.

The world, mercifully, didn't follow England and football didn't die. But the manner of England's playing in 1966 had a profoundly negative effect on the English game from which that country suffered for the ensuing 30 years and from which, to an extent, it still suffers. The England manager of the day, Alf Ramsey, decided that he didn't have wingers up to the task of winning a world championship. So he devised a playing system that dispensed with wingers. This meant a new route to goal. Instead of feeding the ball to the flanks from where pinpoint crosses could be made to the forwards – which England did so brilliantly years before with wingers like Stanley Matthews and Tom Finney – the ball would be pumped to the front men more directly from deep; from defenders like the superb maker of the long pass, Bobby Moore, and the full backs Ray Wilson and George Cohen. The system worked like a charm. Tall and springy forwards, Geoff Hurst and Roger Hunt, would rise to pick off the lofted ball and able sniffers Martin Peters and Bobby Charlton would scurry about behind them to pick up the loose crumbs. It all worked and England won the World Cup. The team was nick-named 'Ramsey's wingless wonders'. The playing method, later to be labelled 'route one', had been born.

Though the rest of the world was largely unimpressed, seeing the Ramsey game as nothing more than a coach's short-term solution to a dearth of good wingers and creative players, that was not the case in England. There, the majority of clubs immediately aped the system. They began playing a game characterised by the early long ball to the forwards and bypassing the middle of the field, where players would roam aimlessly and unemployed. The English

game became ugly, at least for me; excruciatingly dull and internationally a failure. Four years later England failed in the defence
of its title. The World Cup was won by a gloriously skilful Brazil
whose methods diametrically opposed those employed by England
in 1966. 'Route one' had been exposed as a dud. Harold Wilson,
the British prime minister who had called an election to coincide
with the end of the World Cup, was thrown out of office. Yet
English football went into denial. Jack Charlton, England's towering centre back, memorably said after the tournament: 'We have
nothing to learn from the Brazilians.'

The mistake of building a shrine to the Ramsey dogma proved
costly: since 1966, England has not won an international trophy
of note. On three occasions since, it failed even to qualify for the
World Cup. It managed some notable club successes in the European tournaments, but generally they were by teams like
Manchester United, Liverpool and Nottingham Forest, which
employed playing methods unlike those of Ramsey and his long
ball game. It was not until the mid-1990s, when foreign influences
were allowed to infiltrate the English game, that football in its
motherland began to show a willingness to learn from its pupils. A
breath of fresh air blew through a game which had been left
stranded in the cocoon of 1966.

I make these observations in this book partly to explain my views
on English football and, hopefully, to dispel the notion that I am
somehow prejudiced against England or things English. I was
never anti-English. I was only ever anti-English football, and then
only when that football was characterised by primitive methods
that relied on graft and muscle at the expense of skill, intelligence
and artistry. It was a particular type of football that I preached
against; the fact that it was prevalent in England is incidental.

This is not just some romantic obsession driven by my central
European cultural instincts and the urge to see the whole world
play pretty football. My convictions are also rooted in the fact that
football which puts technique and creative acumen at its forefront
is also the most successful. It is not an idealistic but a pragmatic

notion. As I write Brazil, which is an embodiment of the football I prefer, has won five World Cups. Indeed, no team which relied on brawn rather than brain, on muscle and graft at the expense of technique, has ever won the World Cup, save for England in 1966 and perhaps West Germany in 1954. Real Madrid has won nine European titles, four more than any other, primarily with sublime skill. Teams of ability which rely on players with individual class have won most things in football.

My zeal in all this is driven, above all, by an interest in protecting and furthering football in Australia. This is a particularly difficult mission because of Australia's British heritage; by extension, Australian society has a tendency to build shrines to most things British. Yes, the colonial mentality is still very much alive in my country. Whenever Australia takes inspiration from a foreign source, Britain has a head start. When it comes to football, this is bad – simply because the British, and their way of playing football, have a very poor track record of success in the international foot-ball arena.

So why are we copying it? Goodness only knows – but we are. In the early 1970s the Australian Soccer Federation wisely felt that it was time to look at a long-term plan for broad technical development. It decided to hire a director of coaching: a man who would devise a scheme by which the Australian coaching fraternity could be educated under a uniform system of technical method and licensing. The first candidate for the job was the brilliant German Dettmar Cramer, under whose guidance Japanese football had risen to a peak where Japan, a Third World football country, won the football bronze medal in the 1968 Olympic Games in Mexico. Cramer accepted the approach, but for some mysterious reason he was overlooked and an unknown Englishman, Eric Worthington, got the job.

Worthington, a decent man with his heart in the right place, went about devising a system of coach licensing which essentially remains in place today. Educated in England, Worthington wrote English methods into his curriculum and preferred to work with men who empathised with his dogma. There was a period of many years when every state director of coaching in Australia was an immigrant from the same British school. This was the case with the head football coach at the Australian Institute of Sport, Jimmy Shoulder. And again, when Shoulder stepped down in the mid-80s, his successor, Ron Smith. Australian football, on a developmental level, was being run by the English on English technical methods.

There were a number of things wrong with this, among them the fact that the football community in Australia was decidedly un-English: the fans, officials, coaches and players of most of the clubs at the top end of the sport had a different heritage and were inspired by the football schools of Yugoslavia, Italy, Greece, Czechoslovakia, Hungary, Germany, Holland and even South America. So here we were with our young players being educated on a British philosophy of football, while our elite teams played European-style football. With every intake of new young players, the club coaches had to start from scratch and engage in a process of re-education. Here is an example: players who were taught not to dribble at the Institute, had to be encouraged and re-taught to dribble once they joined their professional clubs.

There is a claim that, for all this, the Institute produced a high volume of excellent players who went on to become millionaires and contributed greatly to our successes at international level. This is true – but only to a point. Most of the good players Australia produced in the past two decades or so – and there have been many – were primarily products of their unique environment. They were most often the children of migrants, with parents who instilled in them the football ethic of their own culture and upbringing. Mark Viduka is the son of a Croatian: he was brought up on the football values of that heritage. It is blatantly evident in the way he plays. The same goes for Ned Zelic. And Paul Okon, the son of a German father and an Italian mother, never set foot in the Institute. Neither did Harry Kewell, the son of an Englishman.

Australia's current players are, above all, the children of our living diversity and multiculturalism. They grew up in a society that is accepting of migrant values, yet which expects its incomers to adapt to its own norms. In a sporting sense, this means that our football players stay faithful to the technical priorities their fathers taught them but are compelled to marry those priorities with the values – the mongrel underdog competitiveness – that are at the core of Australian sport and its historic successes. Australian soccer players have an imported bent for proper technique (or passing the ball straight, in football parlance) but they mix it with our inherent capacity to work for the team cause and to fight. If, in tennis terms, you imagine the mental qualities of a Lleyton Hewitt married with the artistry of a Marat Safin, you will get my drift. This is what makes Australian players good, and valued by coaches around the world. And it is a concoction not common among Australians in most sports other than football.

I was just 20 when disillusionment began to set in, after I watched the 1966 World Cup. It was then that I came to realise, with a shudder, that not all in football was beautiful. In that World Cup, Pelé was kicked to near extinction, first by the Bulgarians and then by a Portuguese defender called Morais. In between those two matches Brazil played Hungary at Anfield, resulting in a 3-1 win by the Magyars; a match the purists later agreed was the best piece of football in the tournament. I was happy with the result, of course, but have always wondered if it would have been the same had The King, who was out recuperating that day, been playing at full fitness. In any case, a loss by Brazil – when it is playing the way it is meant to play – is a sad thing for most football fans, no matter who the victor.

Though television coverage of the tournament was minimal by today's standards (just three out of the 32 games were shown in full in Australia), it was the most I had ever seen of the World Cup till that time. I expected more, in terms of the quality of the football. It was enough for me to realise that all was not perfect in the sport I had chosen as my primary source of joy. I kept thinking of 1960 – of Real and Eintracht – and saw only that the game had regressed to something ugly, brutal and dull and that, worst of all, it was possible to win by methods other than class and beauty. It was then that I began to develop some kind of football idealism: an attitude to which I was already receptive in that era of peace, love and utopian dreaming. I simply extended that to football.

I was not necessarily of the view that England didn't deserve to win that World Cup. Who deserves and who doesn't in sport is always a matter of subjective reflection and often self-serving regret. What matters is what is on the scoreboard and, in 1966, the scoreboard showed that England had won. But like Eric Batty, what I felt was that football may have been better served if the winner had been someone else: a team, if my English friends will forgive me, that played the game the way I felt it should be played. This did not happen in 1966. True, England – save for Nobby Styles – won the World Cup with decency and in the true spirit of sport. But it had won a World Cup which, for me, had been a sham, at least from what I saw of it. In the semi final between West Germany and the Soviet Union, the tricky and elusive little Soviet winger Chislenko was niggled, kicked and hacked until he could take no more, retaliated and was sent off. With the Soviets reduced to 10 men, they lost and were relegated to the third place playoff which they, in turn, lost to Portugal. Lev Yashin, that towering and immense man in black, the world's most admired goalkeeper, sobbed like a baby in the arms of Eusebio after the final whistle.

With those scenes, football for me had diminished, and I was distressed. In the age of revolutionary human values in which we then lived, and inspired by them, I was reluctant to accept this as the norm in sport. To the contrary, and in youthful defiance, my mind rebelled. Fair play and the manner of winning, as opposed to winning for its own sake and no matter how, came to govern the way I defined sporting values. If you play but cannot win fair and square, with sheer ability and on a level playing field, within the rules of the game and within the spirit of those rules, why play at all?

Years later, as sport became even more commercially driven and expedient, I found more resistance to these noble values.

8

The call of television

Tom Anderson is a gritty ex-footballer now in his more mature years, a Scotsman who played the game in the mould of a classic highlander nourished on wind chill, an undersupply of firewood, and a need to swap warming aggression with any human who happened to saunter by. When he ran, sparks flew from his studs; an opponent's best bet was to take a wide berth if he didn't want to land in the nearest infirmary. He was a journeyman midfielder, the type they later called a 'ball winner', with muscles on his breath and kneecaps the shape of bayonets. He was awfully useful to any coach who wanted a weapon with which to torture a potential match-winner from the other side.

He played for various clubs in Scotland and England before landing in Australia in the mid-60s as one of those 10 quid migrants. I met him when, already in his mid-30s, he was playing for his last club, St George-Budapest. In 1969 Frank Arok, St George's new young coach, immediately identified the ageing Anderson as a key player in his strategy for winning. Arok's way was to tag the highly obedient and disciplined Anderson to a potentially lethal opponent, thereby diluting the opponent's

111

potency. In one game Takis Loukanidis, a towering Greek god of a player feared by all, got barely a sniff of the ball all day as Anderson tailed him everywhere, including to the gents at half time.

Back then, Tom would not have agreed with many of the sissy football ideals I preach. I was, in the 60s, a young idealist with the world at my feet. I had a limitless passion for football and a penchant for intellectualisation, along with a cocky confidence about my place in the new world and my views about how football fitted into that world. Within my limited world view, Tom was merely a well bruised footballer, a man with little formal education, well into his late 30s, who was about to unlace his boots for the last time. Tom was looking for a new deal and a new way to make a living.

I dreamed then of becoming a football journalist, waiting only for that break, that moment when the door would open to a heaven-sent opportunity. And it did. Only the man who walked through it was not me but Tom Anderson. It was Anderson who got that dream break as a football journalist and who became one of Australia's highest profile and most successful football reporters for the ensuing 20 years. Ironically, although he didn't know it at the time, it was I who inadvertently helped him make the lucky break. And it was to be 10 years before I got another chance.

This is how I missed that first opportunity. By the late 60s, I was a man without a career. I was 24 and had chucked in medical technology for the sweeter if less secure joy of rock musicianship. In short, I was a bum singer, tied only to The Rubber Band, with no prospects beyond it. Pop stardom was unlikely, given that I neither sang like Don Henley nor wrote like Bob Dylan. Nor was I ambitious enough about music in any case. I had decided, after a handful of failed auditions as a soloist, that the nervous pressures associated with chasing stardom were life-shortening, devoid of dignifying substance and just not worth it. To hell with that. I retreated into enjoying being a rock and roller just for the sake of it. If it led to something more remunerative, good; if not, I was enjoying myself making good music and bringing smiles to faces. It was better than doing something mundane and boring.

In this curricular statelessness, the only ambition I harboured was to dabble in football journalism. The game was my number one passion and since I couldn't make it as a player, writing and speaking about it for a living were surely the next best things. But to attain the dream journo job was no easy matter; a lot harder than it is today. The only full-time job opportunities in football journalism at the time were with the metropolitan daily newspapers, each of which had one full-time specialist football writer. Beyond that there was nothing. There were five daily papers in Sydney: *The Daily Telegraph*, *The Sydney Morning Herald*, *The Australian*, *The Daily Mirror* and *The Sun*. That meant only five full-time jobs in Sydney, Australia's biggest metropolis. And the vacancy rate was not exactly high.

Since I couldn't score a football job with one of the few established papers, as I have mentioned already, I decided to start out on my own. It was a monthly magazine called *Soccer Illustrated*, a publication with pictures and feature articles as its focus which would fill a nice little hole in the market. Or so I thought. What I soon learned was that you don't start up a business by knowing nothing about business, with no money (start-up capital, I think they call it) and in a puny market. My brother Andrew, who is a fine artist, was to be artistic director while my good friend George Kennedy, then a football writer with a Hungarian language weekly but with no history in English language journalism, and I were to be joint editors. George and I wrote all the text. We recruited another Hungarian enthusiast, a keen amateur photographer, to take the pictures and Andrew designed the pages.

My first articles were published in that magazine. I wrote interview pieces on Johnny Warren, on a young and exceptionally skinny Raúl Blanco (later to be our portly national coach), and on Russian goalkeeping legend Lev Yashin. I still remember nervously meeting Yashin in the lounge of the Hampton Court Hotel in Sydney's Kings Cross; both of us chain-smoked our way through a one-hour chat about what makes a great goalkeeper. Yashin, a most cordial man, was the first international celebrity I interviewed.

With the help of another *paisano*, a Hungarian friend who ran a cottage printing shop in the far west of Sydney, we got the first issue printed and put it on the streets. But it flopped. We sold less than 2000 copies and, under a mountain of debts, we closed the magazine after issue number one.

It was a heartbreaking experience but it didn't extinguish my dream. The desire to break into football journalism persisted. So I kept plugging away. In 1971 I submitted a football article to, among many others, *The Daily Mirror*, a mass circulation evening tabloid in the Rupert Murdoch stable. Expecting nothing, I got a huge shock when a letter came in the mail from the paper's sports editor, Peter Miller, asking me to give him a call. When I did, he offered me a job. The vacancy had arisen because Tony Horsted, the paper's long-time football writer, working under the pseudonym of 'Hotspur', was retiring. It was Tony who coined the name 'Socceroo' and he was a living icon among the small band of soccer writers then in Australia. To get the chance to replace him was indeed a dream come true, and I jumped at it.

But I had a small problem. The offer came in November and The Rubber Band had a contractual commitment to perform on a Pacific cruise ship in January. I told Miller I was in, but I asked that he excuse me for two weeks in January to fulfil my commitments with the band. He refused, so I had to decline the opportunity. When I returned from my gig around the islands, Tom Anderson's byline appeared under every soccer headline in the *Mirror*. He had obviously been Peter Miller's option B. Tom was now a football writer and I was still a singer in a rock and roll band. Thus resumed my long search for the elusive chance to become a daily chronicler of football.

Since then, Tom Anderson and I have become good friends. I did many overseas tours with him, both of us reporting on the Socceroos. He became a regular studio colleague as a pundit on SBS and, though he is now retired, he remains a fixture on SBS' annual telecast of the FA Cup final. One of my fond road memories is of a visit to Scotland, where Australia played Rangers at Ibrox in the bracing November of 1984. The day before the game Tom and I took a slow ride to Loch Lomond. The trip involved stopping at every pub on the way, at each one tasting a different brand of single malt whisky. My memory on how we made it back is but a blur.

Maybe in another vocation Tom and I would have become mortal enemies, or at least bitchy rivals. But the dominion of media work in football, in those days, was narrow. Those of us in it were like a family. Although there was some competition among siblings, essentially we were all on the same side. And when our great game was under threat in this land of rugby and cricket, we pulled together. Hence the lasting friendship.

Though I had missed out on the *Daily Mirror* opportunity, through no fault of anybody's, I maintained the dream. And while it was many years before I could get another crack at working in the football media, my chance to break into general journalism came fairly quickly. This time I grasped the challenge with both hands and worked obsessively to make a success of it. I knew that if ever I was to become a football writer, I first had to learn to be a journalist.

It was 1971. I had been floating about as a musical bum, taking the odd short-term job to make ends meet when gigs were less than frequent. I worked as a hamburger cook, storeman, process worker on conveyor belts; anything that paid. It was then that I met Eva, a stunningly beautiful and sweet little girl of 18. I was a front man in a band, she was in the audience, she took a fancy as did I, and 18 months later we were married. But I was a bum and not a good investment in security terms. Then I got a gig on the ABC mail desk. This entailed sorting mail, putting envelopes in pigeon holes and delivering the post to odd spots around the ABC's disparate offices. Not long after making my start in this less than stimulating vocation I was transferred from the central mail desk to the editorial offices of *TV Times*, a glossy weekly magazine then owned and published by the ABC, much in the mould of the BBC's *Radio Times*. I was to be the resident copy boy, the fetch-me-this and fetch-me-that messenger who ran errands for anybody in the office who required instant service – including buying ham and cheese sandwiches for the hungry journos swamped by the pressures of deadlines. The buzz of being in an editorial office infected me straight away. And this time I kept my goal clearly in view: I wanted to be one of the journos.

But to achieve that at *TV Times* took some doing. The editor, Chris Day, was not partial to training up copy boys to become journalists. He preferred to hire experienced, ready-made professionals. And there were other hurdles thrown in my way. I was then a long-haired scruffy specimen of the 'peace generation', something that didn't sit well with my immediate boss, the magazine's business manager. He was an ageing Tory by ideology and we had a few social arguments about the Vietnam War, the rights of Aboriginals and various matters that concerned the future direction of humanity. During my lunch break on one particular day I took part in an anti-war demonstration, a Vietnam moratorium march down Sydney's George Street, and returned to the office proudly sporting a moratorium badge on my T-shirt. The next day, without a reason given, I was transferred back to the mail desk.

I was devastated and thought my big chance at breaking into journalism had been snuffed out. I moped for a few days and then decided that I wasn't going to give up without a fight: in those few days, I grew as a man. For the first time in my easy-going laid-back life, I decided that if I wanted something I would fight for it, even if I did not succeed. My languid and selfless prioritising of the collective good, driven by youthful hippie influences, gave way to the birthing of individualism: a steely resolve to get what I wanted and to fight to the bitter end to get it.

From the far distance of the mail desk, I persisted in badgering and nagging the editor, Chris Day, to give me a break; to put me on his editorial team at whatever low level. I despatched letters and sample articles to him, all the while flattering him and trying to convince him of my passionate desire to be part of his brilliantly run newsroom. Mostly, the response was silence – until I co-opted a supporter of some influence. He was Bill Craig, a sweet and decent elderly man who had a rapport with me and was sympathetic to my ambitions. He was the 'programs editor' of *TV Times*: the man in charge of the magazine's program pages. In response to my lobbying he promised to 'push the thing' with Chris Day. The process took over a year. But at the end of it I was hired as a sub-editor on the magazine's program pages: a 'proggy sub' – my first job in journalism.

The job did not require great journalistic talent. What I had to do was turn the networks' publicity-slanted press releases into objective, readable guides to what shows were scheduled when. So 'the most wonderful movie ever made' was changed, with my pen, into an 8 pm Movie Western, titled *Warlock*, starring Anthony Quinn and Henry Fonda. That was it. Not much to it, really. But it was sub-editing: what Chris Day called 'separating shit from clay'. And it gave me a foot in the door of the trade. It was low grade and lowly paid ($60 a week was my salary) – but it was journalism. Each morning I swaggered past the desk of my ex-boss, ignored him with a turn of the head and strolled on to take my chair at the 'subs desk'. He was a business manager. I was a journalist.

The experience served many purposes, but paramount were the lessons regarding the spiritual core of journalism: to stick to the facts, to tell the truth, and to write without fear or favour. Suddenly, I found a link between my cathartic experience at the Wentworth Park pub with Laurie Hegyes all those years ago, and what I now wanted to do. It was a small thing – editing program pages in a TV magazine – but I was now in a vocation where publishing fact and unbiased truth was my job.

I grew up idolising not just footballers but also football commentators. The first of them was György Szepesi, a legend among radio sports callers in Hungary. Given that television didn't exist when I first came to be poisoned by football – when Hungary was making all those conquests abroad – it was not hard to idolise him. Szepesi drew fabulous word pictures of the play so brilliantly we felt we were inside the stadium: through his lips, we 'saw' every sensational goal Puskás scored, every dribble by Hidegkúti, every glorious pass by Bozsik and every thumping header by Kocsis. Szepesi was more famous than any politician or movie star in Hungary and as famous as any member of the Golden Team. Later, he became president of the Hungarian FA and a member of FIFA's executive committee. A CD of his commentary on England vs Hungary in 1953, the famed '6-3', is one of my most guarded possessions.

As I got older, I turned my admiration to the great English language television commentators like Kenneth Wolstenholme, the ex bomber pilot who became the pioneer and benchmark for BBC style commentary in the 1950s and 60s. And there was Hugh Johns, who did much of what Wolstenholme was doing at the BBC's rival ITV network. And later my ears ogled at Brian Moore, John Motson, Barry Davies and a young Martin Tyler. When I first heard these people, it was unthinkable that one day I would not only meet all of them (including Szepesi) but actually earn a living doing what they were doing.

By the early 1970s I was dreaming of and toying with the idea of becoming a commentator. I would take my transistor tape recorder to games and imagine that I was a Wolstenholme, rabbiting on, annoying the bejesus out of every spectator around me. Even earlier, in the mid-1960s, I hijacked another toy – the PA system microphone at St George home games – from the heavily accented club president, Les Bordacs, who was glad and relieved I did. That was my first attempt at public speaking. People said I had a nice microphone voice and an easy-on-the-ear accent and, in the area of match-day presentation, St George got a small head start on the other 'ethnic' clubs. More importantly for me, it was a confidence builder.

In 1972 I got my first chance to dabble in real football commentary. It was purely amateur but it had actual people viewing it and listening to it. That year the St George club, in yet another pioneering act, decided to buy an amateur video camera and recorder. The idea was to record the team's games so the coach could analyse them. Mike Johnson, the St George coach, asked me to commentate on the recordings. In those days, way before video cassettes and mass consumption VCRs, this was a cumbersome task. Setting up the recordings took hours, and included the frustrating task of lacing the tape in the machine via an obstacle course of curves and counter-curves, often to find later that it had been botched and the game didn't record at all. But after some trial and error we got it right. My brother, Andrew, manned the camera and I commentated. So there we were, perched conspicuously on the hill at Hurstville Oval: camera on tripod, Andrew bent over the view-finder and me on a chair waffling into a pencil mike. Spectators would stroll past on the way to the hot dog stand, giving us mighty stares, wondering if we were inter-stellar aliens. It was the forerunner of the soccer OB, or outside broadcast. Nothing else in football was being recorded for television at that time in Australia.

Mike Johnson loved our work and was most appreciative, partly because he was under pressure at the time, given that the team was not performing. Even the male fans who stayed loyal because of their devotion to Johnson's beautiful, statuesque wife were getting thoroughly fed up. Andrew and I did our bit but at one point we, too, were so disillusioned with the team that we thought of chucking it all in. Johnson begged us to continue. And we did. In 1972 we 'covered' all of St George's games, home and away, and I commentated on all of them. It was grounding from which, a few short years later, I was to greatly benefit.

Around this time, my latent urge to return to Europe and resolve an identity crisis once and for all started to become irresistible. I had been a migrant in Australia for 15 years and had become a citizen. But I remained unconvinced that Australia was where I wanted to spend the rest of my life. I loved the country and, without knowing it, had already been spoilt by its freedoms, its good standard of living and its amicable, easy-going ways. But I still felt European and held European values. Besides, Europe was the world centre of football.

What hastened my decision to go was a collapsed marriage. In 1973, after just 15 months of marriage, Eva and I decided to separate. I was devastated by this and, with a heavy heart, moped around for a couple of years in the hope that we would reconcile. We had no children and had settled on the assets so there was nothing keeping me in Australia except that hope. When I finally became convinced that all was lost and there would be no reconciliation, I decided it was time to make the move. Ironically, years later, Eva and I would reconcile, re-marry and rear two beautiful children. And, in a further twist to the irony, it was my decision to leave at that time that made the reconciliation possible.

In July 1975 I took off on a Thai International flight to Rome and then on by train to Hungary, with breathless anticipation about what I would find and what impressions I would form after 18 years of absence. When the Hungarian customs officers boarded the train at the Austro-Hungarian border, they almost had me wondering why I had bothered. They were rude and arrogant and treated the passengers – Hungarian and non-Hungarian alike – like dogs. Thankfully, this experience did not taint my general impressions of the country which were overwhelmingly pleasant.

The country I had left in that grim winter of 1956, in the dark haze of post-revolution – its morale crushed by bullets, mortar and steel – was now back in full blossom. The people were smiling and by and large appeared content. The shops and supermarkets were laden with food and there was a general sense of wealth. All this, while in nearby communist countries – most notably Poland – people were queuing for hours for a loaf of bread. The reason for the relative prosperity in Hungary was something called 'Goulash Communism', an economic concept which attempted to mix market economy elements into a communist system. János Kádár, whose government introduced it in 1966, called it the 'New Economic Mechanism'.

To me, it appeared to have worked, at least for a time. Certainly, the people seemed to think so and, much to my astonishment, many of them stoutly defended the regime: essentially the same regime that helped put down the brave quest for freedom in October 1956. Indeed, János Kádár was the leader installed by the Soviets after the revolt had been crushed and the revolutionary prime minister, Imre Nagy, executed. But when I attempted to voice my opinions on Kádár during a dinner with my Budapest-based relatives, I was shouted down by a cousin for daring to criticise 'our János Kádár'.

It dawned on me that the lessons of 1956 had been learned by the governors, both in Moscow and in Budapest, and the chains had been loosened in an attempt to ensure such uprisings would not happen again in the Soviet empire. The revolution had been ruthlessly crushed, to be sure, and its key players shot or hung like criminals. But once the broom of retribution had been put away, the government, with Moscow's blessing, gradually introduced reforms. The people no longer lived in humiliation, as they had under Stalin, and above all, their bellies had been filled.

This surely had its effect on a global scale. In 1976, Chinese leader Mao Tse-tung died and his reformist successors put in train the massive changes that have since turned that country into an economic colossus. In 1986, Soviet leader Mikhail Gorbachev launched his perestroika, an attempt to water down the country's command economy structure and allow market forces to inject new life into it. In each of these cases, I believe, inspiration had been taken from the example of Hungary, the first communist country to 'go to market' and keep its citizens contented. And so began the slow collapse and ultimate disintegration of communism, so dramatically expressed in 1989 by the tearing down of the Berlin Wall. Short term, the Hungarian revolution of 1956 was soundly defeated. But by 1989, it was clear that, long term, it had been victorious.

My impressions of Hungary, circa 1975, were generally pleasant. And from a soul-search perspective, this first return visit was educational, revealing and beneficial. When I strolled on the banks of the Danube and walked the Parisian-style boulevards of Budapest, I felt eerily at home. Migrants who have done this can relate to such a feeling. It is difficult not to feel at home when you land in a place where even policemen speak the language of your birth; where the advertising hoardings are in your mother tongue; where the scent wafting out of every eatery is what you have always smelt in your mother's kitchen; and where you linger in parks and squares that were your playgrounds as a child. I had lived my first 11 years in Hungary. And during my next 18 years in Australia, I lived – as most migrants do – a schizoid existence, traversing the distinct borders between my Hungarian and Australian lives every day, as easily as crossing the street. So when I landed in the old country, it was like entering the family home. Everyone else was just like me.

To a point. Unlike the long-term locals, in Hungary I was still an *émigré*: someone who had been away in the West for nearly two decades, fattening myself on the riches of a rich country, spoilt rotten by its squeaky clean democracy and its well protected freedoms. This penny dropped for me during that visit, persuading me to cast aside any germinating temptation to reinstate Hungary as my permanent home. As much as I greeted the opportunity to 'come home' gleefully and with excitement, I realised that I could not live there. I knew that I had been away too long; that in the war of affections and allegiances being fought on the battleground of my mind, Australia was winning. I kissed and hugged my cousins, uncles and aunts, and waved the Old Country goodbye.

The place that Hungary, and my Hungarian-ness, holds in my heart did not change. It couldn't and it can't. These things are in one's blood and they stay there forever. You don't cease to be a Hungarian when you become an Australian. Migration, and human emotion, doesn't work that way. These are not things over which one has any control and why would one want to? By heritage – save for our Indigenous people – we in our multicultural polyglot Australia all hail from somewhere. I don't see myself as any less an Australian than those whose background is different to mine, including those who carry Anglo-Celtic genes. Sure, I laugh at Hungarian jokes, eat Hungarian food, search for Hungarian medal winners at the Olympic Games and root for the Magyar water polo team whenever it plays. But that's no different to Anglo-Australians rooting for England whenever it takes on Argentina in a war over some chilly group of islands in the South Atlantic. And on those rare occasions when Australia plays Hungary in football, I always barrack for Australia.

From Hungary I headed for England, the home of football, where I hoped to be able to work and get a daily fix of my beloved sport. The length of my intended stay was open ended: I made my family no explicit promises regarding when I would return to Australia. I ended up staying the best part of two years and loved every day of it.

As soon as I arrived I busied myself by connecting with football in every way I could. I was now back in a genuine football country and intended to make the most of it. The first thing I did was buy a second hand MGB sports car – a red one – for £350. With the then exchange rate of the pound against the Aussie dollar, it was a steal. I drove it straight up to Luton, around an hour from London, where Luton Town was playing Plymouth Argyle in a second division league match. My chief reason for going to the match was that Noddy Alston, one of my favourite Socceroos, was then a Luton player and I wanted to see how the local boy made good was making out. I arrived 10 minutes into the match and was disappointed that Luton was already trailing 1-0; worse still, Alston was on the bench. As the minutes ticked towards half time, much to my amazement, the Luton fans began to chant: 'Alston, Alston', urging the manager to bring on the man they considered some kind of match winner. Early in the second half, as things began to get desperate, Alston was brought on to much elation. And there I was, marvelling at all this: an Aussie – well, sure, an expat Aussie (Alston was by birth an Englishman) – but an Aussie none the less, being hailed as a saviour and a hero by an English crowd. Luton lost but that was not relevant. The welcome to Alston stunned me and made me feel all warm inside; I drove back to London feeling satisfied that I had had a happy first engagement with football on my return to Europe.

More was to come. Living in London in those days was no hard life for a genuine football fan, especially a neutral explorer of the game like me. London had 11 professional league clubs across a number of divisions and one could attend a game of some sort in that city almost every night of the week. At various times, if I felt like it, I went to Brentford, to Crystal Palace, Fulham, Charlton, Millwall, Leyton Orient or West Ham, not to mention Arsenal, Chelsea, Tottenham or Queen Park Rangers. This was as good as it got: I was having the time of my life.

For a bit of divine inspiration I sought out and found my journalistic idol Eric Batty, the *World Soccer* columnist. He was delightfully receptive and invited me to a West Ham training session where we talked, exchanged football ideologies and found some common ground. He said, 'I am off on a trip to the Continent to check on some real football. Why don't you come with me?' Of course, I jumped at the chance. So within days Eric and I, in his car, set off across the Channel to explore football in Germany, Holland and Belgium. It was the way of things in those days. This was well before cable or satellite television, not to mention the internet. If you lived in England you saw nothing of football other than English football. Even the newspapers covered nothing of football – not even results – other than English or Scottish. So if you were English and wanted to sample how the game was played elsewhere, you had to take the trip to see it. Eric Batty's speciality was to monitor and report on modern tactical trends; he could not do his job cocooned in the confines of English club football.

In a seven-day spell we took in four games in three countries. We started in Germany at Mönchengladbach where local club Borussia took on Real Madrid in a pre-season friendly. Madrid was parading Günther Netzer, a German who was a leader of that country's golden generation of the '70s. Another, Berti Vogts, was with Gladbach as was Rainer Bonhof. Next stop was Amsterdam for a European Championship qualifier between Holland (runner-up in the previous year's World Cup) and Poland, which had finished third. The full line-up of stars from both countries was on view, the biggest of them Johan Cruyff, who played a superb match leading the Dutch to an emphatic victory. Then it was on to Bruges in Belgium where Club Bruges met Real Madrid in a European Cup match; the next day, we headed to the nearby small town of Lokeren for a UEFA Cup clash between Lokeren and Barcelona. I recall noting that Cruyff, now playing for Barcelona, had an unusually quiet game, barely touching the ball; this was just four days after his conquering display for Holland in Amsterdam. I read later that Cruyff was in a pay dispute with Barcelona, which rather explained things.

It was a dream come true for me to have that trip with Eric Batty, given that I idolised the man and had read just about everything he had written in the previous 15 years. But not all of it was fun. Batty suffered from chronic depression and nothing was more likely to send him into one of his dark moods than seeing football he didn't like. This happened after the Gladbach-Madrid game where the Spanish team was a sad reflection of the great Real of Di Stefano fame — which had done so much to fashion Batty's convictions on football through the 1950s. 'The game is dead,' he muttered as he popped two anti-depressant pills.

Batty had an engrossing passion for the game, the like of which I didn't sense in anyone, except perhaps my good friend Johnny Warren. To him, any team that didn't play what he called 'real football' was the anti-Christ and he refused to discuss its merits as a football outfit. To anyone who challenged him he would say: 'Don't argue with me about football, son. I have seen Di Stefano!' On good days he would ring me up and we would chat about football for hours, trying to diagnose its ills. On one occasion he called me after returning from one of his football guru treks to central Europe. He said he had found the new Netzer: it was Antonin Panenka who, a year later, led Czechoslovakia to victory in the European Championship. His winning penalty in the shootout against West Germany in the final, chipping the ball arrogantly over the head of the great Sepp Maier, became the stuff of legends.

One of the first games of football I attended as a European resident was at Loftus Road in late August, 1975. I had settled in as a boarder with a nice Polish family in Chiswick, west London, and Queen Park Rangers' home ground was my nearest venue. I thought I'd go along to the game between QPR and West Ham, but I wanted to make sure I got in free. So I wrote to Lou Gautier, editor of the Sydney-based *Soccer World* and asked him if, in exchange for me filing the odd report from London, he would consider giving me press accreditation. Lou obliged in spades, writing me a letter of authorisation which made me *Soccer World*'s 'European Correspondent'. So there I now was, not only able to wangle press entry to just about every game in England, but officially a 'football correspondent' to boot. As it turned out, from the press box at Loftus Road, I saw not only one of the more memorable games of my life, but also the start of the best season in the history of QPR.

As you may have gathered from previous chapters I was not exactly in love with the broad English way of playing: the long lottery passes and the rest of it. But QPR – vintage 1975 – was different. It was managed by Dave Sexton, one of the more academic English coaches, a man who took note of how the game was being played outside England. Rare among coaches, he spoke with an educated accent, and wore clothes that suggested he may have actually attended school at some time in his life. He had assembled a bunch of technically skilful players, most of whom were the antithesis of the muscular, bustling runners and aerial battlers that characterised English football. The king of them was Stan Bowles: Stan the Man – an errant urchin, womaniser and chronic gambler who just happened to be the best British player I ever saw. On his good days, he was up there with George Best, with his outrageous repertoire of tricks and powers to create incisions in the meanest defences. On his off days, he wasn't there because he just didn't show up. Rangers played skilful, eye-catching football at breakneck speed week in, week out. And that season they were undefeated at home in 21 games, finishing runner-up to Liverpool in the old Division 1. I was sold: QPR became my club. I filed back to Sydney a story on which the editor pinned the headline, 'At last, an English team with skill'.

That said, I also had a soft spot for Liverpool who were in the midst of their long hegemony: yet to win their first of four European titles in eight years, but also playing the type of 'real football' I liked. And I just loved their cultish, tribalistic fans, whose colour, passion and Scouse sense of humour still makes them unique – even in the unique realm of English fandom. I remember catching the train one evening to Selhurst Park for a Crystal Palace-Liverpool match and engaging in conversation with some Liverpool fans sitting opposite. When I inquired as to what their thoughts were of Everton, their rival Merseyside club, the biggest and meanest looking of them leaned slowly across, tightened his scarf and said: 'You so much as mention them scum in our company again and you're a dead man.'

Thus I lived in England for near on two years: loving my life, loving the cultural offerings of one of the world's great cities, loving the pub life, the eccentric colour of its people and, above all, loving being immersed in the football.

But it was not all a bed of roses. I had arrived an insecure and futureless adventurer, and the London experience helped make me a man. My first few nights were spent in a two-pound-a-night hotel near Kings Cross station. Outside my tiny matchbox of a room was a puddle of urine, and at night I could hear the rats chomping on the organic debris left by the previous tenant. It was the lowest point of my life and I thought of turning around and coming straight home.

Pining for what I had lost and left behind, including my short-lived but blissful marriage, was not helping. But I chose to hang in. It was a time to be strong and, as the male ego would have it, to be obsessed with being strong. Going home was one thing; being defeated was quite another.

I worked at all sorts of jobs: builder's labourer, storeman, kitchen hand and collector of empty glasses in suburban bars. But what kept me together, above all, was the football. Once again, the beautiful game intervened to give fuel and life to my insecure existence. Three, four, five times a week I would go to a game to keep myself sane. The most memorable – and soothing – was on 5 November 1975, my 30th birthday.

I had been sitting in my room in Chiswick feeling lonely and unloved. One's 30th is a significant birthday, after all. It is when one turns a kind of corner: faces up to mature responsibility, having left behind the silly years of bopping nonsense and fun. Such a day needed celebrating but I had no family nearby, no friends and no one to celebrate it with. I went to the papers, found the fixtures list and discovered that there was a UEFA Cup match at Upton Park that evening. So I hopped on the tube and headed east.

West Ham was playing Ararat Yerevan, a club from the then Soviet state of Armenia. The stadium was packed. Someone near me referred to Yerevan as 'the Russians' whereupon he was shouted down by a swarthy Yerevan fan, no doubt ethnically Armenian. The offender was asked, 'How would you like it if I referred to Glasgow Rangers as English?' West Ham was chasing the tie after handily drawing 1-1 the first away leg. At the break, the Hammers led 2-0. This was the West Ham of Alan Devonshire, Alan Curbishley and Trevor Brooking. They were coasting. But minutes into the second half, the Armenians got one back and it was 2-1. Now the picture changed. One more from the visitors and they would go through on away goals. Suddenly the stadium rose. Fans stood erect, including one old timer next to me who said he had been coming to Upton Park since 1922. The throng broke into song, bellowing 'I'm Forever Blowing Bubbles', the club's theme song. All sang, not just the young hooligans and rowdies behind the goal, but all the Hammers fans, young and old, women and men. The team lifted and won 3-1. It had been a cold November London night. But it was one of the most warming experiences of my life. I had a good birthday.

More than a year later, my life in London was going swimmingly. The Fleet Street-based publisher I was working for had arranged my work permit, and I had no immediate plans to return to Australia. But two things happened that were to change my life again. Firstly, through a series of letters and telegrams, Eva and I had agreed to reconcile. Secondly, I won an audition to become a football commentator on Australian television.

This happened in early 1977. That year, football in Australia was to take on its boldest venture yet, launching the National Soccer League, the first national league of any sport in the country. By March 1977, it was ready to kick off. The launch of the league breathed new life into football. This might sound familiar, but it was all about a break with the past and taking the sport into a new realm. And although these were the same old clubs, with the same supporters, the new halo hovering over the league impressed a good chunk of the mainstream, including bits of the media. The Channel Ten network was sufficiently excited to take up the rights to the Philips League – as it was labelled in its first season – and mounted a weekly one-hour program called *Philips Top Soccer*.

This was revolutionary. The show was programmed in prime viewing time, at 9.30 on Saturday nights: a daring move for a commercial television network driven only by the quest for ratings. Football, or soccer, had a little bit of history on Australian television but no history of it ever rating. The show's line-up basically consisted of two matches of the week: one played in Sydney, the other in Melbourne, edited down to around 25 minutes each. The show had no hosts: only two commentators and a couple of reporters doing short post-match interviews.

Away in my London domicile I had no idea this was going on. Luckily, my close friend George Kennedy – he of *Soccer Illustrated* fame – knew of my commentary ambitions and sent me a telegram, alerting me to the fact that Channel Ten was auditioning commentators. So I grabbed my portable tape recorder, went to Loftus Road to do a dummy commentary on a game and despatched the tape by express post to John Frank, the CEO of the new league, who was co-ordinating the auditions. Within days a telegram came back from George, saying they liked the tape and that I should contact someone called Bob Gardam at London Weekend Television. LWT was the network that produced *The Big Match*, a slick weekly football show hosted by Brian Moore. Bob Gardam, then regarded internationally as a pioneer in multi-camera match coverage of football, was its match director.

Channel Ten had hired Gardam – on a short-term contract – to come to Australia and train up the Australian directors on how to cover football. Australia had no match directors trained on anything much other than rugby league, Australian rules or cricket. When I called Gardam in London on a Friday, he was already packed to leave but still had to direct a game the following day: Chelsea v Nottingham Forest at Stamford Bridge. Gardam asked me to come along and do another audition.

When I arrived, gasping for air and quivering like jelly, I was thrown into a world I had barely dreamed of. Gardam introduced me to Brian Moore who was in the crew van sipping on a cup of tea, doing his research in preparation for his commentary. The three of us had a five minute meeting in which Bob explained the bare essentials of the call: how and where I would start, where the replays would come in and so on. Then he left me with Brian, who was an utter gentleman. He gave me all his tips on the tricks of the trade, including the trappings, and allowed me to borrow a copy of his research. Importantly, he clued me up on how to cover replays, which were done blind in those days because the matches were not transmitted live. The commentator had to recap the incident – usually a goal – purely from memory and the tape editors later inserted the slow motion replay to match the commentator's exact words. This was tricky business. If, for example, the commentator got wrong the name of the man who crossed the ball, he looked like a proper goose.

It was a late February day in London, decidedly chilly. I began to shake even more as Brian and I climbed the ladder to the gantry where the cameras and commentators were positioned. Brian and I were to do a parallel commentary. His would go to air while mine, recorded on a separate track, was for audition purposes only. The floor manager gave me a warm cup of coffee and I settled in my chair, donned the head-set and tried to come to terms with the reality. There I was, a few metres from Brian Moore, commentating on a top match in England at Stamford Bridge. This was a chance I couldn't afford to botch.

The call generally went well but with one embarrassing blip, well into the second half, which I thought might have cost me the job.

I began tentatively, but only because of something on which I hadn't been briefed: the director's voice, with his unending instructions to his cameramen, was forever present in my headphones. This can be a real nuisance and a distraction when one is trying to commentate: some baritone blaring in your ear, 'Camera 3, frame tighter. No, tighter! Four, give me a close-up of the referee!' But I quickly learned to live with it, realising that this might be useful to commentators who may want to be aware of what shots are coming up next. In football commentating, even live, keeping one eye on the monitor is essential: one needs to be totally aware of how the director is designing his coverage and what the viewer actually sees.

As the match went on I began to relax, grow in confidence, and the words started to flow. Until one hairy moment. Deep in the second half, a Chelsea player was brutally fouled from behind. The game stopped as the player rolled on the ground in agony, the referee was engulfed by a throng of protesting players and physios came running onto the pitch. This was new to me and, suddenly, with no football action to describe, I froze. There was a long

pregnant silence which must have lasted an agonising 20 seconds.
Bob Gardam, this time addressing me, screamed in my ears: 'Les,
cover it, cover it'. But I couldn't. In the confusion, I had forgotten
the name of the player who had gone down and, not being able to
see the number on his back, I couldn't identify him. I stayed silent
until play resumed again. The whole thing would have lasted no
more than a minute. But in football commentary that length of
time is an eternity. I was sure I had cooked my golden goose.

I didn't see Bob Gardam after the game. By the time Brian and
I descended from the gantry, he was gone, off in a speeding cab to
Heathrow, with two reels of tape containing my commentary in his
bags. Ten very slow days later came another telegram from George
Kennedy: 'You got the job. Come home. Buy a ring for Eva.'

What a sweet message! I felt as though all my Christmases had
come at once. The lady had decided, after nearly four years, that we
should reconcile. And I was finally being offered a gig as a professional football commentator. Of course I was coming home.

The timing was extremely tight. I was told on a Monday that
I had the job, and the first match I had to call was the following
Saturday in Sydney. My London employers were shocked when
I told them I was leaving in two days to return to Australia. But
they understood.

Despite my delight, it was not a happy homecoming. My father,
who had been ill for some time, died on the very day of my arrival
back in Sydney. He was 63. So there were no parties or celebrations
over my homecoming; only the quiet of bereavement and the dull
practicalities of unpacking and settling into yet another new life.
Plus, of course, the softness and comfort of being reunited with Eva.

The day after my arrival I was called in to Channel Ten to meet
with Peter Skelton, the executive producer, primarily to discuss
contract and money. At no time before my decision to return from
London was money ever discussed. Not that I gave a damn. I would

have done it for nothing. The job was a part-time one anyway and I always knew I would need a full-time gig as my main source of income.

Next, I was flown first class to Melbourne where Bob Gardam was having his last rehearsal with the crew, doing a dummy OB of a state league game. I called the second half; the Melbourne-based commentator called the first. All went well, apart from Gardam suggesting I put a touch more 'energy' into the call. Whatever that meant.

The only other event scheduled before I took up the microphone was the official press launch of *Philips Top Soccer*. It was held at the fashionable Gazebo Hotel in Sydney's Potts Point. The MC was Peter Skelton, my new boss: a suave, elegant, softly spoken man with a genuine keenness for making the bold venture work.

That streak in his personality – the capacity to break away from safe television programming and take risks – was a trait I became better acquainted with later, when our paths crossed again at SBS. But even on this day, at the program launch, he made a huge impact on my public and private future. It concerned my name. Remember, at that time I was still Les Ürge. You probably won't be surprised to hear I was never truly comfortable with the name. The surname had already caused discomfort when I was a kid in Hungary. The name in Hungarian means a small field animal that feeds on grain and burrows itself in holes, probably 'mole' in English. So you can imagine what an easy target it made me for the school bully boys: 'Go on Ürge, crawl back into your hole'. Etcetera. Much to my distress, the move to an English speaking country didn't lighten the handicap. In Australia, though the name meant something totally different, Ürge, not to mention Les Ürge, could be an equal source of embarrassment. It could all have been avoided had the name been pronounced properly: there's a big difference between 'oor-gay' and 'urge'. But getting Australians to pronounce my name properly would have required tongue surgery.

All this changed when Peter Skelton stepped onto the stage at the Gazebo and prepared to introduce me as the new star signing for the program. Before he could finish the first sentence he fell silent, jumped off the stage and, pulling me aside, whispered in my ear: 'Les. Your name. Your name. We've got to do something about your name!' Without a moment's hesitation, I blurted out: 'Les Murray. Call me Les Murray.'

The reason I chose Murray had nothing to do with any ancestral link I may have with a Scottish clan. The reason was something my father had said to me some years earlier: 'If you ever anglicise your name, change it to Murray because it also works as a Hungarian name.' And it's true: it does, even if Murray would be a less than common name in Hungary. In Hungarian, if a surname ends with 'y' or 'i', it means 'of that place'. Thus, the name Dunay or Dunai means 'of the River Duna' (Danube). Now, it so happens there is a famous river called the Mura in Hungary; it forms part of the borders with Austria, Slovenia and Croatia. So the name Muray means 'of the Mura'. Add another 'r' in the interests of Anglicisation and, presto, you have Murray. That's how I got the name 'Les Murray' – and Peter Skelton was the first to utter it. It was, of course, just a stage name at first; I remained officially Les Ürge for some time. But as my public profile grew and more people knew me as Murray than Ürge, I changed the name by deed poll. Les Ürge was no more.

Finally, on the Saturday, I reported to the Sydney Sports Ground for my first commentary engagement. I arrived three hours early, researched to the eyeballs. After two hours of boredom, memorising every name and fact in the research, we finally had a production meeting where I was introduced to a tall, bulky Englishman called Mike Hill. He was to be my assistant. This was a bit of a surprise, given that I had no idea I was to have an assistant. I later found out that Mike had run second to me in the auditions. John Frank, the league's CEO, favoured him for the job but he was overruled by both Gardam and Skelton. So, rather than assistant, he was actually a deputy, ready to step in if I was sick or had to be absent for some other reason. The match was between Sydney Olympic and South Melbourne, the two Greek-backed powerhouses of the league. There was a big crowd on hand, as there was at all venues in the opening round of the new league that weekend. I was well primed for the commentary and it went beautifully. Apart from describing one incident as an 'almost near miss', it was as good as I had hoped. Skelton reviewed it as faultless.

The show rated around 14 per cent for Ten, an encouraging figure for the 9.30 slot on a Saturday night. Skelton was happy. But sadly, the ratings didn't build, and those of us working on the show were not surprised. It received no promotion whatsoever, either on-station or off. At the time, Ten was the broadcaster of a high profile mid-week rugby league knockout series, an event which received wall to wall promotion on the network. We figured the network wasn't putting its heart into *Philips Top Soccer* and was reluctant to promote it for fear of offending rugby league. It was what Johnny Warren called the 'sheilas, wogs and poofters' mentality at work.

Though I commentated through the entire season, and received no criticism from Peter Skelton or anyone else, for the following season I was overlooked. With season two approaching, I had not heard anything from Ten about preparations. So I rang the match director, Eric Steen, and asked him what the plans were. He said, in a hushed voice: 'We've decided to give Mike a go this year.' Mike was Mike Hill, my 'assistant'. I had been shafted. My dream lasted one year.

That was not the only change to the program. Because the ratings had slipped, the show was not paying for itself and Ten put the knife to its costs. From parading two six-camera full game productions each week, the show was reduced to single camera highlights packages, with Mike calling the main Sydney games. At the end of that season, the show was killed. There ended Channel Ten's bold experiment with covering football. It was to be the last time a metropolitan commercial TV station covered football. The National Soccer League was off the air and had no television coverage until a new kid on the block – SBS – arrived two years later.

In the meantime, my commentary career was rescued immediately after the Channel Ten program died. Out of the blue, I got a phone call from Steve Doszpot, then the main mover and shaker of Canberra City, the NSL club in the nation's capital. Steve was an old acquaintance from my St George days, another Hungarian expat, who migrated to Canberra and basically founded Canberra City. He told me the local commercial station, CTC 7, was about to give live coverage to all of City's home games and was looking for a commentator. Canberra City was the only locally based team of any sport that was taking part in a national league. The capital still had no Canberra Raiders, Canberra Cannons or Brumbies, so its football team was top profile. I got the gig. I flew to Canberra every second Sunday, did the game in the afternoon, and flew back that night. It was easy, gave me some handy pocket money and – importantly – kept me alive and warm as a football commentator. But beyond that, I had no visible prospects in television.

Then SBS came along, bringing another major transformation to my life, and to the fortunes of football in Australia.

9

Football finds a friend

By this time, I was well settled and content in my private life. Eva and I remarried (yes, I married the same woman twice) and had two beautiful, healthy baby daughters, Tania and Natalie, born barely a year apart. I was happy in my day job – chief features sub-editor at the Sydney evening daily, *The Sun* – and saw my future in television as, at best, a sideline or a professional hobby. I also had my own football column on *The Sun*, so kept my profile up as a football man. Believe it or not, I even had a music record review column, so the paper drew heavily on my twin pasts as a football nut and a rock and roller. I was not searching for new opportunities. But suddenly, one came. And with some caution and trepidation, I took it up.

In early 1980, championed by Prime Minister Malcolm Fraser, the Australian government set up a second government-owned national television network, in addition to the ABC. Its mission was to be multicultural in content: a perceived natural extension to a multilingual radio network, the Special Broadcasting Service (SBS), that had been established five years earlier. This perception was wrong – but more about that later. The network was going to be called the Independent Multicultural Broadcasting Corporation, or IMBC. It was going to be heavy on foreign language content, which included Hungarian. I got a call from a man called Ulf Honold, who said he worked for this network which had yet to go to air. He said my name had been given to him as an Australian who was fluent in Hungarian and that there was some work available in subtitling Hungarian programs into English. So I was recruited as a moonlighter on this new network, trotting up to its headquarters in the evenings, three or four nights a week, translating Hungarian movie dialogue into English. Eva, who was fluent in Polish, was hauled in under the same deal.

One night, as I was walking down the corridor from the tea room back to my subtitling booth, I bumped into Peter Skelton: the same Peter Skelton who had given me my break as a football commentator with Channel Ten three years earlier. He had been ousted from Channel Ten and was now working for this new network as a production consultant. He was pleased to see me, especially since the station was about to mount its first live sports telecast, the National Soccer League Grand Final, and didn't have a commentator. His plan had been to import one of England's top callers, to make some sort of a splash, and he tried them all – John Motson, Barry Davies, Hugh Johns and Martin Tyler – without success. He said he was desperate and asked whether I could do it. Naturally, I said yes.

This was on a Friday evening. The game was on the Sunday afternoon in Canberra. On the Saturday morning, I was flown to Canberra and billeted in the Park Royal along with the rest of the crew. At three o'clock that afternoon there was a production meeting, called by the match director, Brian Morelli. Morelli was already a legend among sports directors. He worked for Channel Nine and had been the creative pioneer in the revolutionary way Nine was covering cricket. The reason he was the man to call the meeting was that Peter Skelton, playing it as safe as he could, had hired the entire Channel Nine cricket unit to cover his network's first football match. This, in hindsight, might appear silly. But, in truth, there was no outside broadcast unit in Australia then that had any experience in football.

At the meeting I was told that Johnny Warren was to be my co-commentator. I knew Johnny well; he had been my friend for years. But we had never worked together in television. Still, we had a football wavelength thing going and I was confident it would work. It did: the telecast went off like a dream. Brian Morelli and his crew adapted to football brilliantly. Their camera shots were perfect, the replays were inserted in the right places and Johnny and I bounced off each other as though we had been doing this for years. Heidelberg beat Sydney City 4-0 in a buoyant final and it was as good a live football match broadcast as SBS has done to this day. The next day, *The Sydney Morning Herald* had a review on its back page, lauding it as a breakthrough in sports broadcasting. It was an excellent piece of publicity for the network which had only been on air three days.

For me, although the event was a major thrill, it did not lead to anything at the time. I went back to subtitling and ambled about waiting for the next opportunity to make a football career in television. But only in commentary. Presenting was not on my radar, partly because I had already been rejected by the network as a potential presenter. Earlier, the network had hired an agency to recruit presenters and I applied. They wanted a presentation team with a new look and of a mixed, multicultural nature. I went to the interview, as did Eva. She made the comment that the man who interviewed her was some kind of loser. He wore socks of two different colours. In any event, we were both rejected. But I knew the opportunity would come again because the network had already isolated football as its main strategic sporting niche and there weren't too many football commentators about apart from me.

The man responsible for the vision to turn SBS into 'the soccer station' was Bruce Gyngell. Not that there was such a thing as SBS Television then. The bill to establish the IMBC had still not passed through parliament and, in fact, never did. It was simply called Channel 0-28, because it transmitted on the VHF channel 0 and the UHF channel 28. Gyngell had been a larger-than-life figure in Australian television. It was his face which first appeared in Australian homes in 1956 when he famously greeted the viewers with the words: 'Good evening. Welcome to television.' When 0-28 began transmitting 24 years later, in October 1980, it was Gyngell again who greeted the viewers, this time with the words: 'Good evening. Welcome to multicultural television.' Gyngell had been hired to run the station in this start-up period, and it was he who set its policies on programming and content.

Two things conspired to persuade Gyngell to run with football as its signature sport. The first was that the game wasn't being covered to any significant degree elsewhere on Australian television: the ABC ran a late night highlights program on football bought from the BBC. That was the full extent of it. The lack of football on Australian television before SBS would today astonish viewers. The 1978 World Cup was covered by the ABC but in the form of highlights packages and on a four-day delay. The tapes would be shipped from Buenos Aires to Sydney via London. The ABC didn't think the event warranted the costs of satellite delivery. The 1974 World Cup got four live games but only because the Socceroos were participating. The 1970 World Cup was not covered at all, not even on radio. I listened to the BBC's descriptions of it on short wave radio. And when football was covered it was almost always English. For Australia, the Serie A, Spanish football, Brazilian football, the European Cup may as well have not existed. Juventus may have been the name of an ancient Roman general, for all Australians knew. A whole generation of Australians were growing up in the belief that Bryan Robson and Terry Butcher were the best players in the world. They had not seen nor ever heard of Beckenbauer, Cruyff, Platini or Maradona. SBS was about to fill not a hole but an expansive quarry in the market.

The second reason football was SBS' chosen sport was that it was the game of the world. And SBS was the station of the world. That was its charter, its raison d'être. Its first advertising slogan was 'Bringing the world back home'. Its nightly news bulletin was called *World News*. It was natural, then, that the world's most popular and important sport would be the station's primary sporting focus. Football was a perfect fit for SBS. Besides, it was the sport of the migrant communities and, though the network was never set up just to placate those communities, SBS felt it had a responsibility to respond to their needs. One wondered, for instance, why an Italian migrant with a love for football should have to put up with watching Everton and Liverpool every time a football match was put to air but never see his beloved Juventus or Milan.

Bruce Gyngell had a sharp, clear understanding of why SBS was brought into being and how it could change and improve Australian society. His vision for the network did not necessarily sit well with the ethnic communities who had lobbied hard and successfully with the Fraser government to establish a multilingual TV service. Many of them saw it as an alternative to the Anglo-centric ABC; an extension of SBS Radio, which was nothing more than a multi-lingual service, listened to by first generation immigrants. What Gyngell wanted was a service that would open to Australians a window that had previously been shut: a window to the world and all of its cultural wonders. Before Gyngell's SBS, Australian television was strictly monocultural. If a Martian had landed in Australia and switched on a TV set, he would have got the impression that the earth consisted of three places: Australia, England and the United States.

It was this that Gyngell wanted to put right. That is why, in the early days, SBS had zero imported content from Britain and the US, sourcing its movies, drama, documentaries, music programs and sport strictly from the non-English speaking world. Not everybody understood this and the station received many complaints from the larger ethnic groups about the allocation of programming. The Greeks, for instance, complained that there were far more French movies than Greek on SBS, whereas the Greek community vastly outnumbered the French community. What they didn't understand was that SBS programming was driven not by community interest but by general interest. SBS was for 'all Australians' and that was always at the core of its charter.

All this applied to the network's coverage of football, which was sourced from a multitude of countries: Brazil, Argentina, Italy, Spain, Germany, Portugal, Holland, Belgium, Yugoslavia, the USSR and many more. There, too, the station was hit with complaints from various communities blaring: 'Why are you showing Brazilian football? There are far more of us in Australia than there are Brazilians'. Again, it was a case of misreading the station's mission. It showed Brazilian football not to please the Brazilian community, but because it was good. SBS used only one criterion in choosing what football it would import: it had to be good.

In the early years of SBS, though I was not an executive and was merely a part-time commentator, I became very much involved in the selection of the football we would buy. This was not because I was such a big football expert but because the executives in charge of this activity knew nothing about football and sought my advice. Luckily, I understood early the Gyngell mission and helped translate it to football programming. It was difficult at first because this kind of football was so unheard of, so lacking in general awareness by Australians, that the audiences were miniscule. But little by little, year by year, they grew. Eventually, SBS saw fat results for its long-term investment in football. The reality is, football in Australia got extremely lucky with the arrival of SBS television in 1980. Never mind its decision to cover football. Far more important in this success story was SBS' capacity for patience and persistence. On any other network, football would have been taken off the air, or buried in a 2 am slot, as soon as it became obvious that it wasn't rating. And I doubt if such long-term persistence would be possible today, even on SBS. These days, with extensive media diversification and much broader choice for content by the consumer, SBS lives in a far more competitive environment and needs to respond to far greater competing pressures.

But let's turn back to how it all began. Months before the network started transmitting in October 1980, the station execs bought a bundle of football material from overseas. Some of this stuff was months – even years – old. But no one cared, and the execs probably didn't even know. After all, how would the Australian audience, which didn't follow any football except the local and the English, know whether a match between Flamengo and Corinthians in Brazil was played a year ago or yesterday? It was the quality and the different brand of football that mattered. Immediately after the start of transmission this material was put into a weekly show called *International Soccer*. The show was hosted by Vladimir Lusic. Vlado was the quintessential 'ethnic', almost a living and breathing caricature of the 'new Australian'. If there was such a thing as the 'face of SBS' in those early days of pushing the multicultural thing, Vlado was it. He had a thick shock of hair, piercing brown eyes under threatening eyebrows, a thick Zapata moustache, a deep baritone voice and a heavy Croatian accent. He was an SBS news reporter who had put his hand up as a lover of football. That qualified him to moonlight as the station's first soccer host.

I was also moonlighting, as part-time subtitler come football commentator. Some of the games brought in had English commentaries on them, but others didn't. On the games that didn't, I was to supply the commentary off-tube. Off-tube commentary meant not being at the venue but describing the action as if one was, while viewing the game on a monitor in a small, dark audio booth. This was not such a common thing in those days and many viewers were fooled. One friend phoned me and said: 'Geez Les, you've scored a good gig, travelling the world: in Buenos Aires one week and Rome the next.' The first off-tube commentary I did was a World Cup qualifier between Italy and Yugoslavia played in Turin. My daring producer, John Rowley, had an idea. He pre-recorded an on-camera introduction, with me wearing headphones and – because it was cold in Turin at that time of year – a ski jacket. He then inserted the intro into the top corner of the screen at the start of the game as the players were warming up, creating the illusion that

I was at the venue. Nobody complained, and it appeared that everyone had been happily sucked in. Everyone except the Head of Television, Alex Baz, who rang Rowley at home and boomed: 'Don't you ever, *ever*, try that again.' My career as an off-tube caller of football lasted another 15 years. I took many voyages around the world and never once moved out of my small audio booth on Sydney's north shore.

It was a craft I taught myself. Nobody coached me, basically because there was nobody in Australia more experienced or senior than I in football commentating. One of the secrets I developed was to watch only 10 or 15 minutes of the game on tape before I recorded the commentary. I had to watch some of it so that I could identify players I had never seen before. But I didn't want to watch too much because I wanted to maintain an element of natural surprise in the call. I made a point of never seeing a goal before I commentated on it. I knew, from research, in exactly what minute the goals would fall and carefully avoided seeing those moments in my preparation. This didn't always work out. On one occasion, I commentated on a goal that was so brilliant I screamed my intestines out in elation. It was as natural a response to a great goal as any commentator could give in a live situation. The audio engineer stopped the tape and muttered in my headphones: 'Sorry. Can we do that bit again? Your voice was distorting.' I screamed back at him in disgust: 'Oh yeah? And what would you have done if this was a live game, fucking imbecile?'

Because I was calling so many different games involving such a variety of teams from such an array of places, good research was critical. Getting that wrong could lead to disaster. As it did on the occasion of the 1981 Toyota Cup in Tokyo between Flamengo and Liverpool. The tape of the game came in with a very ordinary English commentary in an American accent, so we decided to re-stripe it with mine. There were no team captions on the tape so I had to research the line-ups myself. Liverpool was no problem: I knew most of their players. But for Flamengo I used the existing commentary as my guide to identifying the players and the coaches on the bench, assuming that our American friend had done his research. So the Flamengo goalkeeper came out as Defensor, rather than Raul and, worst of all, the Flamengo coach was identified as Coutinho. What I didn't know at the time was that Claudio Coutinho, who indeed had been a successful coach at Flamengo, was dead, having drowned in a scuba diving accident 10 months earlier. The coach on the bench was his replacement, Paulo Cesar Carpeggiani. The following week, in *World Soccer*, Andrew Dettre reviewed my commentary performance under the headline: 'The ghost of Coutinho walks in Tokyo'.

The story illustrates the vastly different times in which we lived and how things have changed. Nowadays, you can buy an entire season of football games and they will be delivered to you in slick packages, complete with graphics, commentaries, music – the lot. In those days, if we bought a game all we got was a roll of tape with pictures and crowd effects on it. Often, they didn't even have replays of the goals. The packaging was done entirely by us. Research was a nightmare. There was no internet, no Google search engine to easily locate information. I relied on foreign language publications and even a network of foreign-speaking contacts with football knowledge as my research sources. If I had to commentate on, say, the Yugoslav derby between Red Star and Partizan, I called a friend in the Serbian press who gladly rattled off the line-ups, the officials, the size of the crowd, even the weather conditions. Whatever Italian, Spanish and French I understand today, I began to learn from scouring newspapers and magazines in those languages, figuring out, by a process of logical deduction, the facts of the game. It wasn't that hard, just painstakingly slow. If, for instance, the name Trapattoni appeared after the word *Allenatore*, then I knew that in Italian *allenatore* meant coach. And so on.

A challenge for me, not shared by sports commentators on other networks, was the matter of pronunciation. On other stations, 'wog' names were pronounced as they were read, with no care given to their accuracy. This is still largely the case and, frankly, it is unprofessional and a disgrace. But for us, it was different. Because

SBS dealt with content – especially football content – that involved many foreign names, and because it had a culturally sensitive audience, we had to take special care with pronunciations. And we did. Right from the early years, SBS became known for pronouncing foreign names properly. George Donikian, SBS' early frontline newsreader, took special care and was very good at it. Mary Kostakidis, who took over from George and still reads the SBS news, is equally good and takes equal care. She will rarely go to air with a difficult name, without checking with a native of that tongue. When it comes to Hungarian, she usually rings me.

This seemed revolutionary in Australian broadcasting at the time but the formula was simple: taking care, and respecting the person whose name you were pronouncing and, especially, the members of the community – the language group – concerned. I still get phone calls and letters from viewers correcting me on pronunciations; I listen to them and try to get it right the next time. Sometimes I'm accused of being over the top with all this: maybe, being a 'wog' myself, pronunciations come easier for me than for other broadcasters. But it's in my nature to try and get these things right and I wince every time I hear mispronunciations on television like 'Shut-up-over' instead of Sharapova. I remember one commentator at the Seoul Olympics in 1988 referring to a Turkish weightlifter as Smith because he couldn't, or was too lazy to, learn how to pronounce his name. I was surprised he was ever allowed to work again but he was. As head of sport at the network, I will not tolerate slackness in pronunciations from my colleagues. It's not hard. SBS, because of its large subtitling unit, has very good language resources; foreign speakers who can set you right on pronunciations are just a phone call away.

Happy and content with being a commentator, I had no designs on being a presenter or an on-camera person of any kind. But within a couple of weeks of SBS' inception, an unforeseen opportunity kick-started my career as a presenter. The Socceroos were on tour in Europe and their game against Greece was being beamed in live from Athens: SBS' first live coverage of an international match via satellite. John Rowley went along as the producer and took David Fordham, then of NBN-3 Newcastle, as commentator. Vlado Lusic hosted the coverage from the Sydney studio. All was going well until some minutes into the second half, when we lost the satellite signal. Cutting back to the studio host, the normal practice in these instances, only made things worse. Vlado froze on camera, was totally unprepared for the contingency, and the director was forced to switch to a station ID slide. Skelton called me and asked if I could take over all football hostings. Without any training, or even a rehearsal, I began presenting the weekly *International Soccer* program the following week.

Soon my workload at SBS multiplied to such a degree that I virtually had two full-time jobs. I would start my shift at *The Sun* at 6.30 in the morning, finish at 3.30 in the afternoon and adjourn to SBS to do researching, scripting, commentating and hosting until 10 pm. With the two jobs I was earning good money, very useful for a man with a young family. Eva, a full-time mother, tolerated my long hours away from home. And soon, those hours extended to weekends. SBS was now rights holder of the NSL and once the new season began, in March of 1981, I was required to commentate on the Sunday match of the week from location – often interstate – and host a compilation highlights program which went to air each Monday at 6 pm. Every week, I was hosting two shows, and commentating on one overseas and one local game. I also hosted all one-off special events such as European Cup finals, and did all the associated research and scripting for all the games. This went on until 1983 when the newly appointed SBS Head of Television, Ian McGarrity, figured I was too valuable to the network to allow such a draining schedule and offered me a full-time contract. The salary was enough to cover what I would lose by leaving *The Sun*, and that year I left newspapers for good to become a full-time television man.

In the late 1980s, before the birth of the internet and pay-television, the respected English monthly *World Soccer* did a global survey on football television coverage. It was disappointed in the results, which showed that by and large coverage of the game in every country was mono-focused and local-centric: on German television you only saw German football, on English television only English football, on Brazilian television only Brazilian football and so on. The only exception it found was Australia and a namesake program on a multicultural television network. It called SBS TV's *World Soccer* 'the only definitive, comprehensive football program' it could find anywhere in the world. Fifteen years after Eric Batty and I trekked across the English Channel to catch a glimpse of Netzer and Cruyff, not much had changed in England or anywhere else. Except in Australia, where there was this one-hour program that took the viewer on a global voyage of discovery every week.

The roots of the *World Soccer* program were in the first football show SBS launched, *International Soccer*, hosted by Vlado Lusic. It had a simple format: front and back hostings (top and tail, as it's known in the business) and, in between, a selected match from some part of the world, edited down to under an hour and usually re-voiced into English. After I replaced Vlado, it was re-named *World Soccer* and moved to the 5.30 to 6.30 slot on Saturday after-noons, where it stayed for the best part of the following 22 years. It grew to be the longest running sports program in the history of Australian television but, more than that, it had a deep and enduring impact on all aspects of football in Australia, including its technical development.

But first it had to evolve. And the process began almost as soon as I became involved. We decided to reduce the duration of the main feature match and to utilise the huge volume of unshown news highlights we were already getting. We also had access to the brilliant Italian program *Domenica Sportiva*, a two-hour weekly review of the Italian Serie A which goes to air on Sunday nights. This program not only included highlights of all games in the Serie A but had interviews with the big stars as well. Suddenly,

Australian fans who had previously only read about these players in newspapers and magazines were seeing them in action and meeting them as people, speaking in their own languages.

For football fans, this was an astounding break from the recent past. Some of the world's greatest ever players – Maradona, Zico, Socrates, Falcao, Platini, Van Basten, Gullit – were first seen in Australia on SBS. And they were being seen week in and week out. In one of the earliest games I called, Argentinos Juniors, with a teenage Maradona in its line-up, met Boca Juniors and won 5-2, with Diego scoring four of the goals. It was a magnificent exhibition, the like of which was rarely repeated, even on SBS. Maradona was later exalted as a demi-god when, in 1986, he almost single-handedly won the World Cup for Argentina. The rest of the world was astonished by his superhuman qualities. But not SBS viewers, who had been watching him do much the same for his clubs for five years.

We ran results and tables, trying to fill the gap the rest of the media were leaving as they fed their obsession with the rugby sports, Aussie rules and cricket. Later in the series, I came up with the idea of mentioning significant dates such as birthdays. Thus was born the birthday tribute: a closer to the program with a musical montage of a great player scoring goals and doing his stuff. These became enormously popular; people used to record them onto master tapes and run them at soccer parties. We had so much material in the library, some of these closers ran as long as seven or eight minutes. We even had special nostalgia editions and, for a time, we re-ran that fabulous 1960 European Cup final once a year every May. To this day, I have never had as much viewer mail as I did after first screening that match in 1985. One young man wrote: 'My old man would forever eulogise and preach to me about how the game used to be played in the old days and I always dismissed him as living in nostalgic fantasy. Now I know he had been right.'

All this had a tremendously mind-broadening impact on Australian audiences; not just football fans, but many others

besides. Just as Bruce Gyngell had wanted and imagined, a window
had been opened for Australians, and they liked what they saw
when they looked through it. Perhaps the biggest impact was on
the young. The timing of *World Soccer* – 5.30 on Saturday after-
noons – was perfect for the kids. They would play in the morning
in their suburban leagues, go shopping or to the beach with their
parents and be home in time to watch the program. Neville Wran,
the NSW premier, who had a football playing grandson, became a
fan of the world game via this ritual. Don Lane, the entertainer, got
hooked via his son. Who knows how many others there were like
this? Johnny Warren, in his book *Sheilas, Wogs and Poofters*, dedicated a chapter to SBS and titled it 'Australia's best coach'. He was
referring to SBS' capacity to have made a technical impact on
Australia's coaching and youth development. Kids watched, and
saw the high quality football and the different ways football could
be played. They saw the great players – the geniuses of the world
game – and were inspired by them, tried to imitate them. They
grew up admiring role models. Harry Kewell and Mark Viduka
both name Marco Van Basten as their greatest childhood inspiration. Both only ever saw Van Basten on SBS; more specifically, on
World Soccer. For Australians, he was not visible anywhere else.

The same went for coaching and coaches. In 1989, two young
men appeared in my office attempting to peddle a concept they
thought might benefit the Australian game. They were Gary and
Simon Ireland: two brothers, Australian-born football-loving jour-
neymen, who had returned after years abroad searching for the
game's holy grail. They asked me if I had heard of something called
the Coerver Method. I pleaded dumb. They described to me a revolutionary coaching method for young players, developed by the
Dutch coach Wiel Coerver. The concept of it was built on both
individual and collective skill, whereby the skills and moves of the
world's greatest players and teams, through a system of drills, could
be imitated, practised and perfected to produce wonderful young
players. They showed me some tapes. I was impressed and showed
off the tapes on *World Soccer*, persuading the network's corporate

heavies to agree to market them as videos. The tapes sold like hot cakes and the Coerver Method became adopted by various coaching bodies around Australia. It continues to exist today as an important ingredient in the drive to fashion excellence among young footballers. All thanks to the Ireland brothers and SBS' willingness and capacity to give exposure to the Coerver notion.

People remember telecasts of mega events like World Cups and major matches involving the Socceroos as being the key vehicles by which SBS put football into the Australian sporting psyche. To my mind, more than those things, it was the weekly diet of *World Soccer* that did it. Hence its long run. The show survived five SBS managing directors, five heads of television, two network programmers, two chairmen of the board, several dozen directors, four heads of sport – and at no time was its demise even remotely contemplated. Ironically it was I, now as head of sport, who brought about its end. In 2002, in the wake of the enormous success of that year's World Cup – watched by 14.8 million Australian viewers – it became clear that a one-hour weekly program dedicated to international football just wasn't enough. *World Soccer* was replaced by a six-hour mega-show on Sundays, carrying a title even more closely associated with the SBS identity: *The World Game*.

10

It's not a game, it's a mission

Almost as soon as I was given a microphone and a camera, I felt it my place and responsibility not only to present but to preach the beauties of football. Sure, I was a journalist, trained to be objective and balanced in all aspects of carrying out my duties. But this was different: I was now working for a television network whose charter gave it a clear mandate to introduce – as an instrument of multiculturalism – new experiences into the Australian consciousness. It was therefore the station's duty to present the best possible football and it was my duty to accentuate the game's beauties. After all these years, I can say in all conscience that I never did this by attempting to denigrate other sports. I simply did it – and SBS simply did it – by highlighting the things that make football beautiful and the world's most popular sport.

With each commentary or written script, particularly in the early years, I attempted to embroider my words with a sense of passion and protection for the sport that had conquered the world but, puzzlingly, failed to conquer Australia. I felt from the outset that if football was ever going to conquer my country, here was a golden opportunity for me to be an instrument in that process. I make no apology for it. This missionary fervour involved not just spreading the word on football; it had to be the right kind of football. It was only in this area that I encountered difficulties: in the first instance, because I was often accused of bias against teams which I reckoned were playing ugly football and, in the second instance, because I was often accused of being negative, especially when criticising less than able football officialdom. But in each of those instances I was trying to protect the game and influence the propaganda process. I figured that ugly or dull and unimaginative football would never convert anyone. Furthermore, I felt there needed to be the widest possible distinction made between football and other sports, especially the rugby sports, in order to highlight football's distinct character before it could be easily 'discovered' by new fans. If, for instance, football was overly brutal and physical, there was little to distinguish it – apart from its rules and the shape of the ball – from rugby. How, then, would potential converts to football appreciate its distinctive beauties?

On this mission, I found a perfect and priceless ally in Johnny Warren, or should I say: we found each other. By the time Johnny was hauled aboard the SBS wagon we were already friends and he had spent years bashing the football bible. But it was his on-screen alliance with me that made the power of the mission seriously formidable: SBS could not have succeeded in converting millions to football the way it did without Johnny Warren.

The relationship and friendship between Johnny Warren and me is well documented in the book, *Mr and Mrs Soccer*, and in Johnny's earlier autobiography, *Sheilas, Wogs and Poofters*. But it is important that I encapsulate here the key ingredients that made the bond so strong and, ultimately, so powerful. Firstly, though he was not an immigrant, he lived most of his football life among immigrants – mostly Hungarians. So he had become emotionally intertwined with the migrant urge to open Australian eyes to football. He was part of the grand contribution immigrants made to the development of football; on a philosophical level, we were ethnically as one. Secondly, he and I had an identical football ideology. We both saw real football as a game played with intelligence, skill and style, and shunned the boofheadedness of so-called football that relied only on strength, speed, discipline and so-called 'character'. One of his stock jokes was to quote Jack Charlton, the towering England centre back of the 1960s, who famously said of Diego Maradona when he first saw him: 'I like the boy number 10. Good first touch'. He hated the word 'pace' when others used it to describe great players such as Ronaldinho or Thierry Henry, whose technique and capacity to improvise gave them their greatness, not their pace. So we were ideological soul mates when it came to football. Thirdly, we had an equally well developed awareness of the social resistance football had to smash down in order to become an equal with other sports in Australia. And fourthly, we were both fiercely independent and single-minded in the cause.

We were football fans first and last, and couldn't give a damn whether it was Liverpool, Milan, England or Brazil that won, as long as whoever did it won with the right kind of football. About the only team we both rooted for was Australia. Apart from that, neither of us was a scarf-carrying fan of any team. Granted, Johnny had been seen wearing replica shirts of Brazil. But that had nothing to do with any kind of allegiance to the Brazilian flag. It was a statement of his affection for the team which, historically, played football the way Johnny felt the game was meant to be played. In this, too, we were as one. After Brazil was eliminated from the 1990 World Cup in Italy, we went back to our hotel room and got mercilessly drunk.

All this, of course, may not have been enough to form a strong bond if we had been different people on a personal level. But thankfully this was not the case. Johnny and I got on famously in all things: we both smoked, laughed at the same jokes, were politically aligned, loved travelling and smelling the scents of other cultures, and liked the same foods, as well as a drop of wine or Scotch. If we sensed that there were areas in which we were likely to disagree, we left those alone and retreated to talking football.

Our association began with that 1980 NSL Grand Final in Canberra but it was not an immediate start to a professional relationship. Johnny was still doing stuff for Channel 7, working with 'The Moose' – Rex Mossop: your classic rugby league producer, and host of a show on which Johnny's football segment got two minutes each Saturday. Rex once told Johnny, 'If your game ever becomes popular in Australia I'll bare my arse in Martin Place'.

In 1982, Johnny independently presented a kids' football series for SBS called *Captain Socceroo*. But he didn't join the network on contract until 1984. It was then we began our professional affiliation that was to last 20 years, until his death in 2004. In that span we covered five World Cups together, seven World Youth Championships, four European Championships, six South American championships, 18 European Cup finals, 10 FA Cup finals, over 100 Socceroo matches and 750 NSL games. No wonder we ended up eating out of the same football bowl.

Our second home was the SBS studio in the idyllic, harbourside Sydney suburb of Milsons Point. Studio, not studios – because we only had one. And it was neither picturesque nor idyllic. It measured 10 metres by 8 metres. Once you stumbled past the cameras and crew, space was so tight that a performing guitarist would have had to strum the guitar vertically to avoid knocking over some of the equipment. It was there that Johnny and I spent much of our lives between 1984 and 1993, when SBS moved to more salubrious quarters in Artarmon.

Working the mission came at a price. The best football in the world – the type we wanted to show off – was played in parts of the world where it was summer when we had our winter, and where it was evening when – for us – the sparrows had yet to open their eyes. Game after game, year after year, we had to turn up at three in the morning, prepare, and be ready to front the cameras at four. We had no idea who was watching, or indeed whether anyone was watching at all. There were times when the make-up girl never made it and we had to do our own powdering. One time, Johnny slept in and we went to air without him, faced with having to explain how he mysteriously appeared in his chair at half time. Another time, both of us slept in, having had a deep and meaningful the previous night over a full bottle of Scotch. Three alarm clocks went off without as much as a quiver from either of us. Miraculously, we made it — after my front door had been practically kicked down by a conscientious production manager who didn't fancy facing the cameras in my place. The viewers never knew it. Borussia Dortmund beat Juventus 3-1. The production manager, Rob Marin, who was a major Juventus fan, called it a day to forget.

But all that was easy compared with the 1985 European Cup final — the day of Heysel — when we became live broadcasters to a major tragedy that claimed 38 lives. The match we were hosting, played at the Heysel Stadium in Brussels, was between Liverpool and Juventus, distinctly the two most illustrious teams in Europe at the time. Liverpool, with Aussie Craig Johnston in their midst, were trying to win their fifth European title in seven years. Juventus, serial winners of the Serie A and agog with star players led by the magical Frenchman Michel Platini, were chasing a title they had only won once before. The mixture was right for a classic game and a good morning's entertainment. But it all turned bad.

Our studio call was for 4.15 am with the game due to kick off at 4.45. We were to do the usual chitchat, analyse the two teams and how they got to the final, run a few minutes of highlights of lead-up games and throw to the commentator. But as we waffled on, I got the word in my earpiece from the director that there was a delay to kick-off. I was told there had been some crowd trouble outside the stadium and we may have to fill for a while. So we filled. But then came further word that some people had died. The first figure was eight, then it grew to 15 and then to 25. It hit me that a colossal catastrophe was unfolding, even though we were not to learn the full extent of it until the next day. I tried to get a grip. Here we were, broadcasting a showpiece game of football which was turning into the darkest possible advertisement for the game: hooliganism was at work, and now it was killing people. I began to editorialise about how the enemies of football would use and exploit this occasion to beat football about the head. Which, of course, they did. But editorialising at such a time was probably insensitive, and I now regret doing it.

On the line to the studio control room was Gary Thornthwaite, then SBS head of sport, who was in Melbourne having covered a game between the Australian B team and Tottenham Hotspur the previous evening. He saw the bind we were in: there to talk football but having to talk about a tragedy, a tragedy we'd rather not have talked about.

Johnny and I were football commentators, not social analysts. We could have stuck to talking football — but how can you sit there talking football when people are dying? Gary came to the rescue by deciding to feed the Australia B-Spurs game up the bearer from Melbourne and instructed the control room to put it to air as a filler. Conscious of our mission to protect the game, he also ordered that no news vision of the violence be put to air during the broadcast. That was for the News department, he said; this was a sports telecast.

After a delay of one and a half hours, the game went ahead and we proceeded to broadcast it. Predictably, we were criticised in some sections of the media for not pulling the plug. Though I was not party to that decision, I believe Gary Thornthwaite acted properly by broadcasting the match. His decision should be understood in the context of the way hooliganism — rife at the time and much worse than it is today — was constantly eating away at SBS' campaign to have football appreciated. Hooliganism was never 'soccer violence', as the sneering and opportunist media call it. It was just hooliganism: a symptom of a deeper social disease which had nothing much to do with sport. Football was merely the stage: a common reference point the loonies were using on which to play out their hideous form of tribalism. It was in this context that the decision was made to go ahead with broadcasting the match. The violence and the tragedy were indeed news stories. But our viewers had risen at dawn that day to watch a football game — however tainted that game may have become — and that's what we had to give them.

In the mid-1980s, competition between major sports in Australia – especially in the area of marketing – began to intensify. It was at this time that sports such as rugby league, Aussie rules and the new kid on the block – basketball – started running advertising campaigns to grab a bigger stake in the sports spectator and participation market. Rugby league went with the label 'the greatest game of all' and Tina Turner began wailing that it was 'simply the best'. Rugby union stuck to its old claim that it was 'the game they play in heaven'. And Aussie rules was making its leap on the back of the hit song 'Up There Cazaly'. (Neville Wran, at one of those battle-of-the-codes functions, quipped: 'Rugby is played in heaven, football is played here on earth and Aussie rules is played in Melbourne.') But football was neither sufficiently well resourced nor sufficiently businesslike in its thinking to be able to compete. Football's entire marketing vehicle was SBS: effectively the marketing arm of the Australian Soccer Federation.

And it was at SBS that football, quite by accident, got itself a branding label that would make a seductive, unchallengeable statement about the might of the sport. The label was 'the world game'. Over the years I have been credited with inventing this label, though I have never ever made that claim. It is certainly not true that I sat down one day and began scratching my head – like an advertising copy writer would – trying to come up with a clever slogan with which to market football. If I did give birth to the label, it was simply born out of my old sense of mission. Responding to the nauseating claims by other sports to be the greatest, best, heavenly, etcetera, I wanted to use a term that distinguished football – my sport – from the others. It had to be one that flattered the sport but it also had to be objective. I had always thought calling one's favourite sport 'the best' or 'the greatest' was natural – but it is about as convincing as a father claiming his daughter is the prettiest girl in the world. Big deal. The label for football had to be objective, factual and unchallengeable.

As I sat down one morning to write a stock intro for an episode of *World Soccer*, the words flew into my head. The stock intro every week read: 'Good evening. Welcome again to *World Soccer* . . .' This time I wrote: 'Good evening. Welcome to the world game . . .' Similarly, the stock farewell sentence of 'From *World Soccer*, good night,' I changed to: 'From the world game, good night'. I didn't think it would have much of an impact; thought it would probably be dismissed or ignored as just another of my subtle attempts to hype up my scripts and, with the power of suggestion, woo more converts to the true faith. But it stuck. And gradually it became accepted as the standard label that would distinguish football from other sports. Today, football is referred to as 'the world game' not just by its fans but by even its enemies. Of course, once I saw that the label was making an impact, I extended its use to every football program or event I hosted, and by the time I presented SBS' first exclusive coverage of the World Cup in 1990, I greeted viewers by welcoming them not to the World Cup but to the world game. A decade and a half after the birth of the label, when I initiated the spawning of a football website for SBS, I insisted that it be called *The World Game*. And in 2002, SBS launched its most ambitious and comprehensive football program ever, with the title *The World Game*.

Meanwhile, another evolutionary change to the nomenclature was germinating at SBS, this one championed by Johnny Warren. And this change, like 'the world game', would gain widespread and common acceptance over the ensuing two decades. It was the usage of the term 'football' instead of 'soccer'. Like me, Johnny never liked the word 'soccer', and he wasn't enamoured of the label 'Socceroos' either. In 24 years of commentating with Johnny I don't recall him ever calling Australia 'the Socceroos'. Mike Hill, a regular commentator at SBS, even went so far as to religiously call the team the 'Winfield Socceroos' in generous deference to a tobacco sponsor. Johnny, his co-commentator, just referred to the team as Australia. But pushing the word football in preference to soccer in 1980s Australia was less than rewarding. Football was simply not popular enough – hadn't penetrated far enough into the common psyche – so as not to cause confusion among viewers who also regarded rugby, rugby league and Aussie rules as 'football'. That is why, even at SBS, we stuck with the word soccer for some years, calling our flagship program *World Soccer*, not World Football. Imagine the level of puzzlement there would have been in Melbourne, for instance – where there was only one kind of 'football' – if we had called our program World Football. Their kind of 'football' was only played in Australia; so the concept of a program dealing with 'world football' would have been curious to them indeed.

This was more than a matter of SBS editorial policy: it was a hobby horse for Johnny and me. It annoyed the crap out of us that sports which were primarily played with the hands were being referred to as football while the game played with the feet – in which the use of hands was outlawed, and which the rest of the world called football – was being referred to as soccer. The very word suggested a 'second class citizen' status for the game. Football – the real football – was like a black sheep brother in a family of so-called football codes. The media would say: 'It's the start of the football season so, whoopee, we have the full coverage and preview of all football codes.' But football – soccer – wasn't included.

The game was referred to as 'the round ball game', which was equally offensive. Round ball game? Which round ball game? Most ball games are played with a round ball: football, tennis, golf, basketball, cricket, baseball, table tennis, volleyball, water polo, handball and many more. Again, it was a way of sidelining football: setting it aside as some kind of entity foreign to the norms of the rest of 'football'.

We chipped away at this, especially Johnny, who was unconcerned by the confusion it might cause. It was his style. If people couldn't understand what he meant by football, they could work it out. So he would go into an interview where he would be asked: 'When will soccer get its act together?' And he would answer: 'Well, partly when football ceases to be discriminated against.' Little by little, this part of the mission started to hit home. When David Hill became chairman of the Australian Soccer Federation in 1995, he wanted to change the name of the body to Football Australia. He got rolled by the board. But he had put a stake in the ground: sent up a signal that all was not right about the use of this word soccer.

When I became head of sport at SBS in 1996 I made it editorial policy – house style – to use only the word football; I outlawed 'soccer'. I also banned the expressions 'the round ball game' and 'code' in reference to football. I considered football to be a sport in its own right and not a code of anything. Once, in Israel, I was asked to come to the local television station by a local reporter in some panic. He was having a major translation problem with an interview he had done with the Australian coach Frank Arok. He could not decipher a word Arok was using: the word turned out to be 'code'; Arok had used it in reference to football. I thought, 'How will I explain this?' In Israel, there are no such things as codes of football. There is only football, and then there are other sports. So how will the word 'code' translate into Hebrew and still be understood in the context in which it was meant? I advised that they simply use the Hebrew word for 'sport' as a direct translation.

Johnny Warren continued the fight for the use of the word 'football' until his death. When he was already suffering from cancer he responded to a call by the NSW Premier, Bob Carr, to chair a task force and set up a scheme to enhance football development in the state. In his report he insisted, among other things, that the word football, and not soccer, be used in every reference to the project. The NSW Soccer Task force became the NSW Football Task Force and its chief derivative, the Johnny Warren Soccer Foundation, became the Johnny Warren Football Foundation.

In early 2005, a few months after Johnny's death, the Australian Soccer Association announced that it would change its name to Football Federation Australia. John O'Neill, the chief executive of that body and a rugby man by persuasion and background, never publicly uttered the word soccer in reference to football again. Even earlier, two prominent Sydney newspapers, *The Sydney Morning*

Herald and *The Sun-Herald*, declared an editorial policy change. Soccer, in all copy, was now to be referred to as football. If not quite mission accomplished, these were major breakthroughs. Johnny Warren, looking down from above, would have been smiling from ear to ear.

It was a hard grind, working at the mission, and not all of it was rewarding. Covering the NSL for one. This was truly a hard slog that required sacrifice. It meant being away from my family every Sunday, most often to travel interstate. My children grew up minus the tradition of a Sunday family lunch. I would kiss them and be off, meeting Johnny and crew at some stadium or airport lounge, at the ready to cover a game that would attract only a smallish audience and carry a few paragraphs in the next day's fish wrapper. In retrospect, hats off to SBS and its corporate heads for their belief in it. The NSL, throughout its life, always got prime coverage and high programming priority on the network. Right up until the network lost the rights, and the deal was made to take 'soccer' on to Channel 7 in 1998, SBS's faith in the sport never waned.

SBS covered the National Soccer League from 1981 to 1998: 18 years of weekly prime time; free to air exposure that would be seen as a supreme gift to the game today. But in those years, the product was far more difficult to sell; and doubly so for SBS. This was the era of ethnic clubs with ethnic followings and SBS, stereotyped as the ethnic station, appeared the perfect fit as a broadcaster. Later, the notion would arise that the league would be better off on another network as a way of escaping the 'wogs' game' tag and gaining acceptance by the Australian mainstream. This, I think, was uppermost in the mind of David Hill when he jettisoned SBS as a broadcast partner.

But this notion was wrong. Rather than football being tainted and stigmatised by SBS it was, in my view, the other way around. It was SBS that was being seen as the 'wog station' as a result of its enthusiastic willingness to cover the 'wogs' game'. Unlike some of the insecure governors of football, SBS was not uncomfortable with this. The migrant communities were in the throes of changing Australian society irreversibly and for the better and SBS, as an agent of multiculturalism, was happy to be a catalyst in that process. Propagating the world game – the game of the migrants – was precisely in line with the aims of multiculturalism and what SBS had been established to do.

It is also true that Johnny Warren and I saw ourselves as more than just broadcasters of football. We also had a protective instinct for the game and tried to play a role in improving it, often to the annoyance of the game's administrators. For example, in the early 1980s the playing standard in the NSL was dropping and the game was becoming decidedly ugly. The football was overly physical, even thuggish, and the referees were not given the licence to deal with it. In one of the first editorials I did for SBS, I called for a clean-up campaign, advocating harsher penalties, the use of video evidence to determine punishment, and even the deduction of points for clubs that failed to clean up their disciplinary records. After a few more weeks of nagging, the campaign bit. NSL admin-istrators, seeing the league's diminishing marketability, decided to act and the game was cleaned up.

We had a similar influence, I believe, in the introduction of summer football. Johnny and I, along with a number of high profile allies like top coaches Frank Arok and Eddie Thomson, were long-term advocates for switching the seasons of the NSL from winter to summer. The arguments were plentiful and hard to challenge: no competition from other 'codes', better weather for families, better conditions for evening games, better pitches, better football. This took a lot longer: we went on and on about it for years. The seasons were finally switched in 1989, with immediate success and an upswing in attendances. And there were other areas in which SBS had a positive influence, such as the introduction of three points for a win and the admission of a Perth franchise into the league.

One of SBS' earliest innovations, as a marketing ploy, was to place its cameras so they were shooting into the crowd or the main stand. In the early years, club venues usually had only one main stand which was always placed on the western side of the field, ensuring that spectators were not looking into the setting sun. And that's where the cameras would also go to ensure the lighting was right and the players were not appearing like silhouettes against the glare of the sun. The problem with those camera positions was that the bulk of the crowd was not seen. Spectators would always fill up the main stand first and, unless the arena was filled to capacity, the opposite side, towards which the cameras were pointed, showed only a few dozen individuals. At times, it was worse than that. In the case of Brisbane Lions' home ground, at what was then rural Richlands, we ended up with a backdrop of half a dozen grazing cows.

Once summer football was introduced and games were played in the evening, the sun was no longer a problem and we moved the cameras. It was an instant hit, especially with NSL administrators who made it a requirement for member clubs to build camera scaffoldings opposite their main grandstands. Once, when we tried for technical reasons to divert from the new norm and shoot away from the main stand, our match director copped a huge serve from the league's operations manager, Peter Russell; the two of them nearly came to blows.

These were the years when SBS covered football with a kind of saintly zealousness. The station saw itself as a member of an underdog clan: a partner of football in its underprivileged status and its pining for acceptance. It covered the action but it also spoke loudly against the forces that were working to hold the game back, even when those forces were the administrators of the game themselves. This made SBS, beyond being a broadcaster and a television partner, a protector and custodian of the game.

In 1988, the long-serving president of the Australian Soccer Federation, Sir Arthur George, finally decided to step down. His anointed successor was John Constantine, a high-flying young lawyer and *paisano* of Greek parentage. But to everyone's surprise, political manoeuvres installed veteran Queenslander Ian Brusasco as the new chief. In the press conference room at the Camperdown Travelodge after the announcement, Johnny Warren and I glared at each other and wondered what this would mean for SBS. In the era of Sir Arthur, we had our differences with the ASF but by and large we got on well with him; and he considered SBS a valued, if last resort, partner. He knew what it had been like for football in the bad old pre-SBS world of television coverage – or lack of it. We would have felt equally safe with Constantine, assuming that the younger man would follow his mentor's policies. But Brusasco was a mystery and, as it turned out, we had good reason to be uneasy.

At the time, David Hill was running the ABC. Apart from being a man of the Labor Party, which installed him as ABC chairman from where he bounced to become its managing director, he was a high performing and ambitious executive. Unfortunately for us, he was also a born football fan and still an active player. Rumours were circulating that Hill had designs on snaring the football rights from SBS. At the time, the ABC had lost most of its previous hold on sports rights and its entire sports identity had been purged by the big-money muscle of the commercial stations. It needed sports content and looked on enviously at SBS' rich, brand-building hegemony over football. Given that SBS still had a year to run on its rights contract with the ASF, we ignored the rumours. I had a courtesy meeting with Brusasco where I got the impression that he was content with the existing television arrangements and wanted to continue.

In late November that year I flew off to Fiji to cover Australia's World Cup qualifier in Nadi, a trip which had its own story to tell about the perils of sports coverage and its ill-defined legalities. I lobbed, complete with camera crew, with the intent of shooting a news story to bring back to Sydney. News coverage in Australia, of any sports event, didn't require any licensing of rights. Under Australian law you could film any sports event and run up to three minutes of it without incurring a rights fee. But what we forgot was that this may not be the law in Fiji. Soon after settling in my hotel room I got a call from an angry president of the Fiji Football Association, Dr Sahu Khan, who proceeded to tell me that I may as well turn around and go back home because I had not been given the rights to shoot the game. In a panic, I rang my boss in Sydney, Dominic Galati, who authorised me to negotiate a rights fee. I then arranged to meet Dr Khan at a nearby bar the following night. A lawyer with a well-chiselled face, surly eyebrows and a goatee beard, Dr Khan suggested that we Australians thought all Fijians were idiots. I protested that this was not the case, that it had all been an innocent mistake and grovelled apologetically. He eased off and we agreed on a rights fee of A$5000. We shot the match and got the report to air the following night. Australia had lost 1-0 and I was content at having reported on one of the great shocks in the annals of Australian football.

But by now SBS was experiencing a bigger shock. A media release had gone out from the ASF stating that it had signed a rights agreement with the ABC, giving it exclusive rights to the NSL and all home games played by Australia's representative teams. The ASF thanked SBS for its many years of valuable coverage and – blah, blah, blah – looked forward to a long and fruitful relationship with the ABC. This caused utter dismay in the SBS camp: having the ABC as a bed partner for football scarcely looked plausible. Some time earlier, the ABC had snared away from SBS the rights to Italian football. They ran it at 4 pm on Saturdays for one hour, then reduced it to half an hour and, when the rugby union club season began, took it off air. The ABC's evident sports content priorities, and its willingness to snub football, should have sent alarm signals to the ASF. But Brusasco didn't seem to see them. It is my opinion that he was of the trendy mindset among football administrators that taking football off the 'wog channel' and putting it on the agenda of the 'mainstream' was some kind of road to acceptance and salvation for the game.

The way the deed was done was even less believable, and far from noble. Ian Brusasco's chief executive, Alan Vessey, drove up to the

SBS offices in Milsons Point, double parked his car, and dropped off at reception a letter addressed to the SBS managing director, Brian Johns. Signed by Brusasco, the letter gave notice to SBS that the ASF's rights agreement with SBS had been terminated. Johns immediately called a meeting with Galati and me. Dominic and I were suitably livid and we convinced Johns that we should fight. After all, we were still under contract with the ASF and had done nothing to breach it. The matter proceeded to court.

But before a ruling could be made by the court, the return leg of the World Cup tie between Australia and Fiji was beckoning. It was due to be played in Newcastle on 3 December, a fortnight after the first leg in Nadi. As is usual with major sports telecasts, the outside broadcast vans rolled up to the venue the day before the match and were parked inside the stadium, in readiness for the laying of cables and general preparation the following day. This time, however, it was not one but two OB units that had turned up. Both SBS and the ABC were preparing to broadcast the game, each believing that it had the exclusive right to do so. An historic stand-off, unseen before in Australian broadcasting, was brewing. When I arrived at the stadium two hours before kick-off to host the telecast, our ABC counterparts – hosts and commentators – were already there. An hour later Dominic Galati, who was never on time for anything and will probably be late for his own funeral, showed up grinning from ear to ear and informed me that SBS had won an injunction that morning, giving it the sole rights to broadcast the game. The SBS telecast went ahead, Australia won 5-1, Socceroo captain Charlie Yankos had his nose broken in a major punch-up with the Fijians, and we drove home after a wonderful evening's entertainment. The ABC crew was given the night off.

But the battle rolled on. In the courts, the judge presided over the matter of who had the rights to broadcast certain football matches. In the end he ruled that, under the law, there were no such things as broadcast rights. He ruled that the only determining factor in all of this, under the law, was property; and it was up to the proprietors of the property to decide whose cameras would be allowed onto the property and whose would not. In other words, it was up to the owners of each individual venue to decide whether or not SBS' cameras would be allowed in. As quick as lightning, the instruction was sent out by the ASF to all clubs in the NSL who owned or presided over their own grounds, that they should not allow the entry of any SBS equipment and that the only broadcaster permitted to cover the games was the ABC.

The following March, as the new NSL season kicked off, I went to Edensor Park in Sydney's far west. This is the home of Sydney United: the club of the city's Croatian community who had always welcomed me as an ally and a member of the family and where I had enjoyed many years of good times as a friend of football. A large man at the turnstiles greeted me with a big smile but, before letting me pass, sheepishly looked me up and down, making sure I had no cameras hidden in my back pocket. He apologised, muttered something about only doing his job, and waved me on. I went in and took my seat: for the first time in eight years, I was at a football match not as a broadcaster but as a spectator. The game had turned its back on SBS, its great benefactor.

11

Mad dogs and Socceroos

The lessons of 1988 were learned the hard way by the ASF. Technically, despite the judge's ruling, both SBS and the ABC had the rights to the NSL until the end of the 1989 season when SBS' contract ended and the rights were again up for grabs. Both networks bid – and bid hard. At the SBS presentation, attended by Brian Johns and myself, sitting at the head of the ASF's boardroom table was a new president, John Constantine. Brusasco's reign lasted one term and he was dumped at the next election. I told the board that they should beware of wolves in sheep's clothing and that the ABC had no track record of commitment to football – quite the contrary. It certainly could not be compared with SBS and the level of passion it had continually shown for football.

The board appeared to be split on which way to go, but working hard behind the scenes to make their choice easier was the ABC chief executive, David Hill. At the time, football's major sponsor was VicHealth: a Victorian government authority keen to push its anti-tobacco Quit campaign in the ethnic communities. Because of the sponsorship, they had some influence on who the broadcaster might be. We knew this and attempted to do our own lobbying with them. But as time for the decision neared, despite our persistent attempts to get in touch with VicHealth's chief executive, Rhonda Galbally, she failed to return Brian Johns' calls. We later discovered she had met with David Hill who, at the time, was also president of the North Sydney Bears rugby league club. Just days before the ASF was to bring down its decision on a broadcast partner, Hill dropped a public bombshell by announcing that smoking would be banned from the Bears' home ground, North Sydney Oval. It was an historic decision. North Sydney Oval became the first outdoor venue in Australia to ban smoking. But it seemed to us a quit pro quo, so to speak. Galbally backed the ABC bid. Nevertheless, the board remained split: it needed Constantine's casting vote to decide the issue. The president opted for the ABC for the soccer rights.

But it was not to last. The ABC covered the league fully for two seasons: 1989–90 and 1990–91. A couple of months into its third season, there was another David Hill bombshell. He announced that, as part of some cost-cutting measures at the network, the ABC was pulling out of all its commitments to football and was tearing up its contract with the ASF. Bang: soccer had been dumped on again, this time from a great height. Remarkably, netball survived the cost cuts and remains on the ABC network to this day. (In the quirkiest of ironies, David Hill replaced Constantine as the head of the ASF five years later. And it was SBS that helped him do it.)

These snubs to SBS – the acknowledged friend and custodian of the game – were by no means the first, nor indeed the last, by football's governors. Indeed, the relationship between the broadcaster and its so-called partner was a litany of snubs and kicks to the groin. In 1981, when SBS was already broadcasting the NSL and putting three hours of football to air each week, the ASF gave the ABC the rights to the crunch home World Cup qualifier between Australia and New Zealand. An obvious reason for this was the ASF notion that SBS, despite its welcome enthusiasm, was really only a 'Claytons' channel: the TV channel you have when you're not having one.

Way back in 1983, I was asked to MC the NSL end-of-season awards night for the first time, a chore I was stuck with for many more years. All went swimmingly at Melbourne's Southern Cross Hotel: the coverage was slick and all the 'suits' were happy with the way we conducted the night. As the traditional last item of the ceremony, the ASF president, Sir Arthur George, got up to make his speech. He was a brilliant speaker who never spoke from notes but this time, perhaps, he should have done. After rattling off all the achievements his federation and the game had made over the year, he noted – with regret – his organisation's one failure: not being able to put the game onto television. This was greeted with embarrassed silence from all those in the room, including the prime minister, Bob Hawke. There I was on stage – the frontline representative of the sport's first dedicated 'soccer station', compering a ceremony being telecast nationally – and a couple of metres away the top dog of the game was saying the game needed to make the breakthrough of being shown on the box.

I thanked Sir Arthur for his words and closed off the night in a dignified and courteous manner, but I was fuming inside. I felt humiliated and insulted, and said as much to a couple of officials who came up to me after the ceremony. 'Did you hear what he just said?' I asked, seething and spluttering. One of the officials, Alex Pongrass, wary of the damage that may have been done, scurried off quickly to detain Sir Arthur who was about to leave. Very swiftly, Sir Arthur was back on stage at the microphone, issuing a long apology to SBS.

The most enjoyable times in this 25-year labour of love have been covering the Socceroos. Those games were at the cutting edge of the mission: we could laugh or cry with the players, sharing their joys and pains through five World Cup campaigns as they tried – just like us – to conquer Australian hearts. From the distance of our commentary boxes or studios, we believed ourselves to be part of the team, willing the boys on in the breathless hope that they would make it. And though we had many differences with the higher authorities of the game – including some coaches – the players were always on our side, seeing us as their sympathetic window to the fans.

In the period of 16 years spanning 1981 to 1997, when SBS had the rights to almost all the Socceroos' games, we covered over 100 of them – and I was present at most. But even in this period and in this part of our work, we got the odd slap in the face from the ASF. In 1983, to celebrate 100 years of organised football in Australia, the ASF scored a peach of a prize when England agreed to tour down under. The rights went to Channel 7; they were not even offered to SBS. Rex Mossop called the games, feeding off the credibility of Johnny Warren who had gone over to freelance co-commentate on the three-match series.

In 1988, Australia hosted a major four-nation series called the Bicentennial Gold Cup, in which Australia performed with distinction against Saudi Arabia, Argentina and Brazil. The rights, again without being offered to us, went to the ABC. Martin Tyler, in his first encounter with Australian broadcasting, was imported to commentate. In their coverage of that series, the ABC again showed a lack of genuine interest in the welfare of its partner, the ASF. Sir Arthur George neglected to write into the contract a prohibition clause against broadcasting the games live in their originating cities. He later pleaded with the ABC not to go live in Sydney with the final between Australia and Brazil. They told him to shove it or sue. By contrast SBS, even when it wasn't contractually required to do so, never programmed games live in their originating cities unless it was approved by the ASF.

Our serious involvement with the Socceroos – and our love affair with Frank Arok's beloved 'mad dogs' – began in 1984, in a so-called World Soccer Series in which Australia faced five different touring club sides: Juventus, Manchester United, Nottingham Forest, Glasgow Rangers and Iraklis. Frank Arok had just been installed as national coach in what his detractors called a putsch. A year earlier, Arok had been put temporarily in charge for the three games against England while the incumbent, Les Scheinflug, chose to be absent with the Young Socceroos in a pre-World Cup tournament in Acapulco. Arok's effort against England – two draws and a narrow loss – suitably impressed Sir Arthur George and especially his marketing chief, Pete Sheehan, who had invested a lot of his own money in his venture to market the Socceroos and the NSL. As the campaign for the 1986 World Cup approached, the performance of the national coaching staff was being re-assessed by both George and Sheehan, and Scheinflug was nervously watching his back. In early 1983, before the England games, Scheinflug's side had suffered two successive losses against New Zealand and there was a prevailing view that, rather than going to Acapulco, he should have stayed at home to hammer some confidence back into the team against the formidable England. I think the fact that he didn't was a big mistake, and even though Scheinflug steered Australia to a win in the eight-nation Merlion Cup in Singapore in early 1984, it seemed it wasn't enough to convince the heavies; he was replaced by Arok.

Arok, caught in the battle of political wills that was precipitated by his ascension, had a baptism of fire. Anti-Sir Arthur George forces in the ASF resented the intrusion and influence of Sheehan, a mere businessman and not viewed as a member of the 'soccer family'. Then, in my view, came one of the biggest and most damaging administrative blunders in the Australian game's sorry history. Citing a lack of financial compensation to the clubs from Socceroo-driven revenues, the anti-Sheehan faction mounted a boycott of the World Soccer Series with most of the NSL clubs withdrawing their players. The one club which abstained from the whole exercise was St George, which coincidentally was being coached by Arok. The question was: how would the players respond? What would they do? As instructed, Arok reported to the Camperdown Travelodge in Sydney's inner west where the players were to assemble for his first Socceroos camp, and waited. One by one, the players all turned up. Not a single player answered the club boycott. Arok and the players had won a massive victory over the negative forces of politics. The national cause had to come first and they answered the call. The extraordinary episode spawned a steely unity and family bond among the players before a ball had even been kicked. This bond was the foundation of the Arok era which was to last six years and two World Cup campaigns, taking the Socceroos – as an international signpost to Australia's place in the world – to new heights.

To understand the significance of the Arok era, one has to understand the man himself. There were other coaches in Australia who probably matched Frank Arok in tactical knowledge, astuteness of player selection, passion for winning and even – his big forte – psychological motivation. Two things set Arok apart from the others: his sharp intellect and capacity to perform his role on a plane much broader and deeper than just the next match; and his passionate yearning to achieve not just for himself, or even his team, but for the broader good of Australia and its struggling football. It was he who inspired the title of the previous chapter in this book. Answering a question from an ASF board member, who had asked why he was seeking the national coaching job, he said: 'Because it's not a job, it's a mission.'

I will confess to having got along better with Arok than with all the other national coaches during my time in the football media. Part of the reason for that was probably the fact that Arok, though he hailed from the former northern Yugoslavia, was ethnically Hungarian. I spoke to him in Hungarian and we shared a central European concord on football ideologies. But Johnny Warren, who was neither Hungarian nor had any central European roots, got on with him just as well. I suspect it was because Arok was not just an opportunist coach, interested only in a lucrative career, but – a bit like us – was a man on a mission.

This did not mean I could neglect my journalistic duty to be aloof, balanced and a willing critic of the national coach, however much I liked him: I didn't agree with everything he did and often had to say so. But whenever I was critical, he would call the next day and attempt to sway me to his way of thinking. For instance on my first tour with the Arok squad, a gruelling nine-match marathon in 1984 that took in China and four European countries, I couldn't help observing how certain players jumped camp and went on late night revelries and how Arok, who knew about this, largely let them get away with it. When I asked him why, he said: 'I don't want altar boys and pussycats in my team. I want bastards, real bastards, who will act like bastards when facing an opponent on the field'. I still didn't agree with what he was doing but at least I understood his reasoning. And it was not just me. All the journalists had this degree of access to Arok and the workings of his mind.

Arok's crafty mind at work was a sight to behold. None more so than on the trip to Tel Aviv for a World Cup qualifier in 1985. Australia was grouped with Israel, New Zealand and Chinese Taipei (Taiwan) in a round robin, home-and-away series, the winner of which would advance to play Scotland. Israel had eliminated Australia in the 1970 campaign while New Zealand did the same for 1982. So it was no cakewalk. Israel had a good, well-balanced team of quality players who were technically superior to Australia's. By contrast Australia, in Arok's preferred words, were a bunch of 'mad dogs': strong, tall, highly physical – but no match for the Israelis in skill. Knowing this, Arok decided that Australia's best chance of beating Israel was to derail them from their winning game; to somehow entrap them into trying to match it with us in strength and machismo.

The mind games began at the opening press conference at the Tel Aviv Hilton. Asked by the Israeli press which of Israel's players Arok feared most, he fired back without hesitation: 'Shlomo Kirat.' This bemused the local journos who looked inquisitively at each other. Israel had a sprinkling of gifted match winners, like midfielders Rifat Turk and Moshe Sinai, the speedy fullback David Pizanti and the flying winger Eli Ohana. But Kirat wasn't among them. He was a mean looking centre-back who could bruise you with his breath. The Arok message, or bait, was to make the Israelis believe that he respected only their more robust qualities and was intending to match it with them.

There was more of the same at Australia's first training session. Arok explained to the players that he wanted to intimidate the Israeli press contingent and instructed them to go out and kick the bejesus out of each other. He picked two halves of the squad and organised a 30-minute war. Never in all my years have I seen a more violent training game. Sparks flew as players barely missed breaking each others' legs and tackled as though this was a World Cup final. As a ploy – which it was – it was brilliantly executed and it was only divine intervention that prevented serious injury. The local press swallowed the bait and wrote the next day that the Australians 'have come here to kick us off the park and, unless we stand up to them, we are gone'. The following day I interviewed Israel's star striker Zahi Armeli, who said: 'I know the Australians are tall and that they are fearless and strong, but we are not schoolgirls either and if they want a fight, we'll give them one.'

Bingo. On match day at the Ramat Gan the Israelis played minus their usual rhythm and were preoccupied with wanting to match muscle with muscle. By the 50th minute, Australia led 2-0. Arok was in his adrenalin-charged element and tried to raise the temperature by remonstrating with the Italian referee, Luigi Agnolin, telling him in one incident to 'Fuck off!' Whereupon Agnolin, who spoke fluent English, brandished the red card and Arok had to watch the rest of the game from behind a chicken wire fence, far behind the Australian goal. But assistant Eddie Thomson, who took over on the bench, was no fool either when it came to street wisdom and screamed to the players to just try and keep possession and run down the clock. Though Armeli pulled one back for Israel in the 65th, the home side was never really in it. With five minutes left, Aussie midfielder Ken Murphy attempted to hook the ball back into play after it had crossed the touch line and, badly miscuing it, hoofed it high into the grandstand. The referee saw it as a deliberate attempt at time wasting and gave Murphy his second yellow and an early shower. The last five minutes seemed to take an hour in the press box as we puffed away on our second packet of cigarettes. All except AAP's Steve Dettre, that is, who exclaimed: 'God, I wish I smoked.'

It was a marvellous day for Australia, as energising as any I can remember in my years following the Socceroos. But it had its negative effect on Australia–Israel relations, given that the Israelis weren't used to the 'mongrel' elements of Australian competitiveness, something to which the European Arok had adapted very well. He was as 'mongrel' as any Australian athlete has ever been. He wanted his players to be like 'mad dogs' and fashioned them in his own image. But the recipe at times resulted in an overcooked concoction, leaving some bad tastes in the mouth.

When the Socceroos arrived home, at the airport press conference Arok, admiringly, said something about the Australian players having played in Tel Aviv 'like mad dogs'. This was misheard by a Sydney journalist who went on to file a report that claimed Arok had called the Israelis 'mad dogs'. This was shocking to Israel, given the similar references Adolf Hitler had made to Jews in his anti-Semitic rally speeches. The proverbial hit the fan and the story ran all week, both in Israel and Australia. The Israeli ambassador in Canberra was on the phone to ASF chief executive, Brian Emery, demanding an explanation. It was a major diplomatic incident producing some red faces at the Department of Foreign Affairs.

Arok issued his press denials and we all hoped the storm had passed by the time the teams met again in the return leg in Melbourne 12 days later. But no. As I introduced the match from pitch-side at Olympic Park, I had two interview guests with me: on my right, Frank Arok; on my left, Mordechai Shpigler, the legendary ex-Israel international. The telecast was being taken live by Israeli television. As I turned to Shpigler for my first question, he interrupted and said: 'Les, I think we should begin by asking Mr Arok a direct question. Mr Arok, can I ask you to tell our Israeli audience what do you think of the Jewish people and is it true that you think they are mad dogs?' The normally composed Arok turned white; I think he felt a noose tightening around his throat.

He paused to take a deep breath before again issuing a lengthy and decidedly angry denial, repeating that his 'mad dogs' reference was to the Australian players and that he had many, many good friends who were Jews.

Subject closed? Yes. But the series of diplomatic embarrassments had a couple more episodes to run. As the two sets of players lined up for the pre-match presentations we could finally expect a bit of decorum, dignity and respect for our visitors to be restored. Except that what we heard were the opening bars not of the Israeli national anthem but the German one. I stood a few metres from the Israeli ambassador, red-faced with embarrassment. And to our agony, the music played on. The poor soul operating the public address system didn't have a clue about either anthem and, content that he was playing the right tape, let it roll. Brian Emery rushed from his seat to the PA booth and tried to get in but, as a matter of standard security with PA booths, the door was locked. Emery literally had to kick the door down and clamber in to push the stop button on the tape player.

Despite everything, it was a thrilling, classic World Cup match, played in a magnificent atmosphere. The Israelis, having learned from the Tel Aviv experience, were very much in it and the teams turned 1-1 at half time. But in the 65th minute, fate again conspired against Israel. After being ruled offside, Eli Ohana, the visitors' star attraction, copped a racist remark from a spectator. He turned and gave the offender a large bent-elbow sign. The linesman, who was in the same eye line to Ohana as the spectator, assumed the sign was meant for him and reported Ohana to referee Dos Santos of Portugal. Ohana was red carded and had to be escorted off the field in tears by his team-mates. Down by a man, the Israelis fought hard for a win but could not make an impact on the score line. Though revenge on Australia would come four years later, it had been a bad fortnight for Israel.

Australia, meantime, went on to hammer Chinese Taipei 15-0 on aggregate over two games, and New Zealand 2-0, to advance to an historic home-and-away tie against Scotland. The SBS mob was

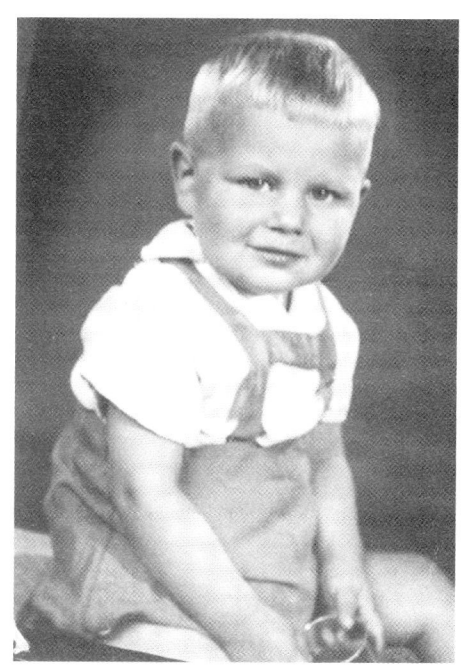

Me at age three.

With Andrew and Joe in Budapest, circa 1955.

A family of refugees, Austria, 1956.

Our first home in Australia: a rented garage in Warrawong, 1957.

Mum and Dad in Warrawong, 1958.

With Mum, Andrew and Joe on Port Kembla beach, 1957.

My very first interview: with Lev Yashin, the legendary Russian goalkeeper, in 1968, for the first and last edition of *Soccer Illustrated*.

László Ürge, the St George-Budapest midfielder in 1969 (*right*). On the left is my team-mate Julius Sztelma.

A professional portrait in 1968, at 23.

That's me, on location with The Rubber Band at Perisher Valley in 1972.

Above: On stage with The Rubber Band in 1971.

Below: A promotional photograph of The Rubber Band in the early 1970s.

Left: Wedding bells – with Eva in 1972.

Above: Wedding bells, second time around – with Eva in 1978.

Below: Nine-year-old Tania (*left*) and Natalie aged 8.

With my hero Ferenc Puskás, in 1985.

My first meeting with Pelé in 1988, in Adelaide.

On the touchline with Johnny Warren in 1986.

Hosting my first World Cup in front of the Villa Miani in Rome in 1990, with Johnny Warren.

On the Tour de France in San Sebastian, 1992.

With the crew on the Tour de France, 1992.

ST. IVES SOCCER CLUB

Doing my bit for junior football in the suburbs in 1992.

With Johnny Warren and Brazilian Ambassador Marcos Henrique C. Côrtes at Johnny's fiftieth birthday bash in 1993.

Getting ready for Australia vs Argentina in Sydney, 1993.

Giving viewers the 'best seat in the house' as I present SBS's exclusive coverage of the USA World Cup in 1994.

Snapped with Dom Galati at the USA World Cup wrap party.

Cup win: SBS gets record audiences for the World Cup, 1994.

On the set of the live coverage of the World Cup in France in 1998 with Tracey Holmes and Andy Harper.

Relaxing at the Hilton Hotel after accepting a Logie on behalf of SBS for 'Most Outstanding Sports Coverage' in 1998.

Doing what I do best: sipping an ale in France, 2001.

With Martin Tyler at
the UEFA Champions
League final at the
San Siro stadium in
Milan, 2002.

Visiting the Estadio
Mané Garrinchea in
Pau Grande in 2004.

With girlfriend Cida
Olson and friends at a
Vasco Da Gama game
in Rio, 2004.

Singing a duet
with Damien
Lovelock in 2003.

With daughters
Tania (*left*) and
Natalie
in 2005.

With Cida in
2006.

On the field in Montevideo for the first leg of the Australia vs Uruguay World Cup qualifier.

The Socceroos celebrate victory after the penalty shoot-out during the second leg of the qualifying match between Australia and Uruguay in Sydney, November 2005.

having the time of its life covering a World Cup campaign – and the Socceroos were winning. Arok had fashioned a national side which he likened to a club team. He rarely tinkered with the line-up, convinced that cohesion for any national team was the number one priority and that you can't build cohesion by chopping and changing. But before SBS could consummate the dream, it was dudded again by the good old ABC which outbid SBS and snared the rights to the first – Glasgow – leg of the Scotland tie. Glasgow being neither Paris nor Rome, I was not broken hearted about having to watch the game from home. Nevertheless, having built the profile of the team through the campaign, and slogged it with the boys in Tel Aviv, Auckland and several Australian cities over an exhausting three months, it did hurt that a possible miracle against a highly ranked European nation was being exploited by another network.

But, of course, the miracle didn't come. Not that the Australians were in any way overawed: they were hammered under a relentless onslaught by the Scots – led by Kenny Dalglish, then among the world's best – but held out resolutely for most of the match. And they were not helped by a Czech referee, Vojtech Christov, who looked graciously on his hosts. The Aussies lost 2-0, so the miracle was left for the return leg in Melbourne. The choice of venue had itself become a subject of some controversy. Frank Arok, wanting to exploit every disadvantage Australia could throw at the Scots, asked that the game be played in 30° Celsius Darwin, to challenge the skill and experience of the Scots who were coming from the chill of a Glasgow December. But the forces of money and politics combined to reject the suggestion. In football's political horse trading it was Melbourne's 'turn' to stage a big international. And then there was the question of revenue: a 30,000 gate at Olympic Park versus maybe 10,000 in Darwin. Brian Emery said to Arok: 'OK, say we take the game to Darwin. And what happens if you lose 5-0? How do we recoup the revenue we have squandered?' What Emery didn't consider was that had Australia beaten Scotland by the required margin, the ASF's revenue from FIFA would have been over a million dollars, just for qualifying. And besides, to suggest Australia could lose 5-0 in Darwin to Scotland was not exactly a vote of confidence by the chief executive in his own national coach or team. Emery, a capable bureaucrat, was not renowned for his creative management skills.

Still, Australia vs Scotland in 1985 turned out to be one of the most memorable games in Socceroo history. Arok considered himself extremely unlucky to have Alex Ferguson as his opposite number. Scotland's legendary manager, Jock Stein, died of a heart attack just a few months before the tie and Ferguson, who had just won the European Cupwinners Cup with Aberdeen, was put in charge to guide the Scots through the last hurdle to the finals in Mexico. Arok believed the younger and more modern Ferguson was a far more formidable foe than Stein. But he had no option other than to attack the Scots and hope that his team of part-timers could pull it off. Arok had a favourite saying: 'You've got to have a dream.' If there was one man among the record 32,000 crowd who believed Australia could do it, it was him.

It was a pulsating game with Australia hitting the Scots hard, coming at them with furious resolve. Only a couple of huge missed chances in the first half saved Scotland, the best of them when David Mitchell slipped his man on the right and his pinpoint cross was headed into the goalkeeper by John Kosmina from a metre out. At half time I interviewed visiting Scottish football writer, Hugh McIlvanney, introducing him as one of the game's most eloquent journalists. He said, 'Well I have to say there's nothing eloquent about the Scottish performance. They are being slaughtered in every facet of the game.' So it continued in the second half, with the match ending 0-0. As the final whistle came, the look on the face of Scotland captain Graeme Souness was not one of triumph but of relief. It had been one of those 0-0 draws we football aficionados hold up as testimony to the fact that football can be dazzling entertainment even without goals. The following day, I faced one of my rugby league-bent soccer-sceptic mates and asked him if he still believed all 0-0 draws were boring. 'No,' he said.

The game achieved its highest ever rating to date for SBS. In those days, the channel was rating a percentage share of one or – on a good day – two. Australia–Scotland peaked at five. The Socceroos may have stopped winning, but we were definitely winning with our football coverage.

We continued to ride with the vintage Arok Socceroos for the next four years, and it remained one of the most absorbing periods of my life as a football television man. In the mind-blowing year of 1988, because it was an Olympic year and the senior Socceroos could legitimately compete in the Games, the team played no less than 28 games. That was the kind of era we were in. Australia played against not only national teams but also touring club sides. Most of Australia's elite players were still home based and the few that weren't were either not called by Arok or simply refused to play. It was in this era that Craig Johnston made his famous remark that 'playing football for Australia was like surfing for England'. And I was personal witness to a conversation Arok had with a teenage Adelaide boy, Tony Dorigo, at Villa Park where Dorigo declined Arok's invitation, saying he would prefer to await his chance to play for England. In the end Dorigo, who married an English girl and became a British citizen, had a good England career and played for his adopted country in the World Cup finals. But Johnston's decision was less rewarding. The greatest achievement of his international career was to play once for England B against Malta B. I make this point because I believe that had Johnston been a regular with the 1980s Socceroos, when he was at the peak of his powers, Australia's fortunes may have been better: perhaps good enough to nudge the country over the line in World Cup qualification.

But I digress. The Arok years were enthralling for people like Johnny Warren and me, partly because of the Arok personality. He was a football missionary with a high intellect. But he was not a mate to the players. He once told me: 'I want the players to respect me, not love me'. When we toured with the team, after the hotel team dinners when the players and the coaching staff had departed either to their rooms or for a night on the town, Arok would join the two of us and we would talk football till all hours of the night, usually until we got kicked out. He would lay out the tactics – either of his team or its opponents – on the table using knives, forks, spoons, wine glasses or salt and pepper shakers, drawing formations and off-the-ball movement. I learned much of what I know about football during those six years.

He could even give good social advice. I was interviewing him after a game Australia lost in Adelaide and I was in a foul mood, as I was after every loss. In the middle of the pre-recorded interview some fan approached from behind and put a scarf of the colours of the opposing team around my neck. I dropped my microphone and turned to boot the young creep firmly in the arse when Arok jumped in front of me saying: 'Don't be stupid. He'll sue you for assault.' He may have saved my career.

His dedication and unselfishness were legendary. He donated 70 per cent of his national team salary back to his club, St George, in return for the club not raising any objection to his dual role. Unlike most before him and all after him, Arok was a part-time national coach, yet he still lasted two World Cup campaigns and more than 80 games. Before the 1988 Seoul Olympics, where Yugoslavia was to be Australia's first opponent, he wanted to go to Europe to spy on the team in a pre-tournament friendly against Switzerland. The ASF declined to fund the trip so he went at his own expense. Needless to say, Australia caused the shock of the tournament, beating Yugoslavia in Kwangju a few weeks later.

The demise of Frank Arok as Socceroo coach was among the saddest moments of my career. It came in the campaign to qualify for the 1990 World Cup. Australia was drawn with Israel, New Zealand and Fiji, the winner of the round robin destined to play Colombia in a final playoff. It began with a shock 1-0 loss to Fiji in Nadi: sheer humiliation for the team which earlier that year beat world champions Argentina 4-1; had returned just two months earlier from the Olympics where it earned a quarter final place; and had beaten New Zealand twice in consecutive friendlies. I was sent to Nadi to report on the match and had gathered much footage of the swaying coconut trees and the easy south Pacific lifestyle to incorporate into a happy story. The footage never made it to air. Arok was livid and in the post-match video session screamed at the players: 'Are you men or mice? Do you have no blood?'

But hell hath no fury like a Socceroo scorned and in the return, in Newcastle, the Fijians were hammered 5-1. They were reduced to disintegration and resorted to the fist, one of them breaking Charlie Yankos' nose. Australia then coasted to an easy 4-1 win over the Kiwis in Sydney before trekking back to Tel Aviv to meet the old enemy. And there, too, the Australians may have triumphed again but for some misfortune. Charlie Yankos' brilliant goal which gave Australia a 1-0 lead will also be remembered as one of the great gaffes of my commentary career. From a good 25 metres out, Yankos hit a curling free kick which sailed around the defensive wall and hit the back of the net. There were no Australian supporters in the stadium and the kick was met with deathly silence. Hearing no cheers, my first impression was that it had hit the side netting, and that's what I said. Then I saw Yankos leaping up in celebration, punching the air. I thought: 'My God, it's a goal.' In the one sentence, I had to retract the side netting verdict and suddenly sound elated by the 1-0: 'Oh, he's hit the side netting . . . no, no, it's a goal, it's a goal, 1-0 to Australia!' The trouble with gaffes like that is that they don't get forgotten after a live game. The goal gets replayed time and again, not just on SBS, but on all networks in news bulletins. By the end of the day you are a national goose. Israel gained a reprieve, courtesy of a penalty converted by Ohana, after a ball driven low by an Israeli ricocheted off Alan Davidson's foot and onto his hand. It was a clear case of accidental hand-ball but the referee gave a penalty.

The 1-1 in Tel Aviv was still a good result: far from a disaster. That came a fortnight later in Auckland. New Zealand, tired of continually losing to Australia, had reappointed as its coach John Adshead, the man who steered the Kiwis into the 1982 World Cup finals at the expense of Australia. By now, New Zealand had nothing to gain from the match. They were already out of it, having suffered away defeats to both Australia and Israel and only managing a draw with the Israelis at home. But Adshead had a point to prove and figured out what would be Australia's one weakness: complacency. The Socceroos lost 2-0, thanks to two excellent goals by a man called Billy Wright, a journeyman striker who has done nothing notable in the game before or since. Arok was judged guilty of either not reading Australia's over-confidence or being unable to find the remedy against it. Johnny and I were scheduled to fly out the next day and were counting on a pleasant post-victory dinner with the team. Now there was little sense in staying the night. When we got back to the hotel after the game we saw the leader of the Australian delegation, Sam Papasavas – who hated Arok with a passion and probably would have been happy to see the back of him – chomping calmly on a steak. That did it. Within half an hour we were packed and at the airport, catching an early flight.

Now there was just one game left, against Israel in Sydney. Australia had to beat Israel, while a draw was enough to allow the Israelis to advance and meet Colombia. It became one of those horrid experiences only passionate fans of the Socceroos can relate to, almost as bad as the dreaded loss to Iran eight years later. In a desperate throw of the dice, Arok made four changes and brought back four expats from Europe, three of whom had not played any significant part in the campaign: Eddie Krncevic, David Mitchell and Frank Farina. At the time Arok figured the risk was worth taking, given that if he had not made the changes and the team lost, he would have been crucified. Later, Arok acknowledged that it had been a mistake to disrupt team unity by bringing back the 'foreigners', one of whom – Krncevic – only arrived back the day before the game.

Given the shortage of time available to build any kind of tactical cohesion incorporating the new men Arok, against all his convic-tions, opted for expediency and played the 'English' game: a stream of early, long balls pumped into the opposing box for the lanky Krncevic and Mitchell, the speedy Farina and a fourth striker, Graham Arnold. 'It won't be pretty,' he warned – and it wasn't. On 40 minutes, Yankos headed out a long clearance from the Australian defence and the ball was lobbed back his way by an Israeli. Yankos and Gary van Egmond, in momentary confusion and each waiting for the other to clear it, allowed the super quick Ohana to steal the ball, round the keeper and put Israel into the lead. The Socceroos now needed to score at least twice to stave off World Cup failure.

By half time Arok was losing his conviction that the ploy of 'bingo football' was working. He brought in more technique and brain by sending Micky Petersen into the midfield in place of Paul Wade and tweaked the formation so the midfield would not be bypassed by aerial missiles. Australia improved but there was no breakthrough as Israel fought bravely to hang on. On 67 minutes Arok introduced the skilful young Paul Trimboli, again to top up creativity at the expense of aerial power and strength. In the 88th minute Trimboli levelled the scores and I screamed into the micro-phone: 'A glimmer of hope for Australia!' With two minutes still to play plus at least three minutes of added time in a game riddled with stoppages, I figured there may be enough time left for Australia to score another. But to my astonishment, the Italian referee, Carlo Longhi, blew for the end after adding just 50 seconds of stoppage time. Arok rushed towards Longhi, frantically pointing to his watch, accusing the referee of having blown early. Oscar Crino, who had a terrific World Cup campaign, strode with intent towards Longhi and was restrained by Arok and others. The refereeing by Longhi certainly was, at its kindest, curious. In one instance, an Israeli player was carried off the field for treatment and the referee, rather than restart the game, waited for the player to return before resuming. That alone must have taken over a minute.

But it was over: both the World Cup campaign and Arok's career as national coach. Distressed, I didn't attend the post-match press conference and lingered for a while in the car park with Johnny and others, reflecting on what had been and what might have been. By then I was well into my 40s, more than mature enough to accept a football defeat as one of life's norms, even if that defeat was to Israel. I certainly didn't begrudge them their triumph. The game was the last in a long rivalry between the two countries that spanned 21 years and 17 games. As joint outcasts in the geopolitics of the game, we became as much friends as we had to be on-field enemies. Some of the Israeli players became personally known to me, as did Mordechai Shpigler, while Nissim Kiviti, then my opposite number on Israeli TV, is a life-long friend who these days spends a lot of time in Australia.

After that, Israel soon joined UEFA, the European federation, and Australia has not played them since. More's the pity. The long history had turned Australia–Israel games into derbies. They were always fierce, highly competitive matches with scores to settle and pride at stake. And they were close: of the 17 games Australia won five, Israel three and nine were drawn. The goals tally was 18-16 in Australia's favour. I would love to see the rivalry reinstated, even in the shape of an annual game, for some kind of trophy designed to commemorate the long history between the two countries.

The car park had emptied and I was about to head home when I saw the lonely figure of Frank Arok descend the stairs leading from the Sydney Football Stadium concourse. It was one of my saddest moments. This man, who had been seen as a national hero for the previous six years and had been a magnet for the media, looked a forlorn soul as he headed home to his delightful and understanding wife Gordana (who never attended his games, believing she would jinx the team). We chatted for a few minutes and I can only remember him saying he screwed up by bringing back 'the big boys' from Europe. He knew he was gone, for no national coach who fails in two successive World Cup campaigns can survive, even in Australia. The ASF went through the charade of advertising the job vacancy for which Arok was welcome to apply. And he did, saying at the interview that the mission had not been accomplished and he wanted to finish it.

But he never had a chance, for I believe the bosses had already made up their minds that Eddie Thomson would be the next man. The late Thomson, whom I considered an excellent coach, had one gift which Arok didn't. He was an excellent networker, cultivating relationships with people in influential places. He had been Arok's assistant with the Socceroos until he resigned after the 1988 Olympics and was appointed technical director by the ASF.

With Arok not considered, there remained just two credible candidates for the Socceroo job: Thomson and the impeccably reputed Slovakian, Joe Venglos. ASF chief John Constantine flew to Bratislava to interview Venglos but on his return, the board decided on Thomson as its choice. It was during our stay in Rome to cover the 1990 World Cup that we learned of the announcement. Johnny Warren and I were disappointed, having publicly supported the Venglos appointment, not because we felt Eddie was not good enough, but because we felt Venglos, with his central European roots and his deep background in football academia, would have been more ideal. When Johnny Warren got a call from a Sydney radio station and was asked if he was happy about the Thomson appointment, he replied: 'I'm very happy for Joe.'

At any rate, a new era was about to begin and the legacy of the Arok age was there to be harnessed by the new national coach. History allows people to judge what that Arok legacy was; it is not my place to rate him as better or worse that other national coaches. But I am convinced that under Arok, the Australian national team underwent a critical transformation and set up the platform from which a new generation of coaches could benefit. It was during the Arok years that the Socceroos gained a true Australian identity, as Arok married his own European influences with the unique quali-ties of spirit Australian athletes possess. Part of his mission was to transform the team from one of a 'colonial' mentality – short on ambition and real hope against so-called pedigree opponents – to one that was prepared to dream and 'have a go'. When he started his first World Cup campaign, the Socceroos would include four or five imported players, those who were born and gained their football

education abroad. By the time he finished, there were none.
Furthermore, in my view no other coach would have instructed his
men to take on and attack the reigning World Cup holders as Arok
did when Australia beat Argentina 4-1 in 1988. He was also the
first to give Australia a distinctive playing style, marrying the
physical 'Britishness' of our traditions with the European influences
of his own. He may not have accomplished his mission, but Frank
Arok left behind a country that had found self-belief on the international stage in the world's most important sport. That is his legacy.

Israel went on to play Colombia for a place in the 1990 World Cup
finals. It lost by a meagre 1-0 on aggregate over the two legs. Who
knows now whether Frank Arok's 'mad dogs' – if given the chance
– might have done that little bit better; enough for Australia to
make the grand stage for only the second time. Now that would
have been something, not just for Australia, but also for all of us at
SBS; for looming over the horizon was a new and illustrious epoch
in SBS' quest to have the world game embraced by all Australians.
It was the start of a process that finally turned the world's favourite
sporting event into one that would also be valued and loved at the
broadest levels in my adopted land.

12

Cups of life

I first met Dominic Galati in early 1981, soon after joining SBS as a freelance commentator. He was still in his teens. I asked my boss, Peter Skelton, who the handsome, Italian-looking young man was. He was a very keen kid, Skelton told me, a mad football fan who had been hired as a production assistant. Within the ensuing 10 years 'the kid' rose to become Head of Sport at the network and gained considerable fame – in some eyes, notoriety – in the TV industry and indeed in football.

Dominic had been a plumber by trade; I don't really know how he was introduced to television. But he was immensely gifted in TV production: a real natural who seemed to be a friend of every button, wire and blinking light that made television work. He was, for instance, the best and fastest tape editor I ever saw. Once, in another embarrassing gaffe, I called the wrong score in a game for almost its entire duration. Fortunately, the game wasn't live. But it still needed a Dominic-type miracle worker to fix the gaffe in the edit suite. I haven't the faintest idea how he did it, but he did: the game went to air with the right score uttered from my mouth.

Dominic was also immensely and impatiently ambitious, seeing

By the Balls

himself as a quick riser to head up the sports department and, one day, the network itself. His bold impatience would get him into trouble many years later and, I think, stunt his career. But in those early years, his brave urge to score goals and give himself a name was of critical value to the network as a sports broadcaster. His way was to cut through the bureaucracy and procedure and get things done: a technique that seasoned senior executives would not even attempt.

The first 'Dominic classic' was snaring the rights to the 1983 World Youth Championship in Mexico. Dominic, barely 21, was by then a sports producer, answering to the head of sport, John Rowley. He and I, through our singular passion for football, became close allies, forever conspiring to present more football on the network. This included getting more rights. It had stuck in our gut that the 1981 World Youth Championship, in Australia, had gone to Channel Ten which did very little with it. Now Channel Seven came into the picture as an interested party for the 1983 titles; it was negotiating but was not prepared to pay the asking price. The senior execs at SBS were lukewarm to the idea of taking on Seven and had given up. But not Dominic, who worked feverishly behind the scenes to steal the rights from under Seven's nose, all the while keeping me informed. I was the only one at the network who knew what he was doing. He waited till the last moment and, when it became clear that Seven was going to walk away, pounced.

With barely three days to go before the opening match, my phone rang at three in the morning. It was Dominic. 'We got it!' he said. 'Got what?' I asked. 'The World Youth, we got the World Youth. I just did the deal. Got it for five grand.' Dominic, of course, had no authority to do the deal. And the rights fee was not the problem. There were much larger knock-on effects. It was a tournament of 32 games, potentially over 60 hours of television. Even if we only showed selected games it would be a major dislocation for the network in terms of scheduling, staff and production requirements. But that stuff never even entered my head. I was just so thrilled we got the damn thing. It would be the first coverage of many, many major football tournaments for which SBS later became known.

I was still working at the Sydney *Sun* at the time and, aware of the urgent need for publicity, as soon as I got to the office at 6 am I alerted the sports editor who put the story on the back page. I also rang some friends in radio to get the word out. A few hours later, after the first edition of *The Sun* had gone to print, a pensive sports editor, Bill Casey, came to see me and asked if I had given him a bum steer. I said, 'No, why?' He waved in front of me a press release received from SBS denying the story. As I found out later, the SBS head of television, Ian McGarrity, was driving to work that morning when he heard the news on radio that SBS was going to have live coverage of the World Youth titles, beginning with the opening game between Mexico and Australia three days later – something of which McGarrity knew nothing. As soon as he got to his office he instructed the publicity department to issue a denial. He would deal with Dominic later. But by lunchtime, the publicity and public discussion was out of control: SBS was appearing to want to renege on a deal that would allow the Young Socceroos to be seen live on Australian TV. It was a perception SBS, the multicultural broadcaster and darling of football fans, could not afford. At 1 pm another press release went out, this time confirming that the coverage would go ahead.

A small on-air team was assembled. I was to host the coverage; and Tommy Docherty, the renowned Scottish coach then working in Australia, was to be my studio analyst. John Rowley, as a contingency measure, had sent ahead David Fordham to commentate from Mexico. But such were the gremlin-infested communications standards at the time that we couldn't get a peep out of Fordham. Mike Hill did the commentary off tube from the studio with the former England manager, Ron Greenwood, as his sidekick and Fordham was brought home.

At the end of the telecast, which went off swimmingly – despite the fact that Docherty and I had to fill for 50 minutes because of a delay to the kick-off – Ian McGarrity came into the studio and congratulated us for pulling it off. He said that at the ABC – his previous employers – this would never have been possible. I am still unaware of what he said to Dominic. When I popped that question to Dominic, he just waved my questions aside, saying: 'Don't worry about it. We got the deal didn't we?' Dominic was to become more famous six years later for his involvement in SBS' biggest ever coup: capturing the rights to the 1990 World Cup.

It is largely forgotten that Italia 90 was not SBS' first involvement in the World Cup. That honour went to the 1986 Mexico World Cup. But on that occasion, SBS was only a sub-contractor to the broadcast. The ABC was the rights holder, but by 1986 the World Cup had blown out to be a 24-team, 52-match tournament. The volume was simply too much for the ABC's liking so, for a fee, the ABC offered to sub-licence the early – bulkier – portion of the tournament to the football network. We jumped at it, of course, and covered the event's first two phases before the ABC took over exclusively from the quarter final stage. The deal was that SBS would cover one game per day live during each of phases one and two, with the ABC running a nightly highlights package at around 10.30 pm. From the quarters, the ABC would take over everything and SBS would cease its involvement.

It was a wonderful exercise from the point of view of football fans: the first time Australian television had dedicated such a huge number of games and volume of programming to the world's most popular sports event. SBS did well out of it, at least from an image point of view. The production format was nothing too flash; nothing like what was to come with SBS' exclusive coverage four years later. I hosted all games, always with Johnny Warren at my side, with an additional second analyst from a rotating pool of coaches or ex-players. What we didn't anticipate was that the dual arrangement with the ABC presented an opportunity for our football production to be compared with that of another station. A reporter from Sydney's *Sun-Herald* visited our studios, interviewing me and some of my colleagues for just such a feature article. This article was scathing in its criticism of the ABC coverage, making us out to be some kind of messiahs of invention. We were nothing of the sort, of course. It was just that ours was the football channel: we treated the game – and the tournament – as though we loved it and cared about it. Peter Wilkins, along with Craig Johnston, anchored the ABC broadcast, and this is no retrospective snipe at Peter, who is a respected colleague, likes and knows his football and is a splendid presenter. It's just that he worked for a station that had no special affinity with football – and it showed.

One handicap – over which we had no control – was that the ABC had sub-licensed the BBC's commentaries and we had to accept them for our games. The problem was that the British commentators were concerned only with their home viewers. This didn't sit well with Australia's multicultural audience. The lowest point came when I felt compelled to apologise to the viewers for a case of contemptible stereotyping. In the game between England and Paraguay a Paraguayan player, following a harsh tackle, went down and began writhing in spectacular agony, obviously play-acting. John Motson, normally the most professional of callers, made a remark that such acts were typical of South Americans. At half time, mindful of the many thousands of South American migrants watching us, I apologised to the viewers and explained that 'our' commentators were in fact borrowed from the BBC: views expressed by them were not to be taken as those of SBS. That, too, made headlines: it was the first time a television host had apologised for his own station's broadcast. But we learned from the experience: we would never again mount a major event broadcast, especially the World Cup, without using our own exclusive commentators. So the problem didn't arise again because since 1990 SBS, at considerable expense, has been steadfast in mounting its own team of World Cup callers. John Motson's unfortunate faux pas was at least partly responsible for Martin Tyler being brought into the SBS stable, where he has stayed for the ensuing 16 years.

Snaring exclusive rights to the 1990 World Cup was one of the most momentous events in the history of SBS and indeed of football's development as an accepted, mainstream sport in Australia. How this was achieved makes an intriguing story. Following the 1986 World Cup, FIFA signed a famous 'three World Cups' broadcasting deal with a vast consortium of the world's regional broadcasting unions, taking in Europe, all of Latin America, Asia and the Pacific. For our part of the world the rights went to the Asia-Pacific Broadcasting Union, the ABU, of which both the ABC and SBS were members. The deal covered the World Cups of 1990, 1994 and 1998. A certain fee, pledged by the ABU to cover all of its territories, had been accepted by FIFA; it was then up to the ABU to determine the share of the fee for each territory. Australia's share, for the first of the three World Cups, was set at $1 million. In Australia the ABC, as previous rights holder and a member of the ABU, held the first option to take up the rights. All member broadcasters accepted the slice of the fee they were to pay; all, that is, except the ABC – which offered a paltry one-fifth of the amount. The ABU tried to explain to the ABC that the fee was not a matter of negotiation; that the total rights fee had already been agreed with FIFA and that FIFA had to be paid. The ABC then approached SBS to share the coverage and the fee. SBS was to be the junior partner in the deal and would therefore pay less than half of the fee. The new total, still falling way short of the asking fee, was put to the ABU by the ABC. The ABU responded by again explaining that the fee was not negotiable: the Australian share of the fee, already agreed with FIFA, was $1 million; if Australia didn't pay its full share, poorer countries like Sri Lanka and Bangladesh would have to make up the difference. ABC chief David Hill, unimpressed, instructed his head of sport, David Salter, to pen an angry 'no' to the ABU general secretary, Hugh Leonard.

Now, with less than two years to go before the World Cup, there was a major impasse. The Japanese public broadcaster, NHK, had been asked to advance Australia's $1 million share so that FIFA could be paid, and it did. As a result the ABU, always sensitive to its instinctively domineering, white-skinned, blue-eyed member to the south, felt bullied and insulted. More importantly, there was now a real chance that the World Cup of 1990 would not be broadcast in Australia at all. Dominic Galati and I began to heavy SBS chief executive, Brian Johns, to bypass the SBS partnership option and sign the rights exclusively. At one point, we both accosted him in the elevator in an effort to persuade him that, regardless of the cost, this would be a ground-breaking deal for SBS. Besides, we noted, it was our charter responsibility to ensure that the football World Cup was accessible to Australians. It was a big ask. $1 million in rights fees carved out of the meagre SBS budget, plus production costs, was a huge risk in those days. To his great credit, Brian Johns came to the party and made a courageous decision. The next day he summoned Dominic, then a senior sports producer, to his office and authorised him to do the deal and pay the money asked by the ABU.

Dominic, armed with a letter of authority, flew to Kuala Lumpur, met with the ABU sports chief, Richard Read, and did the deal over coffee in a few minutes. Before he returned, he gave me one of his trademark phone calls: 'We got it,' he chuckled down the line. And the deal was for not one World Cup, but three. SBS was now the broadcaster of the 1990 World Cup and the next two beyond. The ABU was ecstatic. SBS had saved it from a major crisis and from embarrassment, and the unity of the broadcasting union had been preserved. SBS was a hero in Asia and the ABC's name was mud. A few days later, SBS made the triumphant public announcements; the ABC stewed, issuing statements about SBS' dishonourable behaviour in reneging on an agreed shared bid. The relationship between the two public broadcasters sank to an all-time low.

Gaining the World Cup rights was one thing. How we were going to do the job was quite another. Given SBS' status then as a small, low-budget broadcaster with next to no experience in covering an event of that size, many in the industry thought there was no way SBS could pull it off. David Salter of the ABC publicly said as much. The scepticism motivated Dominic and me even more and, with the backing of our then immediate boss, Ian Hamilton, we drew up plans to cover the World Cup like it had never been covered before, not just in Australia but probably the world. We decided that, given our responsibilities to multiculturalism, the coverage had to be not just of a sporting event but of a cultural festival. For 1990, the flavour of the broadcast had to be that of the host nation, Italy: a country perfectly suited to beautiful pictures with which we could embroider the football. The tournament had to be hosted from location, with an eye-catching Roman backdrop, and other ways needed to be found to show off Italy and the 12 host cities. In this way, we figured, we would attract viewers beyond the dyed-in-the-wool football fans and sell the World Cup to Australians as the mega event that it is.

Returning from covering a World Cup qualifier in Israel, I stopped off in Rome to meet up with SBS chief engineer Brian Bailey for some reconnaissance on studio locations. We found the perfect spot in the enchanting Villa Miani, a 17th century former convent high on the hill of Monte Mario with breathtaking views of the city below. The villa was to be our backdrop for the live coverage and later became as famous around Australia as Johnny Warren and me. On my return, we began to plan for the production of the most revolutionary facet of the coverage. This would be around 40 mini-documentaries profiling the 12 host cities: their histories, their architecture and their culture. Again, driven by the SBS mission to show off the world to Australians, the idea was that in the lead-up to each live match we would show one of these mini-docos. For example, if the match was played in Florence, we would run a story on the Ponte Vecchio, or if it was played in Verona there would be a piece on the Valpolicella, a famous wine of that region, or *Romeo and Juliet*. They were to be known as the World Cup 'city profiles' and proved so popular that they became a fixture on three consecutive World Cup broadcasts and two editions of the European Championship.

It was Ian Hamilton's idea to send me on these voyages as the presenter or story teller for each profile. And these assignments were among the most enjoyable I have done in my broadcasting career: we travelled through some of the world's most beautiful cities, gazing at their glorious sights, eating fine food and drinking excellent wines. It was quirky, but typically SBS, to send a sports head to front a series on history, architecture, art, cuisine and culture. Apart from showing the stadiums, the series had no sports component and was entirely cultural in content.

It was an ambitious, expensive and risky project. Around one year before the World Cup itself, to ensure continuity of weather, a six-man team was assembled to start the shoot in Florence: cameraman, sound recordist, researcher, interpreter, producer and presenter. From Florence we embarked on a six-week criss-cross of Italy, visiting Milan, Genoa, Verona, Udine, Bologna, Turin, Rome, Naples, Bari, Cagliari and Palermo. All the team members – except the producer, Austin Steele, and me – were of Italian background. The researcher, Ugo Mariotti, travelled one city ahead of the rest of the team, making sure that all the venues were suitable for shooting and that all permits were in order. By the time we arrived in each city, the tourist authorities were well aware of us and often welcomed us with a slap-up lunch. The hours were long and the work was hard but it would be a lie to suggest it wasn't a pleasure.

During one shoot, at 7 am inside the Uffizi Museum in Florence, Austin Steele sat me down on a bench and asked me to gaze up admiringly at Botticelli's giant masterpiece, *The Birth of Venus*, so that the cameraman, shooting from behind me, could include me in the shot. Steele kept adjusting my position, asking me to move millimetres to the right, then to the left, taking an eternity to get the shot right. Impatient and in an early morning mood, I was about to turn around and give him an earful when I was hit by a sudden reality check: there I was, sitting on my bum, gazing at one of the great masterpieces of the Renaissance, being paid for it – and

I was about to complain. I bit my tongue and continued gazing.

Our hosts were often generous. Outside Verona, following the Valpolicella shoot, the owner of the vineyard presented each of us with a case of his best. The only problem was that we were due to fly out three days later to Australia, where customs only allowed you to enter with two bottles of wine each. So for the following two nights, Austin and I sat on our hotel balcony in Rapallo in enchanting Liguria, dispensing with the surplus at some speed. Liguria looked better and better with each drop.

Of course, I took every opportunity to sample the football and had a good ally in our interpreter, Tony Palumbo. We were about to leave Genoa on a flight to Bari when we realised that AC Milan was playing Real Madrid in Milan in the European Cup the following day. A generous Austin Steele dispensed with our presence for the opening stages of the Bari shoot as Tony and I took a train to Milan, watched the game at San Siro, then flew on to Bari to rejoin the team.

But the most memorable football sojourn was in Naples where we actually did the stadium shoot during a UEFA Cup match between Napoli and Sporting Lisbon at the San Paolo. Napoli was where Diego Maradona was playing and at that time still in his prime. Maradona was a god in Naples, having already captained the city's team to its first ever league title in 1987, and about to do it again in 1990. Getting anywhere near him, never mind interviewing him, was but a dream for me – or so I thought. To my delight, Tony Palumbo's good work behind the scenes landed us an interview after the game, although we were last in a long queue and had to wait almost two hours after the final whistle. In that time Maradona had his shower and changed, emerging from the dressing room to kiss his wife and two daughters before attending a half hour press conference. Then followed individual interviews with a procession of TV reporters who had lined up in the long corridor between the dressing room and the players' tunnel. By the time Diego got to us, the stadium was deserted. I found him charming and gracious, with a friendly smile, and obviously enjoying the novelty of being interviewed by a reporter from far away Australia. A natural interviewee, he gave clear and succinct answers in fluent Italian (translated simultaneously by Palumbo). Maradona was a champion of the underdog, an underdog mentality being prevalent in the culture of both Naples and his native Argentina. As my final question, I asked him if he ever thought he was carrying too much on his shoulders, bearing the hopes and dreams of all those millions. He said: '*Sono piccolo, ma forte*' – 'I am small, but strong.'

That was the first of two interviews I did with Maradona. Getting the second was more difficult. It was when he came to Sydney to captain Argentina against Australia in a World Cup qualifier in 1993. I stalked his team hotel several times but couldn't get anywhere near him. Having been disgraced by a cocaine drug bust two years earlier, Maradona was now far more cautious and selective with interviews and was generally reluctant to give them. Then I had an idea. I knew that, for all his faults, Maradona was a doting father, obsessed with his two small daughters, Dalma and Giannina. So I bought two toy koalas and had them gift-wrapped, with a card attached to each, and addressed them to Dalma and Giannina. I grabbed my Uruguayan friend, Mario Etchart, as a Spanish-speaking assistant and the two of us parked ourselves in the hotel lobby. We could see Diego in the bar – which was off limits to media – sitting on a stool, sipping mineral water, laughing and joking with his team-mates. We also knew that to get to his room from the bar he had to pass through the lobby. After an hour or so Diego emerged from the bar and headed for his room. We pounced like two hungry lionesses moving in for the kill. Mario asked if he could spare us a few words. 'Not interested,' said Diego as he waved Mario away without breaking his stride or even looking at us. Then Mario shouted: 'But we have gifts for Dalma and Giannina.' That stopped Diego in his tracks. He turned around, humbly accepted the gifts and gave us the interview.

Coverage of the 1990 World Cup turned out to be the most comprehensive and acclaimed of all time, certainly in Australia. And the city profiles were just part of it. SBS had invested a huge amount and pulled out all stops. This had to be a blockbuster: after all, the football World Cup was the world's biggest sports event, bigger even than the Olympic Games. Its global television audiences were then and still are almost double those of the Olympics.

The norm elsewhere was that rights holders covered anything from just the final to selected daily games, but never the full glut. We were to cover all 52 games. Though the live games were coming in at all hours of the night, the SBS prime time schedule was pre-empted to allow for a nightly one-hour World Cup highlights program between 7.30 and 8.30. There were additional daily replays in the afternoons, in all adding up to around 200 hours of coverage over more than a month. The soccer station became the World Cup station and football fans thought all their Christmases had come at once. A new cultural pattern was triggered in Australia: every four years, thousands take holidays from their jobs and become nocturnal, just so they can watch the World Cup.

We went on location, to the lawns of the Villa Miani, to capture the feel and ambiance of the host country. We sent three reporting teams to Italy to roam from city to city, packaging preview stories of the games, interviewing some of the world's greatest players and their coaches. We ran profiles of the stars in an attempt to personalise the protagonists. We captured Sophia Loren at an Italian training session, Carlos Menem bestowing kingship on Maradona, and Madonna nominating Roberto Baggio as the sexiest player in the tournament. And we had the voice of football, Martin Tyler — the best English-language commentator in the world — calling our games.

Even today, people still ask me how SBS managed to snare the exclusive services of a commentator like Martin. The truth is, we got a bit lucky. The acquaintance began at Sydney's Parramatta Stadium in 1988 after Martin, as guest commentator for the ABC, had called the game between Australia and Saudi Arabia in the

Bicentennial Gold Cup. In the stairwell, as Martin was descending from the gantry, he was confronted by Dominic Galati who introduced himself and asked him if he would be available to call some games for SBS. Martin, forever the gentleman, said he would consider it and that Dominic should give him a call when something concrete came up. Dominic, though he didn't tell Martin at the time, had genuine plans to import him permanently to Australia and give him a new career as a commentator on the NSL. This was pie in the sky stuff: Martin was a star commentator in England, rearing a young family. So Dominic shelved the idea. But a window of opportunity opened two years later when, in early 1990, Martin took up an offer to leave ITV in England and join Sky Sports as chief commentator for Rupert Murdoch's satellite network. Given that ITV had the World Cup rights and Sky didn't, this meant that Martin Tyler became free and available to work for SBS on the World Cup. Martin, remembering the conversation at the Parramatta Stadium two years earlier, gave Dominic a call and asked if he could do a few games for SBS in Italy. Dominic returned his call two days later and said, 'Would 39 matches be OK?'

Martin Tyler was hired and became an iconic component of SBS' pioneering coverage of Italia '90. He was worked like a draught horse by the station, calling two games on most days, and often more. He would commentate on one game off-tube in our Rome studios, speed away to do a second at Rome's Stadio Olimpico, and return to his booth to do a third. It was a superhuman effort. On one occasion he did a game in the studio and then, gathering his research, scrambled off to take a taxi to the Olimpico to call a game on location. The taxi broke down, leaving Martin stranded on the side of the road, his only option hitchhiking to the venue. A kind motor cyclist picked him up and, minus helmet, Martin sped to the stadium – the motorbike zigzagging its way through the traffic – and made it on time.

Since then Martin Tyler, though he lives distant from us and has never been in our permanent employ, has become a friend to me and part of the SBS football family. He has called every European

Cup final broadcast by the network since 1990, as he has every FA Cup final, and he became as synonymous with SBS as did I or Johnny Warren.

The workload and daily grind for the rest of the team at Italia '90 was not dissimilar to Martin's. SBS, though its production was glitzy and looked expensive, was doing the event on the cheap. Its chief resource was neither money nor manpower but sheer dedication by all who were involved. SBS sent 18 people to Italy where, for an event of that size, other stations may have sent 200. The team stayed in cheap accommodation, with only Johnny and I afforded the 'luxury' of a shared apartment with no room service. And the hours were brutal.

A little bit of background might be helpful here. Though Dominic Galati and a higher-ranked executive, Claudio Paroli, were both in Rome, most of their work had already been done in setting up the coverage. All that remained was for the content of each individual show to be produced and that was left to me, as the highest ranking football journalist on the team. There I was, 10 years after becoming a part-time commentator with SBS, effectively producing a World Cup. Neither Dominic, nor any of the producers or heads of sport under whom I worked at SBS, was trained in journalism; nor did they ever challenge my knowledge of football. So I was always given a free hand with editorial content, which often included choosing and buying football matches from overseas. By 1990 I had for years already been the producer of *World Soccer*, buying the content, doing the weekly rundowns, commentating on the main game and writing all scripts. So to do what I was doing in Rome was neither new nor hard. Except for the sheer load of the work.

At 9 am each day, production assistant Francesco Palumbo (Tony's son) arrived at our apartment with a pile of newspapers whose main World Cup articles he translated for us. Then we went around to the corner cafe for a quick breakfast. By 10.30 we were at the Villa Miani to pre-record our half-hour lead-in hosting for the opening game of the day. This took around an hour and a half.

At about noon we would stop for lunch at a terrific garden trattoria on the road between the Villa Miani and Saxa Rubra, where the studio was located. It was no long, rambling, boozy lunch either, because we had to be at the studio by 1.30, ready to watch the first game of the day which kicked off at 2.00. But that hour or so at the restaurant was the only quality time we had each day. The waiter, whom we christened Diego because he looked like Maradona, got to know us and was ready with his recommendations of the day and a glass of pinot grigio the minute we arrived. It was Diego who taught us that in Italy, good traditional restaurants don't have menus: if you see a menu on the table it means the restaurant is a tourist dive.

After lunch, we got down to the business of watching the games on two monitors that faced a table at which Johnny and I sat side by side. I would immediately begin to prepare the one-hour highlights show that was to be fed out that night.

Meanwhile, on the live games, our job in Rome had finished at the Villa Miani. From there, Andy Paschalidis took over the hosting from the Sydney studio. Again, this was a cost-saving measure: we could not afford the facilities and additional satellite times that would have been needed to host all the action live from Rome. The kick-off times were spread on a pattern of 2 pm, 5 pm and 9 pm so the action didn't finish until close to 11 pm. Through it all, I was head down preparing the show, with one eye on the monitor and the other on the typewriter. In between, I'd be liaising on the phone with the field reporters Kyle Patterson, Peter Vlahos and Farren Hotham on whatever stories they were chasing. At around 8 pm someone would bring us some sandwiches. After the last game finished we would shave, change and get ready to record the show, which would roll at around midnight. We were never out of there before 1 am. On the way home to the apartment we'd stop off at a shop to buy a large bottle of Grand Marnier, which we consumed over another couple of hours of unwinding and talking football. We'd crash at around 3 am and be up again at 9.00 when Francesco banged on the door.

That was the pattern of our existence for 31 days. There was no sightseeing of the eternal city. On the rest days, we slept. When people ramble with envy about how lucky we were to have been to the World Cup, I am often amused. What they don't realise is that we hardly ever went to the games: they probably saw more of the World Cup from home than we did in Rome. During the 1994 World Cup, which we hosted from San Francisco, it became so obvious that Johnny and I never went to games that a viewer wrote in to SBS offering money so the station could buy us some tickets. Through Italia '90, I attended two games: Italy vs Czechoslovakia and the final. Going to the former nearly got me into a pickle. I was doing a daily report for radio station 2GB which involved a chat with breakfast host, Mike Carlton. That day, I had arranged for Mike to call me on a mobile phone because I knew I would be at the stadium when his call was due. As the time of the call was approaching, Francesco and I were exiting the stadium in a throng of thousands of singing and dancing fans, celebrating Italy's 2-1 win. Francesco borrowed my phone to make a quick call – and disappeared, swallowed up by the mob. For a few agonising minutes I thought I'd miss the report: not a major tragedy, but I valued my professionalism and work ethic dearly and was loath to embarrass 2GB. In the nick of time, Francesco miraculously reappeared just as the phone rang. In the end, the anecdote – not to mention the sounds of the singing and chanting fans in the background – made very good live radio.

Till then no sporting event – never mind the World Cup – had been covered in Australia in quite this fashion. It was entertainment for all, not just for football fans: a major breakthrough in introducing Australians to the might of the world game. To be sure, in football terms it had been a dreary World Cup: the most defensive on record, with both semi finals decided by a penalty shootout and a dour final by a penalty. Its only unlikely hero was Roger Milla, a 38-year-old from Cameroon. But the colour of the carnival – the contest of worlds and cultures – left a lasting imprint on those who had tuned in for the first time.

My mother, then 78, was among those caught in the grip. She rang me after the Italy–Argentina semi final, having sat up half the night to watch it, to tell me that the Italian coach Azeglio Vicini was an idiot for leaving Roberto Baggio on the bench. She was spot on, of course.

The surveys showed an audience reach of two million ('reach' in ratings language mean the number of people who tuned in through the event for five minutes or more). It was not an especially spectacular figure for the time in comparison to say, the Olympic Games, an Ashes series or an MCG grand final. But for football, it was huge. More important was the platform that it established, for beyond the 1990 event, the World Cup audience reach was to enjoy astonishing growth: from two million in 1990, to five million in 1994, to nine million in 1998 and a staggering 14.8 million in 2002. That is what, in business, you would call successful market penetration.

For SBS, and for those of us labouring at the mission, the results were especially significant. In 1990, SBS was experiencing particular frustrations in gaining audiences, not because of what it was transmitting but because whatever it was transmitting was not being received by the bulk of viewers. Four years earlier, the Australian government had forced SBS to cease transmitting on the VHF band; SBS became the first station to transmit only on UHF. To the layman this meant just one thing: in order to receive SBS you had to buy a UHF aerial, otherwise all you got when you tuned to the station was a black screen. A UHF aerial cost around $150 to $200, if you were lucky enough to be in an area where you didn't have to erect a 20-metre mast on which to mount it. So the majority of viewers, apart from football fanatics, resisted the temptation. But then came the World Cup, providing an incentive for people to reach into their pockets: UHF aerials began to spring up like young green trees in a field of grey. The World Cup became a springboard for progress in SBS' quest to be seen. Once again, football had provided the vehicle. Not surprisingly, it was in 1990 that the station began a steady but continuous growth in audiences, a pattern that has continued ever since.

The 1990 World Cup also became the catalyst for a breach that was, till then, unthinkable in public broadcasting: a government funded station accepting advertising and sponsorship money. In June 1989, one year out from the tournament, the Australian government made a decision to allow SBS to receive moneys for program sponsorship 'in relation to the World Cup'. The first sponsor recruited was OTC, the Overseas Telecommunications Corporation, which aimed a campaign at migrants in an effort to increase overseas telephone traffic. The OTC was followed by the insurance company Legal and General. Though the World Cup had been isolated as the only program on SBS allowed to include commercial advertising, the experiment led to the government redrawing the SBS charter in 1991, allowing both SBS television and radio to run ads across their full schedules. In retrospect then, it can be argued that had it not been for the 1990 World Cup, the loosening of restrictions that allowed SBS to accept commercial funding might not have occurred and SBS, like the ABC, might still be a fully government-funded network.

These are the contexts in which the importance of the World Cup to SBS needs to be understood. It was not an event which in itself guaranteed ratings, even though its audiences were vastly bigger than those the station could normally command. Neither was it ever an event that made money. Because of its vast expense, the World Cup was always a loss-maker for the network. But what it gave to SBS – in terms of building its brand and its pioneering identity in an evolving cultural landscape – could not have been bought with a thousand glitzy advertising campaigns. Football had already become synonymous with the network and now the World Cup – the world's most popular sporting event – was also a part of the SBS identity. When people in the street thought football, they thought SBS; and when they thought World Cup, they thought SBS as its natural home.

Italia '90, for all the sweat and the hours, was not the most exhausting World Cup I was to do. Believe it or not, it got worse in the
shape of USA '94 four years later. But at least we got to do it once
again from a pretty location: San Francisco, as lovely a place in the
United States (apart from the cool temperatures) as you could ever
hope to labour in for a month. Not that we were supposed to be
there. Along with all the other international broadcasters, we and
our headquarters were meant to be in Dallas, Texas. That was the
city the organising committee had chosen as the nerve centre of all
television activities. The International Broadcast Centre (IBC) –
where hundreds of TV personnel congregate, ship in millions of
dollars worth of equipment, and set up studios – was to be in
Dallas. But Dallas, with its concrete jungles and forest of box-like
skyscrapers, was not pretty enough for us. More importantly, it told
us nothing about America.

I formed this view while filming the USA '94 host city profiles
in the summer of 1993. That, too, was a most invigorating and eye-
opening tour of discovery, on which I had to do pieces to camera as
if I were a travel guru: on horseback in Forth Worth wearing a silly
hat; at the top of the Empire State Building; at the Boston wharf
where the Boston Tea Party triggered the War of Independence; on
Santa Monica beach in Los Angeles; and virtually any place in the
United States worth visiting or showing off for a horde of drooling
Australian football fans who couldn't get there. One piece I did in
Dallas was from the grassy knoll where – according to some theo-
rists – a second gunman helped cut down President John F.
Kennedy in 1963. I was a teenager when JFK was assassinated, and
a huge fan of the man, so the moment was one of ghostly significance. When the shoot got to San Francisco, I formed the view that
presenting the World Cup from Dallas would have been an utter
waste of time and that, if we were going to present the tournament
as an 'American' event, San Francisco – with the Golden Gate

Bridge dominating the backdrop – had to be the place. So I rang Dominic Galati in Sydney and earbashed him for an hour about the beauties of San Francisco. He was swayed and asked me to find a production house that could handle the project for us.

So that's how USA '94 came to be done from San Francisco. The production house we found occupied a five-floor office building about five minutes drive from downtown on the southern side of the bay, just two blocks from the water. From its roof, the view was breathtaking. There was only one problem: the Golden Gate was not visible. As we faced north-east, the view of the Golden Gate was obliterated by the land mass to the west, as the bay's shore curved from north to west past North Bridge and Fishermen's Wharf. But what was visible, and awe-inspiringly so, was the Oakland Bay Bridge: a massive construction twice as long as the Golden Gate but of a similar design. Indeed, if Oakland Bay is the first bridge you see on arrival in San Francisco, it is easy to mistake it for the Golden Gate. So we figured: what the hell? It's a sensational view and the viewer is unlikely to know the difference. The presentation was met with delighted approval by the audience and the media alike, newspaper reviewers busily reporting what a wonderful job Johnny and I were doing on the roof of a building in front of the Golden Gate. Of course, we never claimed that it was the Golden Gate behind us. But neither did we say that it was the Oakland Bay Bridge. And when the Golden Gate got the credit as the set's main attraction, we never issued a correction.

The only other problem with San Francisco, though it was less visible, was the climate. Mark Twain once said: 'The coldest winter I ever had was a summer I spent in San Francisco', and we soon found out why. Up on the roof where we built our studio, a chill wind howled: the first thing Johnny and I did on arrival was to plead with Dominic to protect us from the wind. He obliged by building three huge tarpaulin walls around the set, leaving exposed only the side that was behind us displaying the view. The second thing we did was to ask our assistant to pop down to the nearest menswear shop and procure us some thermal underwear. Far from being enviably comfy sitting in the Californian sun – as we appeared to be – we spent a month in San Francisco shivering in our thermal underwear through every day of the World Cup. Later, Johnny recalled San Francisco as his favourite of all World Cup venues, ahead of Paris. I mostly recall it as a month in an ice box.

The hours were no better – in fact were worse – than they had been for Italia '90. Because the early games on the program kicked off at noon to suit European television, and a noon game in Chicago meant 10 am in California, we had to be on set much earlier than in Italy and rose at the crack of dawn. Lunch was brought in by the caterers but it was so bad Johnny and I refused to eat it: we usually sent one of the assistants down the road for hamburgers. We would finish earlier, around 10 pm on a good day, but that still left us with no chance to eat out, and we made do with takeaway in the hotel. Our nightly unwinding habits resumed, the only difference being that we switched from Grand Marnier to dry Californian whites.

But worst of all, Johnny and I didn't get to one solitary game in the entire tournament. Because we hosted all games live, with no input from our Sydney studio, we were chained to the set for the duration of the event. In any case, nothing happened in San Francisco. Though officially it was a 'host city' the games were played at Palo Alto, almost an hour's drive from our studio. About the most exciting things we did on the trip were to watch the OJ Simpson car chase (which happened a couple days before the Cup began); attend a Brazilian training session (where the tournament hero, Romario, spent the entire session sitting on his behind watching all the other players perspire like horses); go to a baseball game at Candlestick Park (which we left early because someone in the party was 'too cold'); and, on a rest day, have a long, meandering, boozy lunch in the Napa Valley.

Our worst day in USA '94 – well, my worst day, actually – was the day Diego Maradona was busted for drugs. The usual routine was that at the end of the day, after we had taped the highlights program, I stayed back for a while longer to tidy up some preparation work for the next day. By the time I left, around 10.30 pm or later, I was usually the only SBS body left in the building. As I was packing up and about to switch off the computer, I noticed a flashing headline from the wire services on the screen: 'Maradona tests positive for a banned substance'. I thought it was a hoax but grabbed the phone and called our reporter in Dallas, where the main press centre was, and got him out of some bar. Within minutes, he called me back with the confirmation. The World Cup's biggest news story was about to hit the streets. I thought, 'Shit, what do I do now? I mean, Diego, thanks for the story, amigo, but your timing stinks.' The problem was that the Maradona story would be on every back page and news bulletin in the world by the time our freshly taped program went to air in Australia. Luckily our technical director, Joan Morrison, was still in the building as was producer Joe di Meglio, who had just finished feeding out the highlights show to Sydney. Joan fired up one of the cameras and some lights as I scampered back into my long johns and suit. Between the three of us, we managed to record two short pieces to camera which ensured that the program didn't look dated and that we were on top of the story. We fed the two links back on the bird and some simple editing in Sydney did the trick.

The next World Cup – France '98 – was for me far more enjoyable, partly because it was in France: I am an unabashed Francophile, one who finds Paris the most enchanting city in the world. I could think of few more pleasurable gigs than emerging out of the Metro station each morning under the Eiffel Tower to work in a studio two blocks from the Champs-Élysées. Our facilities were superb and comfortable, working out of our rented premises on the Rue de Chaillot, where we converted an entire floor of an office building into a television station. Again we shunned the IBC, located in colourless Montparnasse, where the studio would have had only a painted wall as a backdrop. By now the SBS urge to broadcast events from location – in ways that captured a permanent postcard of the host country – had grown into an obsession.

The hours in Paris were better, too. The superhuman efforts of Rome and San Francisco could be put behind us: we were given the budget to assemble a bigger crew in Paris, including three sets of hosts. Instead of Johnny and me doing every game, the hostings were broken up into three daily shifts. I would do the first, Kyle Patterson the second and Paul Dempsey the third. Johnny, too, got relief with the recruitment of Andy Harper as the second analyst. This meant Johnny would do the first shift and Andy the second. All this allowed all the on-camera people to go to games. The roster, for instance, allowed me to go to every game that was played in Paris, except the final which I had to host from the studio. The food was better, too. French caterers would come in daily and spread their gourmet fare, complete with carafes of red wine: we Aussies lived for a month almost like the French. None of us begrudged France their win in the World Cup: the event the French invented.

Well, maybe Johnny did. He came back to the studio after the final in an ugly mood. Part of it was because the quickest and most practicable way from the Stade de France to the studio was by Metro, which was packed with foreigners, semi-drunk and with a bent for engaging in competitions of flatulence. But, though he never said so, I suspect his angst was also up because Brazil had lost.

When he arrived back we were due to tape the highlights show but were told by Kyle Patterson, doubling as Chief of Staff, that it would be at least three hours before we were needed and that we should make ourselves scarce. This was around midnight and Johnny and I peeled off to go up the Champs-Élysées for a coffee or two. The Élysées was packed with revellers and all cafes – including our favourite, Fouquet – had closed their doors. So we found a backstreet espresso bar where we sat for a couple of hours, soaking up the post-final wind-down. We got back to the studio an hour earlier than we thought we were required, only to be greeted by Patterson telling us to get ourselves into gear because a 'lynch mob' was gathering outside our office, a reference to SBS colleagues who were ready to go home to bed and had been only waiting for us to return from our leisure time. Johnny told Patterson to 'piss off', reminding him that he had not been late for anything in his life and that it was Patterson who had told us to make ourselves scarce for three hours in the first place. Patterson did piss off and all was well until a few minutes later when director Tony Aslanidis, not knowing he was giving an encore, walked into our office giving us a repeat reminder of the 'lynch mob'. Johnny snapped, took his shirt and tie off, threw them on the floor, and told Aslanidis to 'stick it up his arse' and that he wasn't going on. We were faced with the prospect of me doing a one hour show on my own, hosting and analysing the final, not a happy prospect given that I was no analyst, and neither was I partial to having to explain why Johnny was absent from the most important show of the World Cup. I pleaded with Johnny to see reason and to think of the viewers, of our reason for being there and of the mission. He softened, began to re-don his clothes and said: 'I'm only doing this for you because you are my friend.'

When people ask me to look back on my career and nominate my most memorable experiences in football, my feeling is that they expect me to name the World Cup, or some singular World Cup or even a World Cup match. I decline, because there are other things in my career that have given me even greater pleasure. But there is no denying that the World Cup, and being part of it, is an unparalleled education in the ways in which football mirrors life. It is living and throbbing theatre, reflecting humanity's diversity and how it rejoices in healthy and happy competition among cultures, traditions and tribes. It is the thing that, above anything, moves the world's peoples. Each of us is infected by the carnival of rivalry and exchange, when we rejoice and find meaning if we win but move on with a laugh – those of us who are sane – and wait patiently and expectantly for four more years if we lose. It is sport's pinnacle but, after all, it is only sport.

My most memorable World Cup moment came after the 1998 semi final between France and Croatia. France won the game, despite having been reduced to 10 men after France's Laurent Blanc had been sent off due to a blatant dive taken by a Croatian defender. Johnny and I were in a Paris cafe winding down, surrounded by a horde of French fans clad in blue shirts and incessantly singing 'Allez les Bleus'. Suddenly, a beeline of Croatian fans walked in, complete with red and white chequered shirts animating the Croatian flag. Johnny and I glanced at each other, anticipating that an almighty fight might ensue. But far from it. As the Croatians entered, the French all stood up and applauded them in. The two sets of fans embraced and the French – generous in their moment of victory – shouted cognacs all round. It was sport at its most majestic: football acting as a supreme catalyst of tolerance and understanding.

We marvelled at the World Cup's wonders, and contemplated how wonderful it would be if Australia, a multicultural country, could ever be part of it again.

13

Iran

In my early days in television, the Logie Awards – glitzy Australian showbiz accolades – did not interest me. Not many others at SBS were interested either. We felt the awards were inspired by crass commercialism, rewarding only populism – and SBS was not strong in either. Indeed, in those early days SBS, the 'wog' channel, wasn't invited. Vlado Lusic, one of SBS' genuine 'ethnic' presenters, once led a campaign to force the organisers to give SBS a table. He came to me for a petition signature and I told him I wasn't interested. But almost two decades later, in 1998, there I was on stage with Don Lane, receiving a Logie on behalf of the network for 'Most Outstanding Sports Coverage'. I must admit I felt like 'the king of the world'. But the moment was soiled by a choking inner sadness, for the award had been given for SBS' extravagant coverage of a game which broke the nation's heart. Five months earlier, Australia drew 2-2 with Iran and surrendered its best chance since 1974 to make it into the World Cup finals. It seemed so unjust that on Logies night so many in the football industry had benefited from that calamity, while the players – despite their heroic efforts – were mere additions to the many names and statistics of those who had failed before them.

One of the reasons the failure was unforeseen and shocking was that Australia had been maturing in what appeared to be a golden era in player quality. It began with the 1991 World Youth Championship in Portugal where the Young Socceroos got to the semi finals. They lost 1-0 to the hosts in front of 110,000 fans at Lisbon's Estadio da Luz, to a crackerjack goal by Rui Costa: with Luis Figo, Joao Pinto, Jorge Costa, Peixe and Rui Costa in their team, it was our bad luck that Portugal was also spawning its own 'golden generation'. During that two-week tournament in Portugal, Johnny Warren and I were close witnesses to those promising beginnings. It was a grand young Australian team: Bosnich; Muscat, Popovic, Okon, Babic; Maloney, Kindtner, Stanton, Corica; Seal, Trajanovski. A number of them went on to bag a wardrobe of caps for Australia and were the forerunners of the age that produced the likes of Mark Viduka, Stan Lazaridis, Harry Kewell, Craig Moore and Brett Emerton. Reserve keeper Mark Schwarzer was injured just prior to the tournament and his stand-in, Zeljko Kalac, never got a game because of Bosnich's brilliance. That was the depth of young Australian talent at the time. They began with a stroll over Trinidad-Tobago, a day of toil for a teenage Dwight Yorke, looking skinny and skilful but alone for the opposition, and before we knew it the Young Socceroos were in the quarter finals. As word spread about the young Aussies, an army of player agents gathered, the most prominent of them Israel Moaz who appeared to have a mortgage on Paul Okon. Australian coach Les Scheinflug closed ranks and banned the entry of agents to the team hotel. As I walked up the steps to my commentary position in Braga, a dapper Frenchman stopped me and gave me his card, saying he was keen to talk to Paul Okon but had been unable to get to him. His name was Gerard Houllier, then technical director at AS Monaco, one of the richest clubs in Europe; and where player wages were tax free. I passed the card to Okon but I was too late: he had already been betrothed to Club Bruges, a client of Israel Moaz.

Eventually the Young Socceroos finished fourth, although they each received bronze medals because they only lost the third place playoff to the USSR on a penalty shootout. But their biggest day in the sun was that semi final against Portugal. Given the size of the crowd – 110,000 – and the grandness of the occasion, it was also the biggest game I ever commentated on. The Australians, visibly intimidated, began nervously. The defence held out and Bosnich was at his cat-like best but at the break the Aussies were 1-0 down, courtesy of Rui Costa who, from his left wing-back position ghosted onto the right side of midfield and from 25 metres fired in a viciously swerving shot that whistled past Bosnich. In the second half, Scheinflug introduced Steve Corica and Kris Trajanovski which changed the game: for the last half hour Australia rallied to almost snatch the equaliser. Afterwards, Scheinflug asked me into the dressing room to say a few words to the boys. I told them this had already been a magnificent tournament from them, an achievement beyond all expectations, and that they should be proud of counting themselves among the four best teams in the world at under 20 level. It was one of the hardest things I ever had to do, and a total flop. My words did nothing to console the boys who could only think of having lost and how close they were to going even further. Later, the Australian under 17 team would play in a world championship final, while the senior Socceroos would also make the final of the Confederations Cup. But until 1991, this had been the best ever achievement by an Australian football team in any major international competition. With a touch better fortune they may have gone all the way: it seemed proof that exciting times were ahead for Australian football.

The final, between Portugal and Brazil, demonstrated how close Australia had come. It was a stalemate, with neither team able to score and the match deteriorating into the lottery climax of a shootout, won by Portugal. For us, about the only memorable aspect of this game was that it failed to kick off on time, which is another very SBS-related story. As the clock passed the scheduled time for kick-off, and with the players still to emerge from the dressing rooms, Johnny and I looked pensively at our watches. Below us at pitch side, we could see Dominic Galati deep in animated conversation with FIFA media chief Guido Tognoni. The game finally kicked off, 10 minutes late; we didn't find out why until we caught up with Dominic later. He had found out on the morning of the game that there had been a double booking on the satellite path bringing the signal to Australia, which meant the satellite wasn't available to SBS until five minutes after the scheduled kick-off. With the other client refusing to cancel, the only options left were either to have Australian viewers miss the first five minutes of the action or, somehow, to have the kick-off delayed. Dominic, who knew how to pull strings when they needed pulling, was gallant and shameless enough to give it a try. I don't know what he said to Tognoni or what powers of persuasion he used, but for the first time in my memory, a match in a FIFA-organised tournament didn't kick off on time.

It was, however, the next World Youth Championship, hosted by Australia in 1993, which thrust SBS forward as a major player in domestic football. The ABC held all rights to Australian football until it dramatically dumped them in mid-1992. But by the time the rights went out to tender again, the ABC had changed its mind – and with good reason: the rights to the 1993 World Youth Championship were part of the prize. Dominic Galati went to work to win the rights from the ABC. I was not privy to the negotiations but I believe a number of things helped SBS get over the line: Dominic's close friendship with ASF chairman John Constantine; Dominic's pledge to give exposure to the tournament's major sponsor, Coca-Cola; and squeezing a sizeable pledge in production costs out of FIFA, which helped SBS put in a competitive commercial bid. SBS won the tender and the network was back in 'partnership' with the governing body. Once again, SBS owned the rights to all available high-profile football properties, except the English Premier League which remained with the ABC.

Late in 1992, SBS staged a glittering draw ceremony for the World Youth Championship at Sydney's Darling Harbour. The ceremony was telecast live on SBS and was beamed around the world. I think Dominic's ambition almost ran off course when he suggested inviting Julio Iglesias to be the star attraction. I talked him out of it, and proposed the Indigenous dance troupe, Bangarra, instead. They proved to be a huge hit and particularly impressed Sepp Blatter, then FIFA general secretary, who conducted the draw. Blatter grew increasingly impressed by SBS' devotion to his sport and developed a soft spot for the network.

In December of that year, SBS tried its hand at another bold new venture: a four-match series in Australia between the youth teams of Australia and Brazil, favourites for the world tournament that was to take place in March of the following year. Though the brainchild was mine, the idea's real champion was Johnny Warren. What I wanted was to have a tournament that SBS owned, and was therefore compelled to promote heavily. I wanted to test the impact of SBS' power as a promotion vehicle for football events. Johnny's keenness was rooted in his deep affection for Brazilian football and in his personal crusade to build strong football links between the two countries. We called the series the SBS Youth Challenge and gave it heavy on-air promotion. It was a huge success. The crowds everywhere were large, especially for the final match which – by good luck – was the series decider. An over-capacity 20,000 crammed into Sydney's Marconi Stadium, with another estimated 10,000 watching the game on giant screens in the stadium car park. The series established once and for all SBS' clout in mobilising the football flock. It was a great brand-builder for the station and a tremendous promotional vehicle for the world tournament a few months down the track. Johnny's cause also got a great deal out of it, but sadly that was not to last: despite tremendous goodwill from the Brazilians to keep up a relationship with Australian football, our football authorities showed no interest.

It was no surprise, however, that the World Youth Championship in 1993 was a big hit with Australian audiences. And here, too, Dominic Galati can take a bow. He pulled together a great team: facilities supplier Harry Michaels, a man with a rare passion for football; an excellent team of producers, led by Terry Toaldo; and a fine band of commentators, among them Paul

Williams (making his SBS debut on the tournament) and Englishman Gary Bloom, the first commentator SBS ever imported from overseas. Played in prime viewing time, the tournament had superb ratings. The quarter final between Australia and Uruguay – won by Australia with the world's first 'golden goal' – rated 18 percentage points: the first time SBS had rated in the high teens. Football had scored another great goal for the network.

By now the Australian national team, and indeed all the country's representative teams, were well into the era of Eddie Thomson. Eddie, unlike his predecessor, Frank Arok, was a full-time national coach, able to work with and stamp his authority on all the nation's male rep teams. He had a great rapport and friendship with the youth and Olympic coaches, Les Scheinflug and Raúl Blanco, and was able to stamp his technical influence down the line. I once saw him sit high in the stands at the Sydney Football Stadium watching a World Youth qualifier, screaming instructions to Scheinflug who was about to make a substitution. I considered Eddie a fabulous coach: a man with very little education but one with a keen football brain and a street instinct for coaching. He could read a game like a book. We clashed on occasion, mostly because he thought I was anti-British and, being a Scot, felt targeted. But his teams played nothing like a British style, so in truth we had no argument. In any case, he took criticism like a man and our relationship always remained professional and friendly. Whenever I said or wrote something he didn't like, he would give me a ring and say: 'Let's meet for coffee and talk this over'.

My criticism was of Eddie's conservatism in selections and tactics. He was essentially cautious and, though he liked his teams to attack, he would often pack them with defenders and was not adventurous in picking younger players. His results with the Socceroos, I believe, often reflected this caution: his first 17 games in charge produced just 12 goals. I believe he didn't have sufficient confidence in the players and that his attitude was counter-productive to the growing self-belief that had emerged under Arok. And for the development of football in Australia – a country that had so long been a colonial backwater in the sport – self-belief was critically important.

Appointed in 1990, Eddie Thomson quit the national team after 59 games and just one World Cup campaign in 1996. Despite his impressive win-loss record, not to mention taking Australia to the medal rounds at the 1992 Barcelona Olympics, it seemed to me that he felt pressured by his new boss, Soccer Australia chairman David Hill. After reportedly copping some dressing room heat from Hill during the Atlanta Olympics of 1996, he quit to join J-League club, Sanfrecce Hiroshima. Thomson was the first – and remains the only – Australian coach to make it in a big-money overseas league. His departure was a big blow for Australia: I believe (for reasons I will get to later) that Australia may have qualified for the 1998 World Cup had he remained in charge.

Eddie's premature death from pancreatic cancer at the age of 56 was a massive shock for all of us in the football family. He was a super fit man, an avid jogger who had always looked after his health. But Eddie's death was also tragic because the football family in Australia is an underdog family. Although we had our disagreements, we always pulled together, united by the need to have our game acknowledged and accepted. Eddie had been one of us. Besides, he was a larger-than-life character in the game, a man with a terrific sense of humour; a former street footballer with a genuine passion for the game.

Unfortunately, while he was still national coach, Eddie Thomson was at the centre of a major scandal that not only threatened his undoing but brought the game to its knees. Amid rumours of cattle trading by Australia's coaching staff, the ASF commissioned an independent inquiry. Its outcome, the Stewart Report, accused the national coach of acting as a clandestine agent for representative players and recommended his sacking. A subsequent Senate Inquiry exonerated Eddie Thomson and all the others accused in the report for lack of evidence. But it caused a 'sea change' (the very words used by the independent inquiry's chair, Justice Stewart, to describe what was needed) in the game's governance.

At the height of the turmoil ASF chairman, John Constantine, who was not implicated in any way, did the honourable thing and resigned, leaving the door open for fresh blood to come into the sport at the steering level and chart a new course. Political neutrals and non-football folk hankered for an outsider to take over the ASF chairmanship: someone with no 'ethnic' or any other political baggage. Galloping to the game's rescue came none other than David Hill, who by then had left his job as managing director of the ABC. Hill had been made of soccer stuff, a child migrant from England who was still an active weekend player at the time this opportunity presented itself. That background, plus his Anglo heritage, his lack of history with an administration of ill repute and his track record as a senior manager, made him a heaven-sent candidate. He was seen as the grand saviour of the game.

SBS, which had played its part in covering the Stewart Report and its aftermath, now became the instrument of Hill's ascension: a profound irony I think, given the man's business history with SBS in his television days. SBS' Sunday afternoon *On The Ball* program, a football talk show, presented a series of interviews with all three candidates for the chairmanship: Hill; the NSW Soccer Federation chairman, Peter Gray; and the former chairman, Ian Brusasco. It then ran a viewer poll on which of the candidates the cognoscenti would prefer to take over the ASF chairmanship. The other two candidates did not interview well and Hill, a wonderful media performer, walked in, polling more than 70 per cent of the votes. The ASF stakeholders, who had to vote on the chairmanship, felt compelled to go with the people and Hill became the new chief of Australian football, elected by an overwhelming majority.

Yet David Hill felt no allegiance to SBS, the game's premier public promoter. From the moment he took office, it seemed clear to me that he made it one of his missions to move the television rights to all Australian football properties away from SBS and on to one of the commercial stations. He seemed possessed by the notion that football's way out of the 'ethnic' image incarceration was to end the reign of the 'ethnic' station as its broadcaster. He fronted up to the SBS managing director's office and tried to get him to rescind the rights contract which had another two years to run. His request was politely declined.

I soon came to feel that Hill had little time for me, but it was difficult to fathom why. I had never publicly said anything negative about him, certainly not until much later. I can only suggest he may have resented the considerable power of SBS with the football cognoscenti. And of course I, as the SBS front man, was one face representing that power. Johnny Warren was another, and I don't think Hill had much time for him either. 'Mr and Mrs Soccer' was an imperial label – in reference to we two SBS apparatchiks – that Hill would not have appreciated at the time.

David Hill, while showing immense promise before he became chairman – I supported his appointment – turned out, in my opinion, to be less than a success in his short three years in charge. He was the first 'non-ethnic' to lead the game since the migrants took control of it in 1957, a man of high profile and powerful influence, with a mandate to take the game forward and disentangle it from its web of social paralysis and regression. His motivation may have been in the right place but I believe his personality was unsuited to carrying out a task that needed sensitivity, persuasive reason and tactical cunning. To me, he seemed to have no time for the game's dominant migrant forces nor for the massive historical contribution they had made to the game, and appeared to be on a mission to 'de-ethnicise' it, as was the expression at the time. He banned all ethnically inspired logos, emblems and club colours. In one case, he moved a team, Sydney United, from its community based home venue to one 10 kilometres away. He was focussed on Australianising the game, missing the point that – given Australia's multicultural social makeup – the game was actually very Australian. He appeared to be intent not on Australianisation but on Anglicisation – two very different things. But since part of Australia's national flag sported the British Union

Jack, Australian football fans couldn't understand what was wrong with the blue and white of Greece or the red and white checks of Croatia decorating a few suburban football grounds. I think Hill's strategies had the effect of alienating the majority of the NSL clubs, turning the bulk of the fans against him while not winning any new fans to replace them.

In terms of the game's international politics, and harnessing them to Australia's advantage, I think David Hill proved to be naïve and damaging to Australia's cause. At one point, he publicly referred to Charlie Dempsey, a New Zealander who was the president of the Oceania Football Confederation and a man close to the FIFA hierarchy, as Albert Steptoe. Asked by FIFA to apologise to Dempsey, Hill refused. In the 1996 FIFA congress in Zurich, he proposed a vote against his own confederation – which was about to be legitimised by the world body – and lost it 170 votes to one. What he wanted – not unwisely – was to merge Oceania with Asia. But he tried to ram it through. Australia's place as part of Asia was finally achieved by one of his successors eight years later, Frank Lowy, a man who, I think, proved to be a bit more clever at international football politics.

But David Hill was certainly bold, and unafraid of big decisions. After the exit of Eddie Thomson as national coach, Hill dropped the biggest bombshell of his tenure by appointing Terry Venables as the new boss of the Socceroos. It was seen, as one prominent player of the time described it, as a most inspired appointment. Venables, or 'El Tel' as the press liked to call him, had been a successful coach with Tottenham Hotspur and CF Barcelona. He had just coached England to a semi final in the European Championship. But for reasons best known to his English bosses, his contract wasn't renewed. He was successful; he was English; he was an international celebrity with a reputation that had reached Australia. And Hill pounced and got him. It was a major coup.

I was violently and vocally against the appointment, a response I now regret. I went on the *On The Ball* program with an emotional seven-minute editorial, blackly debunking the ideologies that tried to justify the El Tel choice. My knee-jerk reaction was partly rooted in the fact that Venables was English, and therefore – by definition – of the regressive English technical school. But beyond that, Venables was a foreigner, and this was a time when football in Australia was searching for an indigenous identity as a way of distancing itself from being a colonial subordinate in the football world. Johnny Warren supported my views. He commented: 'I thought we were Australianising the game.'

Venables was on a lucrative contract to Australia but spent most of his time in England, something that was objectionable to many at a time when a substantial proportion of our national team was still based in Australia. But while it is true that Venables cost a lot of money (eventually sending Soccer Australia almost broke) and his 'remote control' management of the team was less than ideal, his short era in charge – less than 18 months – was the most invigorating in Socceroo history. The team, under him, played the most cultured and eye-pleasing football it had ever played. It won all of its first 13 games under his charge and tasted only two defeats in Venables' 18-match career as Australian coach. Yet I think his tenure is generally viewed as a failure: it was under Terry Venables that the Socceroos suffered their sixth straight failure at the World Cup.

For the first time since 1982 – 16 years and four World Cups – Australia had only Third World opposition to overcome to get to the World Cup. In that span the path had been via Europe (Scotland in 1986), and South America (Colombia in 1990 and Argentina in 1994). Now, for 1998, FIFA deemed that the route was to be via Asia. The champion of Oceania – most likely Australia – was to play the fourth best team in Asia in order to make it to France 98. Australia strolled through the Oceania rounds, winning all six of its matches: it scored 31 goals and conceded just two. For its last warm-up before the final hurdle, Australia went to Tunis and won 3-0 over Tunisia, a country with a playing standard and style not dissimilar to whichever Asian foe the Socceroos were about to face. In the meantime, South Korea and

Saudi Arabia won their places through Asia in France 98, leaving a playoff between Japan and Iran. The winner of this match would go to France and the loser would play Australia.

The playoff match took place in neutral Johor in Malaysia. SBS had a direct telecast as part of the build-up to the big one against the loser. We sent commentator Paul Williams to Malaysia and I hosted the telecast from Sydney, with Johnny Warren and another 1974 Socceroo hero, Noddy Alston. I asked Noddy which would be the preferable opponent for Australia – Japan or Iran. He said it didn't matter: either would be easy fodder for the Australians. The television rights to the final home match against the loser had already been pre-sold by the marketing agency, Octagon-CSI. If it was to be against Japan, I was told that Octagon-CSI would collect $1 million. Against Iran, the fee was a lousy $5000. Much rode on the outcome. Japan won a dramatic game with a Golden Goal. Australia's opponent was to be Iran.

As we looked towards the clash with Iran, it appeared that Noddy Alston had been right. The Iranians, though brave, were vastly outplayed by the speedy Japanese and looked decidedly unfit. But we were to learn a hard lesson: never underestimate a desperate Iran with its back to the wall.

On the Socceroos' journey to Tehran for the first leg of the playoff, the team attracted much acrimony from their Asian opponents. Soccer Australia's chief, David Hill, spoke of shipping in fresh water for the boys under suspicion that Asian water was less than safe, unaware of the fact that Iran was in fact a respected international exporter of water. The plush hotel in Dubai where Australia was staying en-route to Tehran, and where Hill made his ill-timed remark, was serving its guests mineral water imported from Iran.

To be quite honest, though, we at SBS were also playing it safe when it came to trusting Iranian capacities to deliver. For the match in Tehran, we abandoned all plans to present the game entirely from location, a complex minefield of technical wizardry where one wrong switch or wrongly patched wire could have delivered a screen with an apology slide to Australian audiences for the duration of a game. It was Australia's biggest game since 1974 and we couldn't afford to take the risk. I stayed home to present the telecast from Sydney and the Australian media contingent in Tehran included only reporter Kyle Patterson, commentator Paul Williams and Johnny Warren from SBS.

Even that small effort was fraught with risk and almost ended in disaster. Johnny Warren, who loved a tipple of duty-free Scotch whenever he travelled (and I was always a willing partner), bought his usual bottle of Johnnie Walker Red on the way into Iran. As he joined the customs queue with a whisky bottle poking out of the duty free bag on his trolley, a posse from the Australian party pleaded with him to abandon the bravado and dump the booze. Iran was a booze-free zone and any digression was met with arrest and jail. As anticipation grew about grotesque scenes where the former Socceroo captain would be led away in handcuffs by darkly clad men, a bearded Iranian customs officer — who just happened to be a former footballer who had once played against Johnny — recognised him, promoted him to the front of the queue, embraced him, kissed him on both cheeks and waved him through.

The game was a classic, a thrill-a-minute epic: one of the most memorable in Australia's long history of emotionally taxing World Cup campaigns. A massive, noisy, all-male crowd greeted the teams. At the anthems the Iranian players stood erect, looking up towards Allah, singing with gusto, in complete belief of their right to achieve. This was as big a challenge, it occurred to me then, as any Australian team had ever faced. Suddenly, thoughts of a stroll against Iran wafted out the window. We had a real job on our hands. But Australia survived it, thanks to a goal by the youthful Harry Kewell and some heroics by goalkeeper Mark Bosnich. The match ended 1-1 which was actually a lot more than survival. With away goals counting double in the event of an aggregate tie, a 1-1 was as good as a win.

Australia was now just a 0-0 draw, or the most meagre of home wins, away from the holy grail: World Cup qualification — something it had not achieved in 24 years. The return at the Melbourne Cricket Ground was by far the most anticipated sports event in Australia that year. Not surprisingly, it was to give SBS its highest audience rating ever: 34 per cent of all available households, or around four million viewers. In the week between the two games the Australian media, including its most cricket-bent tabloids, became consumed by the occasion. It was a graphic and revealing illustration of the latent respect with which the Australian public, and its media, regarded football or, at least, the World Cup. Suddenly, the game of the 'wogs' became a national priority, and that had never been experienced in Australia before, not even in 1974. The self-declared 'greatest sporting nation on earth', accustomed to winning in most things except the world's most important sport, was finally at the gates of Nirvana. Hence the media interest and the massive audience.

SBS covered the team's every move: reporter Kyle Patterson was billeted with the Socceroos. Another reporter covered the movements of the Iranians. The entire SBS crew was booked into our favourite Melbourne abode, the Hilton on the Park. A few days before the match I got a phone call from one of Terry Venables' assistants, Raúl Blanco, asking me to move the SBS team to another hotel. Venables had chosen the Hilton as the team's headquarters and didn't believe in co-habitation with the media: he wanted SBS out. I refused, but gave a written undertaking that no SBS person would go near any of the squad members in the hotel. Venables backed off.

The match was scheduled for an 8 pm kick-off, with SBS due to begin its broadcast at 7.30. The deal between SBS and Soccer Australia at the time required approval from Soccer Australia before the broadcast could go live in the game's originating city. The final yes or no depended on the volume of tickets sold and whether live TV coverage would affect the gate. When I arrived at the ground two hours before kick-off, there was still no word on whether SBS could go live with the game in Melbourne. At 7.25 pm, I got a call on my mobile from Ken Shipp, the executive producer of the broadcast, informing me that David Hill had given the go-ahead. The ticket sales had reached 85,000 and we could go live in Melbourne. As I was reviewing my script, adjusting it to include a welcome to all Melbourne viewers, my phone beeped again. It was a text message from Mike Williams, head of sports production at Channel Nine: 'Good luck, Les. We're all watching.' Now I knew that our audience was well beyond that of the soccer norm; maybe the biggest we would ever have. Channel Nine executives didn't make a habit of admitting they watched any channel other than their own.

The atmosphere at the ground was stirring. All around the MCG, flags fluttered and chants of 'Australia!' reverberated. The MCG had been home to cricket and Australian Rules, and indeed the 1956 Olympics; its vast expanses had witnessed many a big sporting occasion. But surely it had never experienced a charged atmosphere like this. Over to the right, above my left shoulder as I looked into the camera, maybe 20,000 Iranian supporters made their presence felt in vibrant red, white and green. The stage was set for a grand occasion, maybe the grandest Australian football was ever to experience.

Venables, knowing the Iranians were on the ropes and aware of their poor away record, instructed his men to play their normal game and enjoy themselves. He understood well the time-honoured Australian instinct to 'have a go' and 'have a go' is all the tactics the Socceroos needed that night. And they did. In the first 20 minutes, Australia pierced the Iranian defence like a jet fighter would a flock of pigeons. When Harry Kewell finally broke through, the arena erupted like Mount Etna on an aggressive day. We were on our way at last. At the break, Kyle Patterson did a pitch-side interview with one of the Australian assistant coaches and grinned from ear to ear, suggesting that the win – and qualification – was done and dusted. As I back-announced him, I cautioned that the game was not yet over. But the bravado continued in the second half and soon, through Aurelio Vidmar, Australia led 2-0 (or 3-1 on aggregate). The Socceroo momentum was awesome: all Iran could do was take deep breaths and hold on for dear life.

Then something happened. A loony drifter – a Mohawk-coiffured serial pest – who had previously tried to make a name for himself by interrupting major public occasions, jumped from his seat, galloped towards the Iran goal and tore down the net, causing the entire frame of the goal to collapse. The game was held up for seven minutes while the goal was repaired. And the only man in the stadium who understood the likely impact of the incident was Iran's coach: the wily old Brazilian, Valdeir Vieira. Immediately the game restarted he made a double substitution, dispensing with two defensive players and bringing on two attackers. One of them was Bagheri, one of Iran's most celebrated players at the time, whose absence from the starting line-up had till then been a mystery. It was a move Vieira had always intended. He knew the Australians would come at his team like a steam train in high gear and eventually exhaust themselves. If Iran could survive until the late passages with a gettable deficit, like a 0-1 or a 0-2, he would bring on his attacking reserves. That was his only chance. Remarkably, the Australian bench didn't respond to the substitutions, either in changes to personnel or in tactics. Venables apparently failed to grasp that the seven-minute interruption might impede the Australians' adrenalin-charged momentum and prevent them finishing the job with a couple more goals. Now there were just 12 minutes left in the game. In what seemed like a flash, Iran scored one goal and then another, incisively cutting through a naïve Australian defence. Suddenly it was 2-2: a number that would take Iran and not Australia to the World Cup.

As I sat in my studio chair high up in the stands, childhood memories of 1954 came flooding back: I recalled the romantic favourite, Hungary, surrendering a 2-0 lead to lose the World Cup final. An instinct told me it was all over: I had seen this before. I swivelled my chair and turned my back on the game, declining to watch its desperate remaining minutes. It had been Australia's best chance to make it since 1973 and we were blowing it. We had the best team we had ever had; the highest credentialed and paid coach we had ever had; the weakest opponent we could have wanted

– and we were still blowing it. After the final whistle I got a grip, composed myself and threw to a commercial break. Back on air, I had Johnny Warren – who had been co-commentating with Paul Williams and had gone through the torture of analysing the calamity – sitting beside me. I threw him the usual inane question: 'What went wrong?' He muttered something about 'feeling for the boys' and then choked on his words. 'Mate, I can't say anything,' he said. Somehow, we muddled through the remaining long and agonising minutes of the telecast.

The Hilton is a slow, five-minute walk through a park between the MCG and the hotel. As we exited the stadium, we had to negotiate this short walk through a multitude of like-minded fans as thousands of them poured out of the arena. Usually, in this situation, Johnny and I would be stopped and asked for photos, autographs and comments about the game. But, eerily, this did not happen that night. As we walked, we felt a thousand eyes upon on us. But not one person approached. Out of respect for our pain, it seemed, we were being left alone.

Arriving at the hotel, we decided to take a side entrance and avoid the horror of negotiating the throng that had gathered in the lobby and the adjacent bar. Once in my room, I dialled room service and ordered a bottle of Johnnie Walker Red. I was told apologetically that the bar was out of Scotch. I exploded with rage: 'You mean to say this is a five star hotel and you have no Scotch? Well get your fat arse down the road and get some!' Five minutes later, a large bottle of Johnnie Walker Black was delivered to my room, complete with a bucket of ice. I don't know how and when I got to bed. In the morning, I awoke to the sight of an empty Johnnie Walker bottle on the coffee table. My mood was not improved when I picked up the morning paper to read that, at the post-match press conference, David Hill declared that this had been 'a great day for Australian soccer' and that Terry Venables would be re-appointed Australia's national coach.

With years of hindsight, I realise it is unfair to blame one man – Terry Venables – for the calamity. There were many other contributing factors: the many missed scoring chances by the Australians; that a number of the Socceroos, notably Aurelio Vidmar and Ned Zelic, had not been fully active with their clubs prior to the game and lacked match-sharpness; the first Iranian goal having been clearly off side; the loony loser having interrupted the game and deflated the Australian momentum; the Australian defenders' refusal to play to instructions not to use the off side trap.

But I think Venables must shoulder the blame in at least three key, determining areas. One: he selected the centre-back pairing of Alex Tobin and the young and naïve Steve Horvat, leaving out Milan Ivanovic – Australia's most experienced defensive general, a veteran of European Cups with Red Star Belgrade and hundreds of games partnering Tobin in the defensive wall of both Adelaide City and the Socceroos. If anyone knew how to organise a defence in times of crisis it was Ivanovic. Two: he made no response to the Iran coach's two vital substitutions after the goal collapse incident. And three: he made no tactical change after that seven-minute pause in the game, seemingly ignoring the obvious – that the incident would take the wind out of the Australians' sails and give the initiative back to Iran. Most who observed the game now contend that Venables, at that point, should have made the tactical and personnel changes needed to shut out the desperate Iranians and protect the two goal – or even one goal – margin. My conviction remains that with coaches of lesser international stature, like Frank Arok or Eddie Thomson, Australia would not have lost that tie with such a short time to go and holding an aggregate 3-1 lead.

For me, and all others in the SBS family, the darkness of the outcome was not compensated for by the fact that SBS made a killing on the game. The peak rating for the telecast was 34 per cent of households, at a time when SBS was hard pressed to average 4 per cent in the ratings. It was the first time SBS had hit ratings above 30 per cent and the estimated audience, at its peak, was four million people. It was the most watched sporting event in Australia that year and certainly the most watched football match ever. It was a long, long way from the few thousand who tuned in when the station first began its bold experiments with 'wogball' 17 years earlier.

The broadcast, as a matter of routine, was entered for a Logie in the category of Most Outstanding Sports Coverage. My own thoughts were: fat chance. SBS had never won a Logie before on an in-house production. I thought a football telecast had a snowflake's chance in hell of getting up in a country obsessed with cricket and various other sports played with an egg-shaped ball. So I declined the invitation to attend the ceremony. But then I got a call from the head of SBS publicity, John Woodward, who pleaded with me to attend. Later, the penny dropped that he must have known something. The presenter of the award was Don Lane, a veteran variety star of Australian TV and a living legend in the Australian small screen industry. As he announced: 'The Logie goes to World Cup Qualifier, Australia vs Iran, SBS Television', I thought, 'Shit, I have to make a speech'. Acceptors of awards were given 60 seconds to prattle off their thank-yous and acknowledgments. I took seven minutes. In my speech I thanked no one in particular, something that many involved in the production were hurt by. But I kept thinking only of the thousands – and eventually millions – of fans of the world game who stuck by SBS throughout the years, supporting the game and supporting our efforts to bring it to them, and it was them that I principally thanked. I also gave a big collective 'Thank you' to the SBS staff, not all of whom were football fans, yet who had worked doggedly and tirelessly to deliver wonderful coverage. But – for the record – I must single out for special praise Ken Shipp, the project director; producer, Peter Hinchley; match director, Harry Michaels; commentator, Paul Williams; and my good friend, Johnny Warren. I also muttered something on that stage about the selflessness of SBS staff who, I said, were 'not on Channel Nine wages'. This, I later found out, offended some Channel Nine people, notably its chief executive,

David Leckie. That was most unfortunate, for I did not mean to offend anyone at Channel Nine, all of whom had done a superb job for their network and fully deserved whatever salaries they were on. I merely made the point that SBS staff were not salubriously paid for their distinguished efforts. I took the Logie home and for a few months kept it there, so paranoid was I of it being stolen. Later it found its way to the SBS sport memorabilia cabinet.

The SBS euphoria over the Logie didn't last long. We had things to do. Two months later we were in France covering the 1998 World Cup, the most ambitious and comprehensive sports coverage SBS had ever attempted. Our studios were perched on the top floor of a Paris office building, with the Eiffel Tower and a medieval church providing the backdrop and the Parisian flavour. SBS gutted the floor of its existing walls and structures and wired it up to create an actual television station. It was a superb effort, ending in a magnificent broadcast, the very peak of SBS' 18-year endeavours to project football as the most glamorous of all things in sport. Nine million Australians – almost half the nation's population – tuned in. The game was lurching forward: Australians were flocking to discover the World Cup carnival and the unique beauties of the beautiful game.

But there were other forces at play, herding dark clouds over SBS' lofty role as Australia's chosen football broadcaster. While we were in Paris, the word came through that SBS had lost all television rights to Australian football: the NSL, the Socceroos and all other representative teams – all of which we had been covering for the best part of 18 years. David Hill, still chairman of Soccer Australia, had sold the rights to Channel Seven. The news coincided with the beginning of Australian football's darkest era: a period that lasted seven years. Although the Seven television deal was not the major cause, I believe it was a supremely regressive component of the downward slide.

SBS' rights contract was due to run out in June of 1998, with SBS holding a first option to renew. But as anyone in business knows, first options are not worth the paper they are written on. Hill offered SBS the opportunity to exercise its option in a letter from chief executive, David Woolley, sent to the network in December 1997 – one month after the Iran debacle. The offer was for a three-year deal with a price demand in the 10s of millions. This was a laughably distant cry from the amount SBS had been paying in its previous contract, not to mention the fact that accepting such an offer would have very quickly sent SBS broke. I politely replied to Woolley, declining the offer and asking him to get back to us once they had received other offers. I specifically asked him to give SBS the opportunity to match other offers, knowing that no other network in Australia would pay so much for three years. I was hopeful that the best other offer might have been matchable by SBS. But Hill – the businessman – never got back to us, knowing that he did not have to: with our refusal of his first offer, our first option rights had been eliminated. In my view, he had an agenda to take football away from SBS, the 'wog' channel, and pass it on to the commercials.

Hill got lucky and found the perfect target in Seven executive, Alan Bateman. Bateman was of an old Australian television school – one which no longer exists – where industry executives would throw money around like confetti for sports rights, just to beat their rival networks. What they did with those rights never entered the picture: I think they were content to do each other over just so they could have a good laugh once the deals had been done. The deal Hill got from Bateman was $23 million for 10 years: $2.3 million per year. The numbers were impressive but on closer examination were far from value. For a start, a television rights deal for 10 years on any sports property was, and still is, unheard of. In a swiftly changing sports television environment, with the advent of cable TV, pay per view, broadband internet, digitisation and the like, the value of sports rights could rise dramatically in a minute. It was risky to sign away rights for a period as long as 10 years.

Then there was the matter of commitment: how the network would do justice to those rights.

Football – then, as now – had a desperate need for prioritised free to air television exposure. Only that would deliver the kind of market penetration an underdog sport like football needed. If Seven was going to do that, as SBS had done for so long, well and good: so be it. But Seven had no such intentions, for all its expenditure of $23 million. The tragedy was that David Hill did not demand any commitment from the network in addition to the dollars. Asked about programming commitment at the press conference where he announced the deal, Hill answered: 'Seven is a reputable television station and I won't tell them how to suck eggs when it comes to their programming strategies', or words to that effect.

Seven paid the money but proceeded to bury football. It broadcast some games on its Pay TV arm, C7, but virtually nothing on its free to air network. The National League, then called the Ericsson Cup, disappeared from free to air screens. On SBS, this competition had enjoyed a one-hour package at 8.30 on Sunday evenings – the prince of timeslots – simply called the Ericsson Cup. But once Seven took over the rights, Ericsson got no exposure. Within a year, the company walked away from its sponsorship of the National League. Football was once again buried: a second-class sport in a country where it was a second-class citizen. Soon, the football community woke up to the deception – to having been sold down the river – and a movement was spawned with the catchcry: 'Nobody screws Soccer like Seven'. Its stickers are still visible on telegraph poles around Australia's mainland capitals. Australian football, for all intents and purposes, disappeared from TV screens and its television hibernation was to last seven years.

14

Year zero: mission accomplished

By 1995 I had been 15 years in the business of television, all of it at SBS and all of it in football. I was content with my lot and happy in my work. I worked hard, putting in 10- to 12-hour days, but each morning I awoke looking forward to my day. On the personal front there were turmoils that year as Eva and I separated once more and suddenly I became a bachelor again. This brought its emotional pressures, especially by its impact on our two young daughters, and I needed to gather all my resources to remain tranquil and strong so that my entire world would not fall apart. Professionally I was probably the envy of a good number of football fans and had no ambition to do anything beyond what I was doing. My salary was no great shakes compared to that of my counterparts elsewhere in television and I drove a second-hand Volvo. But I wouldn't have swapped my job for any other.

Then, suddenly, things changed. Late that year, Dominic Galati – SBS Head of Sport and my boss for the previous five years – announced that he was leaving the network. Dominic was an ambitious young man, always looking for a chance to climb: when Foxtel made him an offer, he took it. Pay television then was still in its infancy in Australia but its owners – primarily Rupert Murdoch, Kerry Packer and Telstra – were spending money liberally to attract the best executive talent. Dominic, renowned for his effective role in getting little SBS noticed as a sports broadcaster, was snapped up. The day after Dominic made his announcement, the SBS head of television, Sawsan Madina, called me into her office and suggested that I apply for the head of sport position. Madina was a great multi-culturalist, loved what sport had been doing for the network and its causes, and saw in me the embodiment of what SBS was about. Above all, she said, she wanted someone with a genuine understand-ing of the SBS mission: a person who could provide 'editorial lead-ership'. I took this to mean that I was a journalist and, till then, SBS had never had a head of sport with a journalistic background.

I was reluctant. Though I had managerial experience, having supervised sports production and produced two World Cups, I had no ambition to become an executive. What ultimately persuaded me to apply for the position was my concern that SBS sport retain conti-nuity and identity. Dominic had been of 'ethnic' Italian heritage and a true football man. Under him, within SBS' role as the distinctive and alternative broadcaster, the network's sports output always focused entirely on its growing audiences. As an SBS believer, my concern was that all the good work of those formative years might be laid to waste if a newcomer took the position. So I applied and got the gig. In addition to being a presenter and commentator, I was now head of sport: an executive. I was not the first to fill such a dual role in television and I was confident I could manage it. But I quickly realised that I had been thrust into a new world, where presenting and commentating were subsidiary to leading SBS into a position of strength in a cut-throat television market. Now, instead of reading the back pages of the dailies with my morning coffee, I found myself turning first to the *Financial Review*. I was blessed with very able deputies, expert in management: first Caroline Ramsay, who later played a key role in the Olympic broadcasts of

Sydney 2000 and Athens 2004; and then Ken Shipp, who headed up the blockbuster broadcasts of the 1998 and 2002 World Cups and dozens of other major international events.

I was appointed in March 1996, at a time of unprecedented challenges to SBS' position as the 'owner' of football broadcasting in Australia. The 'wog game' was becoming very attractive to others who wanted to cash in on its growing popularity. Nervously I looked towards Euro '96, and the epic challenge of covering this 31-match European Championship from location in London. Could we carry it off without the inspirational leadership of Dominic? We did, and established the European Championship of football as a marquee sports event in the Australian market. But what I didn't anticipate was that Euro '96 would become a turning point in the fortunes of SBS as an unchallenged football broadcaster. On the back of it, 18 months later, came the Australia vs Iran game and its four million viewers. Then there was the World Cup of 1998, again broadcast by SBS, reaching nine million Australians. Now football had become irresistible: mainstream commercial property. The other broadcasters made their moves to grab a stake of the new money.

The next European Championship, Euro 2000, was seized by Foxtel; and the next World Cup, Korea-Japan 2002, became a race between little SBS and mighty Channel Nine. With France '98, the three-World Cup deal – signed by Dominic in Kuala Lumpur 10 years earlier – had expired. Now the rights to the world's most popular sports event were not only up for grabs again but had become seriously expensive. FIFA had farmed out the selling rights in a joint deal with the Swiss marketing agency ISL and the German media giant Kirch Sport, whose remit was not to ensure that the World Cup was seen by the largest available audience but to ensure that it made the most money. ISL and Kirch between them had guaranteed FIFA 2.3 billion Australian dollars for the global television rights to the 2002 and 2006 World Cups, a massive amount that required aggressive selling by the agencies. Their tactic was to create an auction within each territory and drive up the price.

In 1998, when FIFA signed the deal with ISL and Kirch, SBS was still comfortably placed as a monopoly player for football in the Australian television environment. The Pay operators Fox Sports and C7 were trying to muscle in but the World Cup was protected under the anti-siphoning laws for free to air television. I was aware, however, that the tremendous audience growth of the World Cup in Australia, from two million viewers in 1990 to five million in 1994, was being noticed by the other Australian networks for its commercial potential. So I moved early to try and protect SBS' prospects. In Paris, during the 1998 World Cup, I had a private meeting with the then newly elected FIFA president, Sepp Blatter. Blatter had a personal affection for SBS because of the passion and dedication with which the network had host-broadcast the 1993 World Youth Cup, and he received me warmly. Knowing what SBS was doing in Australia to propagate the football cause, he was immensely supportive and gave me the impression that an SBS rights deal was his preference. I have no doubt that he was sincere. But ISL had another agenda. Contemptuous and dismissive of its master client, FIFA, ISL was only interested in the bottom line. SBS had to be clever and financially competitive if it was to retain its place as the broadcaster of the World Cup.

SBS made its first offer to ISL for the rights to World Cup 2002 in November 1998. But it took another three years and five months before the issue was finally settled and the rights to all 64 of the World Cup games were sold. The first SBS offer was completely ignored by ISL. The amount offered was not enough and ISL chose to wait for another offer, all the while lobbying other networks. But there were no other offers and for a long time it looked as though there never would be. As a tactical move, to ensure that the SBS offer was not used as a benchmark to drive others up, SBS took its bid off the table.

In March 2000, nearly a year and a half after SBS had first bid, I was at a broadcasters' conference in Chennai in India. I had dinner with ISL's agent in charge of the Far East and Oceania, Charlie Charters. Charlie was a larger-than-life man of rollicking ebullience and good humour, an ex-journo and war correspondent; I had many late drinks in hotel bars with Charlie during the quest for the World Cup deal. He told me that another Australian offer was brewing and that I should get serious. Because he had told me similar things before, I didn't believe him and dismissed the warning. But a few weeks later, via a friend of a friend, I heard a worrying story about a Sydney dinner conversation where Channel Nine owner Kerry Packer boasted of having signed the World Cup rights. I phoned a friend in Zurich – FIFA's media chief, Keith Cooper – and asked him to look into it. Cooper phoned me back the next day and asked me if some deal involving Nine buying 16 games of the 64-game World Cup made any sense.

Now I knew we were in trouble. The 2002 World Cup was uniquely attractive in Australia as a commercial proposition because it took place in Korea and Japan, in our time zone. Games would kick off at 7 pm and 9.30 pm in eastern Australia, smack in the middle of prime time: a far cry from the commercially dormant 2 am and 4 am of the previous World Cup. Games could be scheduled at civilised hours and make a load of money in sponsorship and commercials. Bold risk-taker Nine, which had no history in broadcasting football, took a gamble and bought a 16-match cluster of games that would kick off at times to suit its programming schedule. We figured Nine would select the princes of games – any that involved Australia (in the event that it qualified), the final, the semi finals and the like – and leave the rest to another taker.

ISL confirmed to SBS that the deal had been done and we resigned ourselves to the reality that the World Cup rights had been lost. We had done our bit in building the event to a level where it had become commercially viable in the Australian market and now we were paying the price. SBS walked away and got on with the rest of its life.

But with only 16 games sold, there were still 48 games to be taken up by another Australian network, and we knew that could only be SBS. Because all 64 games were protected under anti-siphoning, the Pay TV operators couldn't buy them unless all free to air networks rejected them. The other free to airs wouldn't schedule games less attractive than Nine's in competitive prime time hours. And they couldn't cherry-pick the games either because, under law, whoever bought the remaining 48 games had to show them all live. Thanks to a clever piece of lobbying by the then SBS head of television, Peter Cavanagh, the 2002 World Cup had been put on the government's 'anti-hoarding list'. This meant any event on the list had to be broadcast live or offered to the two government broadcasters, the ABC and SBS, for a token rights fee of $1. SBS was the only network willing to show all games live in prime time.

There was another development that played a critical part in giving SBS the 48-game portion of the World Cup. In early 2001 ISL, one of the world's biggest and most powerful sports marketing companies, collapsed. Soon Kirch, its giant partner in the World Cup agency rights, did the same. Charlie Charters, a pucker Englishman by appearance and disposition but a Fijian national, retired to his native Suva. The company that inherited the agency rights was called Infront Sports. Newly formed, it was jointly owned by Robert-Louis Dreyfuss (former owner of Adidas and the French football club Olympique Marseille), and legendary German ex-player, Günther Netzer. Fortunately for us, Infront was a lot less avaricious and cut-throat than ISL.

In September that year, I received a phone call from Charlie Charters. He said he was in Sydney, staying at the Four Seasons hotel with an agent from Infront. Could I meet them for drinks that night? Infront had recruited Charlie as a consultant to help tie up any remaining rights deals in the Far East and Pacific region. I met with Charlie and the Infront agent, Nick Schrader, but found – to my frustration – that the picture had not changed: Infront was just as hell-bent on squeezing us as ISL had been. The price they placed on the 48 games was outrageous, and I left them to their beers. A few weeks later my deputy, Ken Shipp, in Monte Carlo for Sportel, an annual sports TV marketing convention, again met with Charlie and Nick. Charlie presented Ken with a completed long-form contract, ready to sign – but with no change to the asking price. When Ken relayed this back to me, I instructed him to cease negotiating and to set up a separate meeting with Nick Schrader in London on the way back to Sydney. He was to tell Nick, in non-negotiable terms, that if Charlie Charters was party to any future negotiation we would withdraw all interest in the World Cup. I hated doing this because I liked Charlie Charters. He was a real football man: a fun adversary. But his estimation of what the World Cup was worth in Australia, and what SBS was willing to pay for it, had ceased to be fun. He had to be frozen out and Infront complied.

But the clock ticked on. There was no movement until Nick Schrader came to Sydney in January of 2002 to try and wrap things up. We were just five months out from kick-off and there was still no deal that would deliver the World Cup, in its entirety, to Australian audiences. Nick met with the networks, including the Pay TV operator Fox Sports who had begun to lobby aggressively with the government to de-list the World Cup as a protected event for free to air. Ken Shipp and I had dinner with Nick at the Manta Ray, a swank outdoor restaurant on the Finger Wharf in Sydney's Woolloomooloo. The alfresco eatery was non-smoking. In between courses, Nick and I – both smokers – took short walks to the edge of the jetty to have a puff, and managed to agree on a figure that would do the deal.

But there was still a row to hoe. The matter of exactly what Channel Nine and SBS had the rights to – including who would choose which games when – still had to be sorted. This took months, as the lawyers got to work to sort out the mess. I was fielding daily calls from media, all wanting to know whether the entire World Cup would be broadcast in Australia: in multicultural Australia, a game between Croatia and Paraguay had the same community appeal as England vs Argentina. But I could make no comment until everything was legally tied up. This meant that rumours of a truncated World Cup coverage were rife; there was widespread concern that only Nine's commercially chosen 16 games would go to air.

The deal finally settled in early April 2002, just eight weeks before France and Senegal were due to kick off the extravaganza in Seoul. That week, I attended a regional broadcasting conference in Seoul, and hired a local television crew to shoot preview material for a World Cup coverage the Australian public knew nothing about. On my return, I announced the deal to the Australian media. At last, the concerns of the Australian football-loving public were laid to rest. SBS had 48 games; Nine had 16: all games in the 2002 World Cup were to be covered – live.

The eight-week lead-in meant SBS production had to be done quickly and cheaply, while maintaining the standards the network had set in earlier tournaments. But it was not easy. We had lost analyst Andy Harper who, having done a fine job for us in France '98, had been signed by Channel Nine. The network still had Johnny Warren, Kyle Patterson and myself, but a replacement for Andy had to be found. Articulate, intelligent football analysts – with the technical expertise needed to decode a game – did not grow on trees. But Craig Foster, a former Socceroo, had made a guest appearance on SBS to analyse the World Cup flop against Uruguay a few weeks earlier. We brought him in for a few dry runs: he excelled and got the gig. Problem solved. Foster, along with the rest of the production, was a massive success.

Because Nine and SBS shared the coverage (but were not joint broadcasters), there were many comparisons of the respective qualities of the two broadcasts. The reviews came down negatively on Nine, but not because the Nine network was a bad sports producer. Au contraire, Nine was – and is – as good at covering major sports events as any TV network in the world. The problem was: Nine didn't care. With no history in covering football, and probably sceptical about its capacity to rate, their production effort was economical and unambitious.

It was a mistake: the football World Cup delivered Nine some of their most impressive ratings. Had they cared more, and thrown more resources at it, the figures may have been even higher. The final became Australia's highest rating sports program, eclipsing the Pat Rafter–Goran Ivanisevic Wimbledon final a year earlier. The SBS portion of the coverage also rated most impressively. Against a station average rating of 4.5 per cent or so, the World Cup games drew regular figures in the high 20s, even though SBS had the less attractive games. By its end, across the two networks, the World Cup reached an audience of 14.8 million Australians, almost three-quarters of the nation's population: an astonishing number, given that it was a football tournament in a cricket country, with no Australian team taking part.

The 2002 World Cup's success was a fascinating indicator of Australia's social evolution through the last half of the 20th century: it highlighted the impact of migration, of football, and of football's frontline vehicle, SBS. Television audience figures for football events pre-SBS are difficult to gather, but it would be safe to say they were miniscule. The fact is, World Cup audience reach numbers grew from two million in 1990 to nearly 15 million in 2002. This growth cannot be attributed solely to the wonders and beauties of football and the capacity of Australians to embrace it. The appreciation for and awareness of football – and its princely main event – is just one of a myriad cultural layers that have been added to Australian society by migrants, their habits and their customs. Australia had been enriched, and continues to be enriched, by migration. But because migration has slowed significantly in recent years, football's major impact on Australian culture was experienced during the decades immediately after the migrant boom of the 1950s and '60s. The '70s, '80s and '90s were a major settling period for many migrants, during which they raised their Australian-born children, fashioning them in their own image.

SBS played a major role in this settling process. It hastened and helped to legitimise it. The network, of course, had not just prioritised football and sport. It exposed on national television all manner of things that were outside the Anglo-Australian mainstream: language, tradition, identity, emotion, values, music, art, cuisine, fashion and customs. SBS was created to be, and remains, an agent of change. Football was merely at the forefront of the process. But if football is now better appreciated, and the World Cup draws large audiences, then Australia is a better place.

Yet for all that, domestic football in Australia in June-July 2002 – when those World Cup audience figures were being registered – was in a terribly bad place. Its governing body, Soccer Australia, was broke. Its national competition, the NSL, was dying. Football's capacity to take domestic advantage of the World Cup success was non-existent. All this combined to trigger a revolution the like of which Australian football had not experienced since the migrants revolted and carried the game to social relevance 45 years earlier.

Six days after the World Cup ended, Australia took part in the 2002 Oceania Nations Cup in New Zealand, where victory was a ticket to the lucrative FIFA Confederations Cup carrying almost $2 million in minimum prize money. Normally, Australia could be expected to win the ONC at a canter. Only once before had it failed to do so, in 1998, when the European-based Socceroos were not called and an under-estimated New Zealand beat Australia in the final. But in 2002, Soccer Australia did not have the funds to recall its best players from abroad and take them to Auckland. The body decided that overseas based players would have to pay their own airfares and only one – Scott Chipperfield from Basel – obliged. The result was that Australia could not field even its B team, let alone its best. The squad that went to New Zealand was a hotch-potch mix of veterans and untried youngsters.

A few days before the tournament, I pleaded with Soccer Australia chairman, Ian Knop, to reconsider. Missing out on the Confederations Cup, I told him, would be a far greater disaster than another couple of hundred thousand added to his organisation's debts. I argued that running a good national team was the core activity of his organisation, without which it hardly had a reason to exist. If you don't have the money to make beer, I said, you may as well shut down the brewery. Knop said he understood – but fiscal responsibility had to be his first priority.

The ONC was a disaster. In the semi finals, Australia only beat Tahiti in extra time by a Golden Goal. In the final, Australia lost 1-0 to New Zealand. The following year, New Zealand went to France for the Confederations Cup and performed so poorly that the darker forces within FIFA were able to reverse an earlier decision to give Oceania a direct path to the World Cup finals.

Not sending a strong team to New Zealand for the 2002 ONC was to prove costly, not just for football, but for Ian Knop and his regime. The Auckland debacle was followed by widespread media and government condemnation of Australian football's war-torn and historically blunder-prone administration. Within a year, Knop and his entire top brass were gone: replaced by a new regime, a new company and a new order for football.

And I was there, somewhere at the front of the pack issuing a call for the governors to resign. This was new even for me for, though I had a long history of editorially criticising football administrators, I had never before called for anyone to quit. But now things were different. In an angry column on SBS' *The World Game* website, titled Enough is Enough, I wrote: 'The fish, gentlemen, stinks from the head. It is time you all faced it and did the noble thing.'

Within a few weeks the federal government, embarrassed by where its taxpayer-funded subsidies to football were going, decided to act. Ian Knop was later painted as some kind of hero in the transition amid claims that he invited the government to intervene and set up a government inquiry into football. I think this is only partly true. Knop's response to Auckland, and the financial destitution that would surely follow it, was to go to the government with cap in hand and ask for more money. The government told him, 'No, we won't give you any more money. But you invite us to have an inquiry into your game and after the inquiry we might give you more money.' Knop concurred and thus was born the Crawford

Inquiry which was to change the face of Australian football, hopefully, forever.

The inquiry, chaired by David Crawford and with Johnny Warren on his board, began its deliberations in August 2002 and tabled its report the following April. When the inquiry was announced elation filled the land, or at least the majority of the football population and most outside it. For me it was an answer to many prayers. In the first instance, the Australian government, forever ready to jump onto the sporting bandwagon whenever there were votes in it, never previously gave a rats about football. The mere fact that the government was bothering was a sign of changing times. Politicians don't have rocks in their head. They would have seen the World Cup party Australia enjoyed a few weeks earlier and twigged that there were votes in football, either for them or, if they didn't appear to act to clean up the mess, the Opposition.

Crawford's report was damning of the way the game had been run and called for a new direction, including a new constitution and a new board. The heads had been summoned to go. SBS, the friend of the game, proved to be no friend of the incumbents who were running it. Our reporters, led by Kyle Patterson, were, to be sure, reporting the story objectively and straight laced. But this did not seem so by the small group that were left carrying the can of the old order, average men in average suits pleased in an average way by being in power. The wind of change was in the air, the momentum took hold and the wheels turned irreversibly.

Leading the new regime was Frank Lowy, a true child of football and, in particular, that of the central European school. His early years were spent in a Hungarian enclave of Slovakia and his teenage years in Budapest, a world centre of football power and class in those times. The imprint left on him by football – his only distraction as a youth in a time of war, personal tragedy and toil – would never leave him. Even after he came to Australia and was working tirelessly to build his business, he found time for football, breaking away from his chores and speeding through traffic to get to a game.

Such a man was ideally placed to lead Australian football. He was ideally placed for other reasons too: he didn't need or want the job. Lowy was already Australia's second richest man, a globally respected magnate who entertained presidents and prime ministers on his yacht. And then there was his business acumen, influence and intellect. At last, with Frank Lowy in charge, football was on a true winner.

Frank embarked on a ruthless and speedy program of change. Within a year and a half he transformed a game of marginal significance in Australia to one that was broadly respected. He began by appointing a board that was surely the envy of any corporation in the land. Of the seven directors, four were listed among Australia's 200 richest and – by definition – most successful businessmen. He and his regime shut down the previous company and replaced it with a new one – Football Federation Australia (FFA); got a $15 million grant for football from the government; re-branded soccer as football; launched an ambitious new national league; and got Australia into Asia, allowing Australia to become a significant player in the geopolitics of the world game. Along the way, he recruited an able ally in John O'Neill, Australia's one star player in sports management: a rugby man with many tries on the board whose gift in managing sport translated easily into a capacity to manage football as a viable business. The Lowy–O'Neill partnership spawned ground-breaking achievements in its fast-paced early months, achieving things the game had only dreamed of in its preceding 130 years.

Unfortunately, while the game as a business was being hoisted to new heights, I think the core business of football at a technical and performance level was still being neglected. This aberration, inherited from the previous regime, was costly and was also the source of some pain in the relationship between the new administration and its biggest supporter and admirer: SBS.

As I see it, at the centre of all the problems was the national coach, Frank Farina: a stone in the shoe of the mutual goodwill that was meant to exist between FFA and SBS, still the sport's primary broadcasting partner. It culminated in Farina laying the blame squarely with SBS – and me in particular – for his sacking by the FFA in June 2005.

Farina was made national coach in 1999. At the time, Soccer Australia was broke and was forced to replace the expensive Terry Venables with someone less expensive: in other words, a local. The Venables remuneration was now unaffordable and a new budget was called for. Applications were called and four young Turks from the local coaching fraternity applied: Farina, David Mitchell, Eddie Krncevic and Ange Postecoglou. Farina was the protégé and pre-ferred candidate of Soccer Australia president, Tony Labbozzetta. Both had a common Italian heritage and Farina was then coach of Labbozzetta's club, Marconi. But things did not go well. Farina fell out of reckoning in the first round of voting. Somehow, though, he survived. Johnny Warren also came out publicly in favour of Farina. Farina got the job.

Yet years later, in late 2004, when Johnny Warren died, the gesture seemed to be forgotten. Minutes after Johnny's death on 6 November, the cable TV network Sky News, the first onto the story, worked the phones to collect tributes to the great man. It got tributes aplenty, without refusal, from all manner of people, politicians, showbiz icons, business magnates and assorted cele-brities. The only refusal had come from Frank Farina. Dialled on his mobile phone while he was in London at the time, Farina declined the request, saying that he was busy.

Australia lost to Uruguay over two legs in November 2001, denying Australia a place in the World Cup for the seventh consec-utive time. Although, naturally, the issue of the national coach's accountability arose, yet still no one at SBS pointed the finger at Farina. But writing on the SBS website, I said that there should be a technical inquiry into the failure. I also said that the fate of the national coach position should be left until after that inquiry completed its business. This, I suspect, was at the root of the dark-ness that descended on the Farina–SBS relationship. My comments implied that the national coach's performance as a strategist over the two legs may have been questionable, and that may have seemed like a direct threat to Farina. Later, Johnny joined in, calling for a new technical direction: a real plan for the national team and the appointment of a high calibre technical director to oversee Australia's technical performance, including that of the national coach. But at that point there was no suggestion from either Johnny or me that Farina was to blame for the Montevideo loss. Yet after that, things only got worse between Frank Farina and SBS.

At the heart of the problem was the unique culture of Australia's small, narrow football media contingent. The number of journalists who make a full-time living out of football in Australia can be counted on two hands. The members of this small group are generally accommodating of the personalities within the game. In other countries, where football is a national priority and seen as a national property, the performance of a figure like a national coach is not only ruthlessly scrutinised but is fair game. But not in Australia, where journalists avoid criticising a national coach for fear of alienating them as a source for quotes or exclusives. Any media organ that dares to criticise a national coach finds itself isolated and vulnerable to the suggestion that it has an undisclosed agenda to knife them. In my view, this is what happened to SBS in the case of Frank Farina after Uruguay. No other media organ had the balls to come out and criticise him for the flop.

Things went downhill from there. In mid-2003, SBS reporter Andrew Orsatti posted an opinion column on the SBS website in which he suggested that Farina was the wrong man for the job and that he should never have been appointed national coach. This seemed to be 'red rag to a bull' stuff for Farina. Farina refused all interviews with him. This only became a problem when SBS signed a television rights deal with the FFA in 2004: Orsatti was the SBS man nominated to interview Farina before and after each game played by the Socceroos. In April 2004, Australia was to play the Solomon Islands in Honiara in the first leg of the final of the Oceania Nations Cup. Boarding the plane in Brisbane, Farina refused all friendly overtures from Orsatti. It was clear that the relationship between Farina and SBS was just about unsalvageable.

Still, we tried to remain professional and get on with our jobs. Under his contract with FFA, Farina was obliged to agree to interviews with SBS. We weren't too worried about the personality stuff.

In February 2005, Australia was to due to play South Africa in Durban. Ahead of hosting the early morning telecast, I was asleep by 10 pm. At around 11 pm, the phone rang. It was an FFA official, similarly dragged out of bed, saying: 'Les, we have a problem'. Farina had refused a request to be interviewed, both pre-match and post-match, by Andrew Orsatti who was on location as SBS' match reporter. I told the official we would relent on the pre-match interview so that Farina's preparation was not disturbed, but that he would have to do the post-match interview, as per letter of contract. This post-match interview went live to air on national television. But Farina gave Orsatti one-word, monosyllabic answers and the interview was as uninformative and lacking in entertainment value as humanly possible. Farina didn't once eyeball Orsatti. I despatched a standard complaint to the FFA, who promised that Farina would be pulled into line, and we left it at that.

Six weeks later, on 26 March, Australia played Iraq in Sydney. It was the most high profile of games. The FFA had just announced that Australia was about to leave the Oceania Football Confederation and was defecting to Asia. Iraq was an Asian opponent whose significance was doubled by the Iraq war and Australia's involvement in it. The game was the first sporting contact between Australia – part of the 'coalition of the willing' – and the new, post-Saddam Iraq. The Australian prime minister, John Howard, was in attendance. So was Mohamed bin Hammam, president of the Asian Football Confederation, and a very good size crowd. It was more a major diplomatic event than a football match.

Australia won 2-1 but played badly. At the end of it, I think Frank Farina was a distressed man. Here was Australia, now just eight months out from facing another final crunch test in a World Cup qualifier against an elite South American foe, and it was flopping. Farina must have been feeling the pressure.

In the post-match interview with Orsatti, Farina attempted to repeat his earlier Marcel Marceau imitation. Out came the one-word, monosyllabic answers once again which I felt were aimed at embarrassing Orsatti and SBS. I was astonished and angered that Farina had not been pulled into line by his bosses: after closing the telecast, I rang my man at the FFA and gave him an ear-burner, complete with expletives. I then headed downstairs to the television compound for a routine post-mortem with executive producer, Noel Brady. I was stopped on the way by commentator Simon Hill, who told me that there had been some kind of altercation in the players' tunnel in which Farina had allegedly threatened to punch the reporter. Brady confirmed the story, telling me he had sent Orsatti back to the tunnel to collect the names of any witnesses to the incident. The news spread quickly: my phone ran hot with messages from an army of newspaper reporters. I rang my boss, SBS head of television, Shaun Brown, to alert him. His instructions were to say only that an incident had occurred; that SBS would investigate it but would not make a statement until after those investigations were completed. I also took the decision – with Australia due to play Indonesia three days later – that SBS would no longer seek interviews with Farina until the entire issue was resolved.

The next day a shaken Orsatti reported the matter to police. The story was growing, and so were the headlines. That afternoon I was to attend a reception for bin Hammam and the AFC entourage, hosted by Frank Lowy on his boat. In the morning I received a call from the FFA and was told that Lowy, as a matter of protocol, did not wish to have the Farina–Orsatti incident raised at the reception. Months later, after Farina was sacked, a newspaper report alleged that at the boat reception I had asked Lowy to fire Farina. This was a fabrication. The incident was never mentioned on the boat. Nor did I at any other time ask Lowy for Farina's sacking.

Noel Brady was conducting the internal investigations and took statements from four SBS staffers who had witnessed the incident. All concurred. According to those accounts Farina, following the 'interview' with Orsatti, left the scene and went into a room near the players' tunnel for a press conference. Orsatti, stirred by Farina's apparent attempt to embarrass him yet again, waited for him in the tunnel. When Farina re-emerged Orsatti confronted him, asking him if he was serious about conducting an interview in such a way. According to the witnesses, Farina at that point put one hand on Orsatti's throat, pushed him against the wall, and swung his other arm in an attempt to punch him. He was hauled off by a couple of bystanders, one of them FFA media chief, Stuart Hodge. Farina then walked off, as Orsatti shouted after him words to the effect of: 'We're both on the same side, trying to promote football'. Farina turned and moved back towards Orsatti, but was again stopped and led away.

Noel Brady completed his investigations a few days later and his report, complete with signed witness statements, was sent to John O'Neill at the FFA, which was conducting its own investigations into the incident. The police were also investigating. There was no action taken against Andrew Orsatti because in my opinion, and that of my management colleagues, he had not done anything unprofessional. Given that the incident occurred while Andrew was on SBS duty, the station would give him total support. Then I received a call from the investigating police officer who wanted to meet me on neutral turf away from SBS. We agreed to a breakfast meeting in an eastern suburbs cafe on 7 April. I was met by two detectives who reminded me of how ugly things could get. They told me that within a matter of days, Farina could be charged. In other words: if Andrew had any inclination to withdraw his complaint, he had to do it soon. Later that day, before jetting off to a broadcasters' meeting in Munich, I spoke to Andrew and told him what the police had told me. I didn't attempt to influence his decision, but I could sense that his anger and his determination to push ahead with the charges had subsided. I think he was nervous at the likelihood that he would go down in history as the young reporter who brought down a national coach. Andrew asked for a couple of days to think about it.

I was already in Munich when I received a call from Nigel Milan,

SBS managing director. He had received a call from Harry Michaels who asked him for permission to mediate between the two men and bring the matter to a peaceful resolution. Harry is an independent television producer, the hired match director for SBS' coverage of the Socceroos, a football fan and a long time associate of SBS. Nigel said it was my decision but encouraged me to give Harry the go-ahead. I called Harry and told him to go for it. Within a couple of days Harry rang me back saying that the 'peace meeting' had been set: it would take place in his office and when it was all settled, there would be a public statement. I monitored the affair daily from Munich and on the day of the scheduled meeting I rang Andrew to see how it had gone. He was over the moon. He said Farina had been very nice and very friendly to him and had apologised unreservedly: Andrew and Harry were heading off to a celebratory dinner. 'You beauty!' I said, as I hung up.

The next day, on *The Sydney Morning Herald* website, there was a report that the Farina–Orsatti affair had been resolved, that complaints to the police had been withdrawn and that Farina and Orsatti had apologised to each other. Apologised to each other? I hit the roof and rang Harry Michaels, telling him that a 'mutual' apology was not what had been expected. I didn't think Andrew had anything to apologise for. Harry told me they were the terms, and that was the statement which Andrew had agreed to and signed. There was nothing I could do: it was a personal matter for Andrew to deal with as he chose. I was glad that the messy affair would now go away, but disappointed that the statement carried the suggestion that Orsatti, an SBS employee, had provoked Farina.

Soon the FFA put out a press statement, expressing its pleasure that the issue had been resolved but noting that its own investigations into the affair were continuing. When they finally concluded, the FFA issued a statement saying Farina had been cautioned and that he had been asked to undergo counselling.

Only a good performance in the high profile Confederations Cup in Germany would save Farina his job. But the team flopped, losing three straight matches, and by 29 June he was gone. There

were some media whines from Farina's backers, most of them uninformed rugby columnists, but they soon piped down when the
FFA announced that his replacement would be one of the world's
most celebrated coaches: Guus Hiddink.

Farina had been in charge of the Australian national team for
five years and 11 months. His record reads 60 games played for
34 wins, 10 draws and 16 losses: impressive figures at first glance
– but they cannot be taken in isolation. Twenty of those 34 wins
were against weak or mediocre Oceania opposition. Most tragically,
in his six years, Farina presided over the most talented generation
of players Australia had ever produced, yet the Socceroos of 2005
were not half a goal better than the ones he inherited in August of
1999. It is true that conditions were not always ideal. During his
early years in the job, management of the game was poor and there
was no money available for proper preparation in a perennially
elusive World Cup campaign. But at the end of Farina's tenure it
became clear, to me at least, that he was incapable of technically
advancing the team, even after the advent of the Lowy regime
allowed him to spend as much money as he liked to build his
strategies.

For me, the Farina experience was the most unpleasant in my
long years as a football journalist, broadcaster and executive. Once
he was gone, we could resume broadcasting the Socceroo games as
professionally as we liked. The commercial relationship between
SBS and the FFA became a delight. It was refreshing to be able to
work – at last – with people I considered to be real professionals.
And in Frank Lowy we had the first chairman of the game's governing body who actually valued SBS as a broadcasting partner. To him
SBS is not the 'wog channel' but a national, free to air network
whose singular, unrivalled passion and commitment to football is a
lethal marketing arm of the sport.

This needs to be seen in the context of modern sports broadcasting. In the past, there were content suppliers and there were
broadcasters – and the two never met, except when their lawyers
sat down to sign rights agreements. A rights fee was paid by the

broadcaster who then programmed the content, while the content
supplier went off to bank its money. That's where the relationship
began and ended. But these days, a broadcast rights deal needs to
be a genuine business partnership with a mutual agenda to build
the product – in this case football – as a brand. Content suppliers
today do not look just at the rights fee. They also need to be satisfied that the broadcaster will do the right thing by the product: will
program it to their satisfaction and will paint it in the right image.
Conversely, the broadcaster – which sees itself as a sponsor and a
commercial backer of the product – will seek support from the
supplier and a commitment that the content will be of a sufficiently
entertaining standard to ensure maximum audience return. If there
is genuine will and effort from both sides, there is a real partnership.
It is this principle that was lacking when Soccer Australia signed
that disastrous 10-year TV rights deal with Channel Seven in 1998:
a deal which proved to be so unproductive for both parties that it
was torn up three years short of its intended life.

Lowy and O'Neill, unlike their predecessors, were sophisticated,
modern businessmen who understood the way these things work in
the modern world. In November 2004, they agreed to a two-year
rights agreement with SBS for all home games involving the
Socceroos. The money had to be right, of course. The ABC had also
bid, and bid aggressively. What swung the deal to SBS was the fact
that SBS was prepared to program the games live, in prime viewing
time, while the ABC was not. SBS, as a committed free to air
partner of football – in the same way that Channel Nine, for
example, was a committed partner of cricket – was the ideal choice.

Signing the rights deal with SBS was, by then, just one of a score
of monumental steps the Lowy regime had taken since April 2003:
year zero for a sport reborn, a new era of hope for the game. It was
then that David Crawford brought down his report and his blueprint for a football revolution. And, as we on the sidelines all knew,

Lowy's sharp intellect, business acumen, gift for diplomacy and strategy, and yet genuine understanding of the football emotion, did the trick. One gets queasy contemplating what Crawford's design for change and progress may have become had the keys been handed to a different man.

Lowy, in keeping with both his own convictions and the Crawford blueprint, would be a non-executive chairman of the new administration. This meant his role – and the role of his board – would be strictly one of governance, leaving management of the sport to managers. Lowy had neither the time nor the desire to run the game himself. Having scored his $15 million grant from the government, his first priority was to appoint managers of the highest managerial skill and calibre; whether those managers had the remotest understanding of football, or even any affection for it, was not important. His view was that football, as a business, now needed to be run by proven businessmen and not petty politicians. Within Lowy's seven-person board, only he and one other were genuine lovers of football. The reality was that proven managers with a direct emotional link to football were nigh impossible to find.

Hence the appointment of John O'Neill. Lowy knew O'Neill well, as a former banker and an immensely successful sports administrator: O'Neill was the man who had turned Australian rugby from a sport of piffling amateurism into an international commercial giant.

Relishing a new challenge, O'Neill moved swiftly to turn football into a real business and shift it from the past into the present. Within months the sport was re-branded, re-emerging as a challenging entity in a new time. A new national club competition, the A-League, was launched to bumper crowds and stirring excitement. Australia's World Cup prospects took a revolutionary turn with the appointment of Guus Hiddink to lead it. And the political guile of Lowy transported Australia and its football into Asia: smack in the middle of a continent galloping swiftly forward as the international game's major force of the future.

These were great achievements. But as I watched admiringly, I also had some concerns. I wondered whether, in the midst of the great leap forward in branding, marketing and commercialisation, enough attention had been paid to football and international competitiveness. When the Crawford revolution was looming, and Lowy beckoned, I identified several core areas of football that needed immediate and critical attention by the new order: the need to create a viable national league; Australian football's technical development; and the national team.

With remarkable skill, the A-League was put together in lightning quick time. We had the swift divorce from Oceania and the shot-gun marriage to Asia. There were brilliant strategies implemented in marketing, re-branding and revenue-raising.

But the matter of the national team – whose performance was the prism through which the broader public would ultimately judge the new order – was mishandled. And technical development – the long-term future of the game – was almost entirely ignored. In part, this was because these challenges demanded specialised skills and sensitivities with which the new administrators were not familiar and for which they had not been trained.

Understandably, O'Neill imported managerial talent from outside football to assist him in the implementation of his programs. Nevertheless, the result was that there were few football people – and even fewer of any substantial calibre – at the centre of the body that sat in football's seat of governance. This would have its consequences.

The first of them impacted on the national team and its critical need to qualify for the World Cup of 2006. In commercial terms alone that task represented a gain – or loss – of over $10 million in revenue in appearance fees from FIFA alone. Then there was the potential to earn multiples of that: in sponsorship, television rights, merchandising and the like. A fortune hung on the question of whether Australia would make it to the big stage. Well aware of all this, the governors put no financial cap on the investment. The national team was given everything and anything needed in order to prepare. The trouble was that the money was handed over to men whose technical acumen did not match the managerial talents of their governors. In charge of the campaign was Frank Farina, who had failed in the same mission four years earlier, triggering the transition to the new era of Lowy and O'Neill.

Not surprisingly, it ended in disaster. By the end of the Confederations Cup in June of 2005, with Australia losing three games on the trot and ejected from the tournament barely four months before it was to face its crunch foe on the road to Germany 2006, Farina had been sacked. The Farina technical regime, inherited from the pre-Crawford era, represented an age of modest ambition and colonial defeatism, and not the Lowy-inspired era of daring risk and a sense of achievement. That Farina should have lasted nearly two years into the Lowy era surprised a lot of people, including me. In early 2004, when SBS contemplated its rights fee offer for the 2006 World Cup and evaluated the event's potential advertising revenue, I was asked by my superiors for an opinion on whether Australia would qualify. Australia's presence would have an obvious impact on revenue potentials for the network, so my answer was critical. I answered with an unhesitating 'yes', so confident was I in Frank Lowy's capacities to achieve the goals he sets for himself. I told my superiors that I trusted Lowy to get Australia to the World Cup and they took me at my word. The offer was made to FIFA's agents and SBS – despite facing stiff competition from two rival free to air networks – won the bid.

The SBS gamble, partly because of my bravado, was skating on thin ice for some time after that. Farina remained in charge for the ensuing 16 months. I watched the modest performances by the Socceroos in that period and grew increasingly jittery about Australia's capacity to make it to Germany. Had there not been a change of coaches in June 2005, I privately opined, Australia's chances would have been dead. But though he acted late, Lowy finally lived up to his reputation and the trust I had in him. Guus Hiddink, Australia's new coach, was a proven achiever in all of football's relevant realms: at club level; at national team level; and, most importantly, at football's third world level, having steered South Korea to the 2002 World Cup semi finals. Typically, the Lowy–O'Neill team had aimed high. Hiddink's appointment was unchallengeable: all those who had opposed the Farina sacking suddenly piped down. And SBS regained its confidence in the risks it had taken.

In the areas of technical and player development – the keys to Australia's football future – a major culture change was also critical. But the new governors were unaware of this. In the years immediately preceding the Lowy takeover, Australia's youth teams were regularly finishing last or thereabouts in international competitions. Worse, they were being described by FIFA's technical assessors as teams strong on physical and psychological qualities but well behind the pack in technique and tactical sophistication. Translation: our kids were seen as honest plodders and triers, and the world was laughing at them. Player agents were describing the situation as scary. The era of the 'golden generation' – quality players like Ned Zelic, Paul Okon, Mark Viduka and Harry Kewell – had come to a close. The first-choice Socceroo 11 had an average age of nearly 30. Successful football teams – World Cup winners – tend to have an average age of 28.

It was a crisis. And its origin was hidden in Australian football's history. In the 15-year period between 1980 and 1995 there emerged a generation of young Australian players who took the established football world by storm. Suddenly, Australia – till then an importer of player talent – became an important exporter of footballers. By the mid-1990s, there were more than 100 professional Australian players employed overseas, mostly in Europe and some with elite clubs, all attracted by higher salaries. This was weird, given that Australia is a country of less than 20 million and one where football is seen as a minority sport. Many attributed this phenomenon to the institutionalised coaching apparatus that existed in Australia through those years. But this was a misreading of the reality. These high quality young players were, primarily, products of Australia's cultural and social evolution.

Many of the football migrants who had poured into the country in the 1950s, '60s and '70s now had Australian-born football playing sons. These kids were playing football in a way that reflected the technical values of their parents: Australia's most elite young players of that era had racial roots in the Balkans, southern Europe, central Europe, South America and even the Middle East. Some, like Craig Johnston, Harry Kewell and Craig Moore, were of British stock, but even they came to be swayed by the cultural colours of their team-mates. And SBS also played a critical role in this process. As Johnny Warren argued in his book, *Sheilas, Wogs and Poofters*, SBS put the world's best players and teams into the shopwindow, so that our impressionable players and coaches had international role models.

But by the late 1990s these influences were beginning to wane. Assimilation ensured that the football migrants had a diminishing role in player development. The football migrant intake was now small and the old migrants were no longer rearing sons. The 'ethnic' clubs were dying and kids of ethnic parents were no longer being pushed to play for them. The talent supply line was drying up.

Suddenly, Australia was relying entirely on the large numbers of kids playing football on Saturday mornings and – more importantly – on how they were being coached. For two key reasons, this meant Australia's capacity to yield quality footballers was in real trouble. Number one: development coaches in the institutions gave no credit to the positive cultural influences the migrants had on football kids and, therefore, didn't foresee the death of these forces. Number two: their coaching methods, across the board, relied on archaic and long-discredited British technical principles that encouraged only speed and muscular directness, suffocating skill and invention.

The symptoms of this malady were quick to arrive. There were no new Zelics, Kewells or Vidukas on the horizon. And the crisis is not going to go away in a hurry. The problem is cultural: deeply rooted in the national psyche. The traditional Australian sporting code is characteristically defined by noble, frontier-rooted values like courage, competitiveness, work rate, commitment and an undying will to win. As admirable as these values undeniably are, they are of little use when applied to the technical education of children, at least in football. In fact, they are destructive. The evidence can be found on suburban grounds each Saturday morning where prepubescent boys and girls are asked to ape the ways of adult warriors. Little kids are being compelled from the sidelines by shouting parents and coaches to kick, rush and fight. The primary need of the children – merely to play – is forgotten. So destructive is this culture that Australia's more astute junior coaches are now banning parents from the sidelines at youth league games. Uninformed commands to run and kick are destructive to the child's learning of technical processes. At that age, rather than running, a child is better advised to stop, hold the ball and think before deciding on his next move. And contrary to kicking, the child is better advised to put his foot on the ball, look around and make a telling pass.

Most kids in Australia don't take up football at the age of six by choice but because their parents – comforted by football's reputation as a risk-free, non-violent sport – enrol them into it. Of the hundreds of thousands of kids who play football on suburban grounds and in schools, the majority are lost to the game by the time they reach their mid-teens. They are exhausted by the relentless pressure to compete and win. Most of them never experience the sheer joy of playing.

When asked to address children at junior club or school gatherings I always emphasise to the kids that the essential difference between football and the other so-called football codes is the fact that in football, the ball is round. It bounces true and rolls true. This is not the case with an oval shaped ball. In football, because of this distinction, the ball can do all the work for you, provided you can bring it under your command – with your feet. It follows that the primary requirement of a footballer – way ahead of size, speed, strength or bravery – is ability to control the ball.

It is this principle – central to football cultures everywhere else in the world – that is lost on Australians. We insist on breeding musclebound athletes, setting aside as irrelevant the need for players to build technique.

15

My friend is dead

Can this supremacy of toughness over technique be broken down? I don't know. If he were still here today, I would ask my friend Johnny Warren. After all, he was a true blue Australian.

In the first place, I'm sure Johnny would join me in shouting that Australia is a submissive football culture, deep in the throws of a colonial mentality, paying undue homage to motherland influences that are beyond their time and regressive to our football interests. He would say that we should listen to the 'wogs', allow them to influence us. Johnny never used the word 'de-ethnicisation' though he did campaign for football's 'Australianisation': something he defined as the increased use of Australian players and coaches; giving our kids a go; and being pro-active in shaping our own football identity. In his view, the 'wogs' had to be part of that process of inclusiveness.

The bond and friendship Johnny and I enjoyed for over three decades is already chronicled in the book, *Mr and Mrs Soccer*, and in Johnny's own biography, *Sheilas, Wogs and Poofters*. Besides, it was thoroughly exposed on television for 24 years. So it needs little introduction in this book. But I cannot avoid reflecting on the partnership, given the prominent and powerful role it played in my story and my life.

The friendship was unique, with many elements to its chemistry. (And, by the way, let me make it clear that if Johnny and I had a common weakness, it was our love of female company.) One of the elements was my Hungarian heritage. Johnny spent a lot of time with Hungarians in the 13 years he was with St George-Budapest as player and coach, and built a healthy affinity with them. He respected their intellect and business acumen (not that I claim to be a champion in either), loved their sense of humour and was deeply influenced by the Magyar brand of football romance. In his heyday as a player he was tutored by no less than five Hungarian coaches: Joe Vlasits, Denis Adrigan, Laurie Hegyes, Gyula Polgar and Frank Arok. Even Rale Rasic hailed from Vojvodina, a Hungarian enclave in northern Serbia. Johnny became a good friend of fellow Socceroo, Atti Abonyi: a Hungarian-bred Australian, who taught him a smattering of Hungarian. He called me Laci (pronounced Lotzy), the Hungarian diminutive for László. I called him Öreg, Hungarian for 'old' but a label of warm affection among Hungarian males, much like 'mate'. So my heritage alone ensured that we would hit it off well.

Conversely, the small community of Hungarians admired him. St George-Budapest adopted him when he was just 21 and made him captain of the team in the hope that its fan base would be broadened to include all Australians. When he was rejected and labelled a sheila, a wog and a poofter by his Anglo-Australian kin, he was treated like a son by the Hungarians.

Though Johnny enthusiastically reciprocated the club's loyalty, and worked passionately to help it achieve its aims, it is not widely remembered that the long association ended in betrayal and the breaking of his heart. In 1975, shortly after Johnny had coached St George to another league championship, he had a conversation with some club officials in which he asked what more the club could do to convince the St George community that it was not there just for Hungarians. A mischievous club staffer overheard the conversation, twisted Johnny's words to imply that he wanted to rid the club of its Hungarian-ness, and relayed them to the board's Hungarian-born members. Johnny was fired. I was living in London at the time, and simply couldn't believe it. In the aftermath, the club's fortunes took a slow dive. Today, it struggles to exist in the lower echelons of semi-amateur football.

Yet Johnny, though broken hearted, continued his friendships with those Hungarians who respected and supported him, including me. At that time we were friends, but not particularly close. It was the arrival of SBS three years later that kick-started our soul-mateship – which grew to be seen as football's unshakeable custodianship. From the day we did our first broadcast together – the 1980 NSL Grand Final – in a football and television sense, we were inseparable for the ensuing 24 years until Johnny's tragic death in 2004.

Three other elements were necessary in the formula that shaped such a lasting bond: a common passion for football; a common ideology on how the game should be played; and a common gift for broadcasting. Without this capacity to speak the same language, our association would never have evolved into a friendship, let alone the telling force it became in the crusade to have football conquer Australian hearts and minds. That force was led from the front by Johnny, for in many ways we were not equals. Unlike me, he was a well respected former Australian captain and distinguished coach. And, of course, he was a true blue Australian while I was a mere reffo attempting to impose my imported football disease on my adopted land. Whereas my preachings could be taken with a grain of salt, even football's most derisory enemies treated Johnny and his utterances with respect. He had played for and captained Australia, even venturing into the war zones of Vietnam with the Socceroos as part of the war effort, and had earned his stripes as a patriot. As a man who wanted the best for his country, he was unchallengeable.

Yet for all Johnny Warren's dedication, football was not always good to him. Despite suppositions to the contrary, he never made money out of the game. The assets he had before he got sick were built by his own business acumen. There were opportunities for him to make an even more relevant career out of the game than he did but he was denied the chance by a series of let-downs. In 1976 he looked forward to taking on the job of Socceroo coach, but the appointment went to a little known Englishman called Jimmy Shoulder. In the mid-1980s, he anticipated being appointed head coach at the Australian Institute of Sport, a vocation very close to his heart, for he had a great attachment to the cause of youth development. But he was overlooked again. I think it was a huge blunder by the appointers, for had he been given that job, I believe he would have revolutionised our development programs and Australia would be a much more competitive football nation today. When David Hill became boss of the game in the mid-90s Johnny expected to take on a plum job, this time as 'head of high performance'. But again the regime gave the appointment to someone else, who lasted a mere few months. When Basil Scarsella took over from Hill, Johnny was targeted again by Soccer Australia as its football head honcho. Johnny had such faith he would get the job that he bought an apartment in Sydney so that he wouldn't have to commute from his country residence. But the offer never came.

This series of rejections and let-downs, over a span of more than 20 years, was astounding: Johnny had almost universal respect in the game and was eminently qualified for the touted positions. But therein lay the problem. To me it seems the game's administrators rarely inducted ex-players, and never ones as iconic as Johnny, for fear of being over-shadowed.

Nevertheless, Johnny Warren always felt blessed by the life football had given him. To begin with, it gave him a sense of a life purpose. And the worldliness of football gave him a perspective on life that few other men brought up in Australia's isolated culture could have gained. He told me more than once – many years before he died – that if the boss upstairs called, he wouldn't have any complaints about the cards he had been dealt. He was a private man and his personal life was not a terrain he and I explored together. But his devotion to football was total: he had only one spouse – the game – and it demanded complete fidelity. He loved women, but each of his relationships collapsed under the weight of his loyalty to football. 'Don't blame the girls,' he told me in his last days. 'It was not their fault.'

His sense of romance was intertwined with football and his frustrated urge to see Australians play football with catwalk-like style and beauty drove him to despair. He was accused of being a 'Latin lover', not as in a Casanova or a Don Juan but as a lover of Latins – or more specifically – their football. To him, a football game had to be won with style and élan. He made 28 trips to Brazil, so enamoured was he with that country's vibrant, smiling culture and the football rhythms that danced Brazil to five World Cup victories. He wanted a bit of that to make an imprint on Australia's football development. Johnny Warren died before he could realise this dream. After Johnny's last World Cup campaign, when Australia lost 3-0 to Uruguay in Montevideo in November 2001, he stood in front of the cameras laying blame on the archaic technical culture that has repeatedly produced Australian footballers who cannot match it with the best. Uruguay, a small country of barely three million people, had just outsmarted Australia with technical resources and traditions that had won it two World Cups and many other things besides.

Johnny was a great multiculturalist. He constantly pointed to the Socceroos – with their rainbow mix of races and backgrounds – as the only national team that truly represents the real Australia.

Although Australia did not take part, the 2002 World Cup was none the less a massive success with Australian audiences. The day after the final, my desk was buried in newspapers, each with front page headlines shouting Brazil's victory over Germany. Johnny Warren was sitting in my office. Such Australian news coverage of football would have been unimaginable only a few years earlier. I said to Johnny: 'Take a look at this. Mission accomplished.' In his sweetly pronounced Hungarian, he replied: '*Lassan, lassan,*' meaning 'slowly, slowly', we're not there yet.

He was right, of course. A few days later Australia lost to New Zealand in the final of the Oceania Nations Cup in Auckland and, in the wake of the World Cup euphoria, darkness again descended on our game.

Shortly afterwards, Johnny reported to me the extraordinary news that the federal government – led by a cricket-loving prime minister – was launching an inquiry into football and that he had been invited to serve on the board of inquiry. I could hardly wipe the smile off my face: this was such exciting news for the future of football. Sure, the government was probably doing it out of electoral expediency. But so what? Football benefiting from electoral expediency was a rare gift I was more than happy to accept.

Four months later, I was jolted out of my elation by even more unexpected news. In late November 2002, Johnny called to say he would pop into my office to see me about something important. Sitting across from me, calm and self-controlled, he told me that he had been diagnosed with cancer. I leaned forward, listening wide-eyed to his story. He told me the tumour was inoperable and that the condition was well advanced and probably terminal. He said I was the first person, outside his family, to learn of this. Even his mother, already into her 90s, hadn't been told. Johnny was too frightened to tell her. He was calm, but negative and resigned, saying he was not going to fight. 'I am not a fighter,' he said. Shaken and a churning mess inside, I tried to gather my strength to respond calmly and wisely, fighting off the urge to weep and grieve. I figured my distress was the last thing Johnny needed. I said to him: 'Öreg: in the first instance, you are not dead, you are just sick. We all get sick at times and then we try to get better. And in the second instance: actually, you *are* a fighter. You have always been a fighter, as a player and as a man. And you have always won. I think you should fight.' I also told him that I – and SBS – would always be behind him and that whatever he needed from us he would get. We hugged and he left the office.

Johnny overcame his early bouts of negativity and resignation. Family and friends steered him to the belief that the killer disease could be beaten. His mum, when finally told of the news, said to him: 'Son, you have always won the big fights. This is just another one.' He broke the story about his condition in an interview with me on the SBS *World Game* program, where he pledged that he would fight the disease. He went to Houston, Texas, to the renowned Anderson Clinic where Lance Armstrong, the Tour de France giant, had beaten testicular cancer. The word from them was that the cancer was containable, and Johnny responded well to their treatments. In August the following year, barely seven months after he was diagnosed, he asked me to give him some air time so he could speak to the audience about his condition. He told the viewers that he had been given the all-clear by the doctors, that he was on the way back, and thanked all who had supported him. We all rejoiced: our friend – football's best friend – was to be spared.

But the devil that had assaulted him had designs on a counter-attack. The nature of the cancer beast is that it can return and, knowing this, Johnny waited nervously for his next bout of tests and results. His next scan was not due until six months later, and as the date approached, Johnny grew increasingly anxious. In early February of 2004, as I was driving to the office, Johnny called me: it was the worst possible news. He had just received his test results which showed that the cancer was not only back but was even more advanced than before, now spread to his lymph glands and his liver. I had major difficulty in summoning even the most superficial words of encouragement. On the back of his apparent recovery, and renewed hope, this news was devastating to Johnny: worse, even, than the initial diagnosis. We both knew that hope was running out. But I could not exhibit resignation, sadness and grief: I had to be encouraging and positive for my friend.

Johnny, with no other choice, went back to the treatment table: chemo, vitamin injections, celery stick diets and the rest of it. But there was no improvement. In May of 2004 the Turkish national team, bronze medallist in the 2002 World Cup, was in town to begin a two-match series against Australia. The NSW premier, Bob Carr, held a welcoming reception for the Turks at the Sydney

Opera House. Johnny attended. After it he could barely walk from the reception to the car park, needing to sit down to take a breath every 20 metres or so. He was slipping. But, though neither of us knew it at the time, the cancer was not the direct cause of this debility.

The day after the reception Johnny phoned to tell me he was going into hospital: cancelling his scheduled appearance on the Australia vs Turkey telecast. Even accounting for the cancer, the downturn in his health seemed too sudden and swift. But there was a reason. With winter approaching, Johnny had a flu vaccine injection, a risky idea given that the cancer and chemo treatment had vastly depleted his immunity and the vaccine was essentially a live virus. Johnny had pneumonia which, as he said later, was not a clever thing to get when one is suffering from lung cancer. For days, he hovered between life and death. But he survived: by the time he emerged from the hospital he had lost 15 kilos and was spectacularly gaunt and his hair had thinned as a result of the chemotherapy. He looked old.

It seemed to me it was the pneumonia – and not the cancer – that so weakened him that he lost the capacity to fight. I feel it was this that killed him, despite the headlines on his death that he had 'lost his fight with cancer'. Johnny survived for another five months but he was never able to regain his strength or his optimism. In those final months, he set new priorities, channelling what was left of his emotional energy into things that were – for a change – more to do with his personal needs and the needs of those around him.

But he still believed and still wanted to contribute, even though he knew he was dying. Indeed, some of his most cogent contributions to the Australian football mission were made during those last months of his life. He spoke eloquently – again – of Australian football's need to engage with Asia and to abandon its obsession with qualifying directly for the World Cup as champion of little Oceania.

Shortly following Johnny's near-death bout with pneumonia, I got a call from John O'Neill telling me that Johnny was to receive FIFA's Centennial Order of Merit and that FIFA's president, Sepp Blatter, would present him with it. He asked if I could tell Johnny the news and ask him to attend the presentation. FIFA was celebrating its 100th year and as part of the celebrations it was giving a specially minted medal to a selected band of people around the world who had made a foremost contribution to the advancement of football. It had asked Australia's football governors to make a nomination and the FFA, to its credit, nominated Johnny Warren. Initially, Johnny declined the invitation, saying he didn't want to be seen in public looking so gaunt and ill. But before I had a chance to tell O'Neill, Johnny called back to say that he had changed his mind and that he felt it would be unfair to snub the noble gesture out of personal vanity.

It was an emotional ceremony at Sydney's Sheraton on the Park. The room was packed with media, including those who had no interest in football but who had, nonetheless, a huge respect for Johnny Warren. The cameras of all networks rolled and the flash bulbs flickered, capturing the moment in which the governor of the world's biggest sport pinned a medal on a great Australian. Sepp Blatter and Johnny Warren embraced. Johnny spoke of this being his proudest moment, the pinnacle in a life in which he had been awarded by royalty and heads of state, but never before been thanked and recognised in such a way by football. The following day, a dinner was given by the FIFA president in a private room at the plush Park Hyatt, where Johnny was guest of honour, dining with some of world football's luminaries. He was back – in his element: animated in conversation, passionately exchanging views on the future direction of his beloved beautiful game.

Johnny's last appearance on SBS was on the network's *The World Game* program on Sunday, 30 October 2004. He was weak, but in fine fettle. The following day, the FFA held a glittering launch of the new A-League at the Imax Theatre in Sydney's Darling Harbour. Johnny rang me in the morning to say he doubted whether he could make it: he felt so weak he doubted whether he could negotiate the walk from the parking station to the reception. I suggested he take a cab right to the door. 'This is a big day for football,' I said. 'You, of all people, have got to be there.'

Johnny took the advice and showed up. It was a glittering, lavish do. On the podium, Frank Lowy described it as 'a red letter day for Australian football'. The attending guests, packing the place to its walls, were impressed. I didn't see Johnny until after it was over. He was slumped in a large armchair well off to the side of the stage, surrounded by a swarm of suited fans, media men and other assorted guests, all wanting to hear his reaction to the event and hanging on his every word. I managed only a brief word with him, saying that I would see him in the studio that evening where he was due to appear on SBS' nightly *Toyota World Sport* program, to chat about the launch and its significance. He apologised and said he couldn't do it: he had another doctor's appointment. I told him not to worry; we'd do it the next day.

That next day – Tuesday, 2 November – Johnny rang again to say he was off the show. The doctors had ordered him into hospital. The full darkness of what was now inevitable had begun to descend. On the Wednesday, the medical staff at Royal Prince Alfred Hospital told Johnny's family and friends that he would not last the night. Johnny, typically, had other ideas and was very much alive the next morning. But the comeback was brief and proved to be nothing more than a last spurt in his body's instinctive quest to cling to life.

On Friday, 5 November – my birthday – I received a call from the hospital. Johnny wanted to see me. Despite our close friendship, in the two years that he had been sick, I had never visited him in hospital. I knew he hated grievers and bleeders crowding him and that the last thing he wanted, or needed, was for his close friends to be slobbering in his vicinity. So now that he had summoned me, I knew something dreadful was up.

He was in an alarming state, barely able to breathe, let alone talk. The attempted conversation was prolonged by his need to reach for the oxygen mask every few seconds. He said: 'The news is not good. The doctors are not giving me much time. So, just to sort out a few things . . .' It was Johnny of the classic understatement and irony.

There were no expressions of closure that afternoon. Johnny just wanted to sort out a few things.. He knew that I was planning my first trip to Brazil barely a month later, and was delighted. He grabbed his assortment of contact books and began to dictate to me a catalogue of information about Brazil: where I should stay, what I should see, whom I should contact, addresses, phone numbers and so on. Then Andy Harper, another good friend, showed up. He, too, had been summoned. The three of us spoke for a while and, thinking that Johnny and Andy may have wanted some private time, I left. I was in denial: still refusing to accept that my friend would die.

The next day – 6 November, a Saturday – I went to a barbecue at the home of my daughter Tania, a singer-songwriter. A host of musicians and music-loving friends were gathered for a prolonged jam session. I arrived around 2.30. Less than an hour later I got a call from Geoff, one of Johnny's two brothers, telling me that Johnny was fading fast and that 'things were imminent'. I high-tailed it to the hospital which was only around 10 minutes' drive away. Johnny was now unconscious, heavily sedated, minus the oxygen mask and breathing in deep, long, rhythmic beats. When I arrived, one of the chairs next to his bed was made vacant. I sat and whispered to him, 'Öreg, it's me.' His head suddenly rose, his breathing went into an irregular spasm for a few seconds, and he slumped back again. I stayed for the next two hours, stroking his head but staying silent for fear of disturbing his final, peaceful moments in this world. Others arrived: friends, ex-Socceroo team-mates. Eventually, Johnny Watkiss – another Socceroo campaigner and Johnny's childhood friend – entered the room. I gave him my chair and left the hospital, returning to my daughter's barbecue.

Not long after I arrived at Tania's house, my mobile rang again. It was Geoff with the dreaded news. Johnny passed away about 20 minutes after I left. I found an unoccupied room in the house for some privacy, and rang SBS to ensure that Johnny's many friends at the station were among the first to know. Liz Deep-Jones was reading the evening sports bulletin that day and the script of a breaking story on Johnny's death was thrust in front of her while

she was on set. She nearly choked on-air as she read it. I then rang
Maryana, Johnny's estranged wife, to break it to her. The news was
spreading fast. I took one call from a reporter, John Taylor of *The
Daily Telegraph*, and then shut down the phone.

Of those at the barbecue, only Tania and my other daughter,
Natalie, knew what was happening and why I had left the party in
the first place. I had told Tania not to tell anyone else. After the
phone call from Geoff, and the brief minutes of the follow up calls,
I stood as if frozen in the room, unable to decide what to do next.
Tania walked in and saw in my eyes the answer to the question she
didn't need to ask. She said: 'Are you going home or will you stay?'
I pictured the prospect of sitting at home in my lounge room,
all alone, Scotch in hand, frantically working the TV remote to
distract myself from grief. I decided to stay.

At the party, the performances were well under way and I stood
back watching and listening, the words of each song bearing a
surreal relevance to what I was feeling. I know this tends to happen
in times of melancholy: there was nothing new or uncommon in it.
But the music was comforting, soothing; and I was glad I had
stayed. Standing nearby was David Cunningham, Tania's guitarist
and musical mentor, and a friend. Summoning up my courage,
I waved to him and said, 'Dave, let's do something.' We did Bob
Dylan's 'Knockin' on Heaven's Door' and followed it with James
Taylor's 'Fire and Rain', each song bearing relevance in a moment
of loss and finality. Then I went home.

The next day, the Sunday, I had to be back on set to host SBS'
four-hour live football show, *The World Game*. Luckily, I kept a grip
and was light on the booze the night before. Executive producer,
Noel Brady, did a brilliant job at such short notice devising the
tribute program: assembling the guests, the interviewees and the
archival content eulogising Johnny Warren. Noel rang early in the
morning to give me the program line-up, offering me the day off
if I wanted. 'I'll be there,' I said. This was personal. For someone
other than me to host a television tribute to Johnny Warren was
unthinkable. I had to do it.

Philip Micallef of *The Daily Telegraph* also rang me early that day, asking me to write a eulogy to Johnny for the next day's edition. Others did too, but I knocked them back because I had already said yes to Philip. His deadline was 8 pm. We finished *The World Game* program at 6 pm, and I rushed home to write the piece and file it by 8.00. Such an article would ordinarily have taken me hours to write: eulogies are not things one writes quickly. But finding the inspiration to work up a portrait of my friend, and what made him such a unique human being, was easy that night.

Some 26 hours after my friend had died, I finally got some time to myself. I threw off my shoes, cosied up to my bottle of whisky and got thoroughly drunk. My friend was gone and I was in shock because he had gone too soon. I could cope with his passing, as we all must in such times. But the timing was off. For two years, I had refused to believe he would die. Now he was gone, and I was unable to grasp what life would be like without my cohort and my friend.

Johnny Warren's death, despite its imminence, had stunned the nation. The calls were loud for an appropriate commemoration. I rang Rob Joske, Johnny's manager, who was well connected with the state government and asked if he thought a state funeral could be arranged. He called back a few hours later: Bob Carr, the NSW premier, was quick to agree and offered a state funeral – the first ever in NSW for a sportsman. The service received live national coverage on television and was appropriately serene, ceremonial and dignified. But it broke ranks, as Johnny would have wished, with such events. At the end of the service the exit of the coffin from the church was greeted by the beat of South American drums. As I emerged from the church, a battalion of Brazilians, dressed all in white, were beating their rhythms. Behind them a smaller group – Uruguayans, dressed in Celeste blue – were making their own racket, paying tribute to the man they considered one of their own. For the first time since Johnny's death, I began to choke. The demonstration by these South Americans was, for me, the most powerful sign of how widely Johnny was loved and how little he realised it.

Much of the entourage moved on to the Sydney Cricket Ground for the wake. From there, a smaller group went to the Lord Dudley pub in Woollahra. As the beer flowed, the Brazilians again picked up their drums and began beating them. It was around 11 pm when the police arrived in response to neighbours' complaints about the noise. Johnny would have liked that.

16

A fear for the game

Accelerated by his death, the Johnny Warren legacies were more plentiful and arrived more quickly than I anticipated. The first of them struck while I was still on holidays in Brazil in December 2004. By the time I got back, the Sydney branch of the Fairfax press had, by decree, changed the name of soccer to football. Johnny's favourite word became 'house style' in one of Australia's powerful newspaper publishing houses. A few weeks later, the sport's governing body in Australia announced that it would change its name from the Australian Soccer Association to Football Federation Australia. A few in the anti-football press complained but their cries led nowhere. With Johnny's ashes still warm, it was not a good look to pooh pooh one of his most sacred wishes.

The 'I told you so' message by which Johnny wished to be remembered was picking up pace. Soon football's engagement with Asia sprang from being a Johnny Warren dream to legislated reality. In this wish, as in so many others, Johnny and I were as one. Way back in 1989, a young cadet reporter from the Sydney *Daily Telegraph* suggested to me that Australia should abandon Oceania and join forces with Asian football instead. 'Of course,' I replied. The next day's *Telegraph* headlines announced that Australia's most prominent football media guru was advocating defection to Asia. It was worth a headline because Australia, as a nation, was not so Asia-savvy in those days. The notion that this self-styled outpost of Europe should enmesh itself with its northern neighbours – politically, economically and socially – still had some growing to do. And as for football, the maxim of the day was that Australia was better placed being a king in the small kingdom of Oceania than a mere subject in a massive continental realm like Asia. Moving north was not a fashionable idea at the time.

But Johnny's affection for the concept had an even longer history. He was an Asia-phile from as far back as 1965 when he was a young squad member of the Socceroo team that succumbed to North Korea in Phnom Penh. As a player he took part in many battles with Asian teams, led St George to a wonderful tournament win in Tokyo in 1972 and captained Australia in three tournaments in Vietnam during the war years. He took his FIFA coaching badge in Malaysia and formed close friendships with some of Asian football's most important figures, like the long-serving Asian confederation chief, Peter Velappan, and Junichiro Okano, Japan's most revered football figure, the man who was to inspire the immensely successful J-League and chair the organising committee of the 2002 World Cup. Throughout those years he saw the wild enthusiasm with which Asians followed football and always wondered why Australia was not engaging them instead of lining up with its small, rugby-bent neighbours like New Zealand and Fiji.

But his voice was not heard, in Australia or in Asia, until the early 2000s. In 2001 the Asian Football Confederation elected a new president: Mohamed bin Hammam, a Qatari industrialist who brought a new vision to the continent that always had the greatest potential but was not fulfilling it. In August 2002, on a visit to Kuala Lumpur where the AFC is housed, I sought an audience with Velappan (the General Secretary), and bin Hammam. By then, SBS' reputation as a significant media player in football in the region had spread well beyond Australia, and its respectability and passion for football promotion was well known at AFC headquarters. At the meeting in a private room at KL's Marriott Hotel I lobbied strongly that the AFC should engage with Australia and, at a broader level, Oceania. My argument was that Asian football, unlike European, South American and even African football, was not yet a global brand, and that its best opportunity to expand its market exposure was via Australia and the Pacific, who were willing collaborators. It was just a few weeks since South Korea and Japan made their stunning conquests in the 2002 World Cup and the time was ripe for Asian football to cash in.

Of course, I had ulterior motives, which were not lost on either man. On a personal level, like Johnny Warren, I wanted Australian football to expand and profit from a relationship with Asia. And on a professional level, I wanted to nudge forward the suggestion that Australia be given a foot in the door of Asian competitions, such as the Asian Cup (of nations) and the Asian Champions League (of clubs). As regular rights holder and broadcaster of these events, I wanted SBS to gain from an Australian participation in them.

Bin Hammam, a likeable, simpatico and receptive man, listened and – I felt – accepted the arguments. This was new. Until bin Hammam, the prevailing attitude in Asian football circles towards Australia was at best deeply suspicious and at worst one of down-right contempt. The reasons were perverse but, in a way, understand-able. The Asians saw Australia as a powerful football nation, one capable of winning in the region. And they dreaded the thought of a white, blue-eyed nation – reminiscent of the colonial era – domi-nating Asia. But bin Hammam was a man of the 21st century. He saw beyond the old prejudices and searched for a way in which a link with Oceania – and especially Australia – might benefit his con-federation. General Secretary Velappan had already indicated that the AFC was in the mood to test the waters of a thaw with Oceania, starting with exchanges of technical know-how between the regions and inviting Oceania teams into Asian youth tournaments.

A year later, Australian football had its Crawford-led revolution and Frank Lowy was in the chair. To my great delight, and that of Johnny Warren, Lowy made the need for Australian football to engage with Asia one of his first declared priorities. Lowy's fortunes moved swiftly in gaining acquaintances with global football's most powerful men. Before too long, he was man to man with Mohamed bin Hammam: and the two hit it off like a house on fire. Both were astute, wise businessmen blessed with vision, and it should not have come as a surprise that each would see a way of collaborating in quest of a mutual cause. But even I – a classic wishful thinker – didn't anticipate what was about to come. My own view was that the Asians would never accept us as one of their own and the best we could hope for was for some kind of collaboration between the two continents, whereby we were regular invited guests of the Asians.

In early 2004 Lowy installed John O'Neill as his first lieutenant and again, at the new chief executive's first press conference, the long-term vision of engaging with Asia was heavily emphasised. But O'Neill was not truly swayed until he attended the Asian Cup in China in July of that year. There, this rugby aficionado saw what football meant to Asians and realised the commercial potential of a liaison. Now the juggernaut that drove Australia north towards Asia was operating at full speed. In February of 2005 a Japanese member of the FIFA executive committee was quoted in a leaked story as saying that Australia was about to join the AFC. As we in the media scrambled to have the story verified there was no denial from Football Federation Australia. Now we knew that it was true: that one of our wildest dreams was coming true. Eight months later, in Marrakech at the AFC congress, a choked up Frank Lowy accepted Australia's formal installation as a member of the Asian Football Confederation. As Lowy and bin Hammam – a Jew and an Arab – embraced, I reflected on football's extraordinary capacity to catalyse détente and uproot divisive wedges. I was never more proud to be a football man.

The 16th of November 2005 – a Wednesday – dawned with gloomy, clouded Sydney skies. I was concerned by the darkness of it, wondering nervously if it was an omen. I had already had a bad week and needed no subliminal suggestions that it was going to end badly. Only the previous morning, I had arrived back with the small SBS team from Uruguay where we covered the first leg of the World Cup qualifying playoff between Australia and Uruguay the previous Saturday.

That Saturday of the playoff in Montevideo, I was immensely nervous, almost as though I was one of the players. But when I saw them walk out onto the field, I realised I had never seen the Australian players so calm and yet so steely in resolve. As they walked on, they were met with a 70,000-strong chorus of whistles. Some of the players turned and applauded a small flock of Australian fans in yellow shirts who were sitting behind me. Mark Viduka strolled past me: a large, statuesque man, the team captain. He looked like a primed racehorse, blinkered to all that was around him, staring forward as though contemplating nothing but the challenge of the day: intent on putting right the wrongs of the past 32 years and his own two previous World Cup campaigns. I knew then that this was different.

The Uruguayans had brought the kick-off forward to 6 pm from the originally announced 9 pm. The original late kick-off had been designed to make it difficult for the Australians to get out of Montevideo on the night of the match thereby narrowing the recovery gap between the first game (November 12) and the second, four days later. But the plan backfired and was to have a telling effect on the outcome over the two games. The Australians had, in fact, hired a Qantas charter plane and it mattered little to them what time the game ended. On the final whistle they would head straight for the tarmac and be off in the comforts of their own aircraft, complete with massage tables and all the in-flight medical amenities known to man. The Uruguayans failed in their own attempts to hire a charter and were reliant on a late scheduled flight to Sydney, via Santiago and Auckland, mostly in economy class.

The sun shone in Montevideo as the minutes ticked to the kick-off but the evening was cool with discomforting, squally winds. As the two teams entered the Estadio Centenario, the atmosphere and the vocal hostility to which the Australians were subjected was like nothing I had ever experienced. I had attended World Cup finals, FA Cup finals, European Cup finals, derbies in Milan and Manchester, and even the Monumental in Buenos Aires when Australia played a World Cup playoff there in 1993. They were nothing compared to this. When the Uruguayans sing *Soy Celeste* before a game, one's hairs stand on end.

But on this day the Australians were in control, at least of themselves. The source of their newly found confidence was Guus Hiddink whose mysterious gift for giving his players belief had transformed the personnel in just four short months. Under Hiddink, the players may not have thought they were superior to the Uruguayans but they knew they were being guided by a superior coach, maybe the best in the world. Once Hiddink instilled this new psychology the rest just about took care of itself. The improved tactical planning, the more astute player selections, Hiddink's intelligent responses to each game situation, were just parts of the equation. The root of the formula was the new mentality: it transformed the team from a bunch of talented self-doubters into winners.

This was evident in the early passages of the game, which Australia dominated, and even more so in the late stanza: an agonising last half hour in which Australia withstood a merciless battering as Uruguay, suspecting that 1-0 would not be enough, went searching for the killer blow. It is there that the two-match tie was won. Had Uruguay managed a goal there, I believe the 2-0 would have been insurmountable. But the Australians kept them out: it was heroism in the truest of Australia's Digger traditions.

The very fact that Uruguay thought it so important to score a second goal in Montevideo was at the heart of the script for the return leg in Sydney. After the game I took the small SBS team to dinner at a *parrillada* – a steak house – around the corner from the hotel. Then I went back to my room, poured myself a Scotch and stretched out to contemplate what had been and what might be four days later. Luckily (as it turned out), I had lost my mobile phone which meant I could not be contacted by the Australian media. Those few peaceful hours gave me a chance for quiet contemplation and with each sip of whisky I became more convinced that the job ahead for Australia was doable. What kept coming back to me was the question of why Uruguay so desperately wanted to score a second goal in that first leg. Surely, if they thought 1-0 was enough, they would have shut up shop after Dario Rodriguez's goal in the 38th, closed the game and gone to Sydney for a 0-0. But they went chasing with sweaty desperation. That to me meant they were on the run, and believed that the Australians could turn it around. When I got back to Sydney and the phones began to ring with questions about what might happen in the second leg, I puffed with confidence. 'Yes,' I said, 'the Aussies can do it.'

But on the way to the Telstra Stadium I was nervous, as nervous as I had ever been before a match involving Australia. I was nervous for the boys, for the starved and hopeful Australian public, and for the years of investment SBS had put into football. I felt somehow responsible for all of that. It was I, along with Johnny Warren and a few others, who had led SBS and the Australian public to this passionate interest in football. In this context, if the boys failed we would fail with them. No wonder I was nervous.

By the time we were into our rehearsals and run-throughs the crowd had begun to file into the stadium and the strident noise that was to dominate the night had begun. The broadcast SBS was about to present was the network's most ambitious. There were 23 cameras: more than for the previous World Cup final. Hoping for iconic historical footage, we had a helicopter camera hovering above Homebush to capture the glittering jewel of the lit stadium. At the Plaza Independencia in Montevideo, Tim Vickery was getting into position at the crack of dawn, ready for a live cross so that Australians could get a feel of what Uruguayans were thinking. At Federation Square in Melbourne, a mob was gathering for the big-screen feast, and reporter Christian Jantzen was in position. Down on the sidelines, reporter Andrew Orsatti was getting ready for the biggest gig of his career. It was he, and colleague Mike Tomalaris, who would later have to gather the reactions of the Australian players, whatever the outcome. A voice check with commentator Simon Hill established that there were no problems with my hearing of the commentary. By my side, analysts Craig Foster and Ned Zelic were straightening their ties. In my earpiece, executive producer Noel Brady, was a voice of calm. 'You right up there? Can you hear us OK?' We were ready.

The live telecast began one hour before kick-off. By now the fans were flooding in and the noise was growing. Craig, Ned and I were chattering to the audience, battling to be heard above the noise. But it was to little avail: the crowd was dominating. The sense of their presence and that of the millions of others at home was overcoming us.

And then it was time for the national anthems. The Uruguayan anthem, coming first, was drowned by a concert of boos from the 83,000. Even the PA system couldn't be heard. I had never experienced such a thing in all my years at such games in Australia and later expressed my disgust. As an immigrant to Australia and one who had a natural empathy with visitors, I felt uncomfortable and embarrassed.

That said, it should also be noted that the Australian crowd had been wound up to it. For weeks before the contest, the Australian populist media had been painting the Uruguayans as a nation of grubby cheats, conspiring to do just about anything to scuttle the Australian dream. And of course, after 32 years of frustration, Australian fans were desperate to do whatever it took to help get the boys over the line. So they booed. It was not nice – but it worked.

The decibels, if anything, went up a notch when it was time for the Australian anthem. Jade MacRae stepped up to the microphone and sang with the voice of an angel. But she was drowned out, too. The 83,000 burst into 'Advance Australia Fair'. The stadium was an explosion of unity and national desire, and the mob sang with a passion and a gusto not previously seen at any event in Australia. Thousands upon thousands of Australians were singing and swaying and being silly, and it was football – my sport – that was the medium. If only Johnny had been here to see it.

The match, at least most of it, was a blur. Up at the studio podium, I was a wreck. Once the game started and commentator, Simon Hill, took over the coverage, I threw off the headphones, got off the chair and pounded the floor. My floor manager, Dorian – a rugby man – kept asking if I was all right. I waved him away and lit up a cigarette. In a strictly non-smoking stadium, I was seen lighting up every five minutes and no one appeared to mind. The Aussies, as I recall, began nervously and gave me some mighty frights in the early stages. Alvaro Recoba, the world's foremost expert at pounding in free kicks that dropped menacingly in front of the goalkeeper, was being given repeated opportunities to execute the telling blow. It went on and on for what seemed like hours. But gradually the Australians got the upper hand. What changed things was a canny substitution made by Hiddink on 27 minutes. It was always in his plans to field a line-up that would be solid enough in defence to soak up any early pressure from Uruguay and then, if no goals were conceded, make some changes. What helped him pick his moment was a yellow card given to Australian defender, Tony Popovic. With the Uruguayans using a one-man strike force, Australia had two spare men in defence, so off came Popovic and on went attacking midfielder, Harry Kewell.

Kewell was the pin-up boy of Australian football: a source of national pride for having been a star player in England and the earner of outrageous sums of money at European champions, Liverpool. He was, and is as I write, Australia's highest salaried athlete, and that's saying something in a nation of rich tennis players, golfers, cyclists, swimmers, boxers and cricketers.

Even Kewell's critics didn't dispute that he was a fabulous, exciting, match-winning footballer for his country. And on this night, he delivered again. Once Kewell appeared Uruguay – needing to adjust and fearing Harry's reputation – retreated onto the back foot. He was unleashed on his natural left flank and immediately began to torment Real Madrid's Carlos Diogo, the Uruguayan right back. Within minutes Australia was in the lead and the 0-1 from Montevideo was cancelled. Kewell's trickery had unlocked the Uruguay defence; the wonderfully deft Mark Viduka gave Kewell a glorious pass; Kewell miss kicked his attempt on goal but interfered enough to direct the ball to Bresciano – who shovelled the ball in at the far post. The 83,000 rose in delirium and eight million or more others, watching at home and on various big screens and in public places, experienced a moment of uncontrolled madness.

By 10 or 15 minutes into the second half, Australia's dominance was becoming complete. I looked across to Ned Zelic inquisitively. 'They're fucked. Their legs are gone,' he said, referring to the Uruguayans. It was true. The Australian team management – especially its medical staff – had done an awesome job in ensuring the team recovered in the brief three days between the Montevideo and Sydney games. The scheduled economy class flight taken by the Uruguayans was no match for the cushy Qantas charter accorded the Australians. In addition, the Australians spent the interval between the games at home, on sweetly familiar terrain, while the Uruguayans were in foreign territory, uncomfortable and fearful of hostility. It all told on them. By now it seemed only a matter of time before the Australians would score the second, killer goal, and Ned and I wondered where in the world a Uruguayan goal could ever come from. Recoba and Uruguay's iron man captain, Montero, were substituted, signals that Uruguay was spent and was giving up.

But we were wrong. They held out. As the whistle blew for full time, with the score unchanged, I was still not worried. It just meant the Australians were given another 30 minutes to score their inevitable winning goal. Uruguay were surely so gone they were now only playing for the penalty shootout and its crazy lottery. But even I – a long-time admirer and student of Uruguay as a success-ful football nation, had been fooled. Spent, giddy and gone, the *charruas* still managed to make a game of it in that dying half hour. They kept coming – and at least twice they created scoring chances that could and should have been converted. When Richard Morales, Australia's executioner in Montevideo four years earlier, had the ball on his right foot 9 metres out and with only the keeper to beat, 32 years of my life and all of those failures flashed before me. But he missed, and I reached again for my lighter.

Then came the shootout: an ugly solution to undecided games and about as fair to deserving teams as shooting crap. I have always believed that they are the spiritual antithesis of fair play and all that is noble in sport. A miss kick here or a lucky anticipation by the goalkeeper there could decide the outcome: I had seen many instances in the past where inferior, uncreative, defensive teams played deliberately for the penalties and ended up winning. Sud-denly, it became irrelevant who had dominated the game through its full duration: once the signal went for the shootout, the odds were back to 50/50. I trembled at the prospect that Australia, having at last come this far, would now be robbed by the vulgarity of this expedient mechanism.

But Ned Zelic made the point that even the shootout favours the brave. The inferior team – the more exhausted team – was more likely than the other to be rattled by the pressure of the moment and blow a kick wide or tap it limply into the hands of the goalkeeper, he said. That made me relax a little. As the 83,000 stood in a hush and waited, Harry Kewell walked up to take the first kick. I remem-bered Diego Maradona telling me that only those with the guts to take penalties got the opportunity to miss them. At such moments, many professional footballers will think of their careers and of the damaging label they will have to wear for the rest of their lives should they miss. Harry, whose stature grew like a mountain in my mind as he walked, calmly stroked the ball home in the left-hand corner. No sweat. 'Harry Cool' was, after all, his nickname.

More Australians, just as willing to be heroes at the risk of becoming villains, lined up. Lucas Neill, a rugged defender not known for the more subtle art of stroking a ball into the net, was one. Tony Vidmar, whose dying international career had been resurrected from the ashes and tears of Montevideo 2001, was another. Mark Viduka, the giant, super calm captain, too. He missed, directing the ball wide and my heart stopped. But hope lived because, after that miss, Mark Schwarzer made his second of two critical saves from the Uruguayans.

Now the Australians were up 3-2 with their next – and last – kick to come. Up stepped John Aloisi, rarely a first choice for Australia and even on this night he had come on as a substitute. But his presence proved to be historically crucial. Aloisi's kick, smacked with his left through the narrowest of gaps between goalkeeper and post, launched a nation into ecstasy and Aloisi on a triumphant, semi-naked run, waving his prized shirt above his head like a flag of conquest.

The scene would be the subject of countless television replays. Up on our studio podium, Dorian and I embraced, jumping up and down like two little boys, chanting into each other's ears: 'We're going to the World Cup, we're going to the World Cup'. As we went into our post-match analysis, I kept thinking of Johnny Warren, wondering how much he may have had to do with this. I am not a religious man and am yet to be convinced that there is any kind of after-life. But the Johnny Warren spirit – the embodiment of all of his convictions and beliefs – was everywhere. It would be just like him to have scripted the whole thing, right down to the last penalty, including the Schwarzer saves and having Viduka miss his penalty just to take the piss out of us.

With the telecast over, I scurried to find my girlfriend Cida who was holed up in a lounge somewhere on the other side of the stadium. She's a Brazilian, so she understood how a nation could be overcome by madness over a football match. I just wanted to look into her sweet Paulista eyes, give her a good hug and have a stiff drink. The mission took an eternity as I negotiated my way through a forest of fans, all of whom wanted to shake my hand, slap my back and remind me of what a shame it was that Johnny wasn't here. Cida and I went on to rendezvous with my daughters, Tania and Natalie, at a bar in the nearby Novotel, where I spotted and embraced Rale Rasic and two former Socceroos, John Kosmina and Rocky O'Connor. Kosmina, as tough and macho as the trunk of an oak tree and not known for his sentimentality, was collected and reserved. But I heard later from a witness that, after Aloisi's kick went in, tears had streamed down his face. Football is a strange thing, and it does strange things to the strongest of men.

In the bar there was no respite from the mass delirium. The beer flowed and members of the fandom, all clad in green and gold, wanted to shake my hand, take a photo and talk to me in slurring beats about their experiences on this big night. I didn't quite understand it. It was not me who scored the goals or saved the penalties. I was not Guus Hiddink, the coach who engineered the tactics. But this was a time of joyful togetherness, of a unique and hard-earned celebration, when people will grab at the nearest human or thing that connects them with a grand achievement.

It was 3 am when I got home. I put three blocks of ice into a glass, poured myself a Scotch and slumped onto the sofa. I was tired but couldn't gather the energy to sleep. Besides, I needed a moment of solitude to contemplate what had just gone on. I anticipated that the next day, the papers and morning television programs would crawl with the Australian victory and what it meant. They did. But what it meant to whom? I thought of the struggle, even as far back as those high school days when I argued with snotty nosed prepubescents about the beauties of football. I thought of Johnny and what he would have made of it. I thought of the fans, the real ones:

the true believers who had stuck by this thing; the old timers who had come to Australia with football baggage in the 50s and 60s and laboured at a mission to make their new land understand. I thought of them now, 50 years older, many of them wrinkled, thin and frail. I imagined them smiling, delighted at having overcome all opposition, and satisfied that their beliefs had not been in vain.

The triumph over Uruguay – and what it meant for Australia, for football, and for me – might seem an appropriate note on which to finish this story. But that would be premature and opportunistic, given that it does not round off my life, not even the football part of it.

For a start, Australia qualifying for a World Cup should not be the end of any story. The story of football's struggle to find its proper place in Australian society will not end even when Australia wins the World Cup – something I am certain Australia will achieve one day. It will only end when this country, as a sporting whole, embraces the real beauties of this sport – as Johnny Warren did and as all those other minorities (migrants and others) have done for a century and more. What we have at the moment – and what we had when football mania swept this land on the night of 16 November 2005 – is a country momentarily titillated, not so much by football but by what being on the world's greatest sporting stage can mean for us and our national ego. This does not necessarily mean that football has been embraced: football was merely the medium of a national achievement. There is, of course, no denying that the moment will rub off on football; that more Australians will now pay attention to it – or at least to the Socceroos – and how they fare in the Cup itself. But the effect, however broad, could turn out to be shallow and, post-World Cup, the majority will probably go back to their traditional priorities. Johnny was probably right when he raised an eyebrow at my suggestion in 2002 that the mission had been accomplished. True: much had been accomplished then, and even more on 16 November

2005. But the mission still has some ways to go: there is work to do.

And in this era, the work is becoming more and more difficult. When I was a youngster I was seduced by sport's suburban beauties: the skills and creative endeavours of everyday people, the nobilities of their drive to triumph by fair means in the name of their colour or their tribe and then go home and sleep in peace, win or loss. It is not the way of things any more. Now, youngsters are more likely to be captured by the forces of who wins – not who plays well, and by whatever slick packages of entertainment are sold to them.

It is the way of things today in all sport – including football – the world over. And thanks to the new world of Lowy and O'Neill, Australian football now competes well in this environment.

But what is happening to football at its commercial apex – mostly, in western Europe – makes me fear for the game. In 1998 I was asked to present a paper at the first World Football Expo in Singapore on the topic, 'The Role of Television in Football'. In it I surmised that all was rosy in the relationship between football and television, but warned against commercially driven interference with the things that shape football's beauties, such as its laws. (Bear in mind that football generates billions of television viewers and draws massive amounts of money in television rights fees.) I aimed those words at FIFA and the game's governors everywhere, but I was aiming at the wrong target. What I didn't anticipate then was that it would be the game's wealthy clubs, fuelled by their insatiable appetite for more millions, that would threaten the fabric of football.

The current behaviour of these so-called football 'clubs' is an obscenity. The fact is, they are not clubs at all but businesses: corporations whose raison d'être is not to win football matches or trophies but to become richer. Winning is just a means to the exalted end of making money. And because money helps buy better players and better coaches (and more winnings), the few rich clubs get richer and the poor – unless they are bought by a billionaire oil king – never get a look in.

When I was growing up the world's richest club was Real Madrid, which bought the world's best players and won many things with them. It had its detractors because of its financial might but in essence it was a club, and still is, accountable only to its 100,000 or so members and beholden to a football agenda. These days the world's richest 'club' is Chelsea which, until a few years ago, was on the brink of bankruptcy. Now it is super rich simply because it was bought by a super rich man whose credentials have no relation to a love for Chelsea nor, for that matter, for football. To me, this is obscene. For a start, those years ago, anyone buying and owning a football club was unheard of. Now we have purchasers queuing up to buy football clubs, with no emotional attachment to anything other than money.

The fuel that drives these clubs has no time for patience. It demands instant gratification in the shape of results, and there is now no possibility of seeing teams evolve to the true grace of greatness. The great teams of the past – such as the Real Madrid of the 1950s, or the Benfica of the 60s and the Ajax of the 70s – were not built in a day but meticulously fashioned over years. The ingredients for their technical recipes were carefully gathered and stirred in the knowledge that greatness could be achieved over time. Now the deal is to buy the 'best' coach, give him a truckload of money with which to buy and train good players, and, presto: you have a great team. The problem is, what you have is not a great team but some kind of rattling machine that spits out trophies and, in the process, bores everyone to tears.

This process has the potential to kill the beautiful game. Players and coaches change clubs at the drop of a million and profess loyalty to a shirt they had barely seen before. No player or coach can be believed when he talks of allegiance to a colour when we know all too well that his only allegiance is to his bank account. David Beckham, a handsome man with a sublime gift for crossing the ball accurately, is the world's richest sportsman. Why? Because the image rights to his pearly whites are worth hundreds of millions and sell an awful lot of T-shirts in Asia. Is that football?

Some might say, as my late father probably would, that it has always been this way. That football became a business the minute

– some time in the 19th century – players started being paid and spectators had to pay to attend a game. But not quite. True, football has been a business for a very long time. But until recently, the core agenda was sport. And in many cases, it mattered how you won: not just whether you won.

The avaricious football clubs of the world are not entirely to blame: they have a willing ally in a modern society that builds shrines to results and is all too ready to prostitute itself for the sake of a victory. The American Football coach, Vince Lombardi, once famously said: 'Winning is not everything. It's the only thing.' That utterance is probably the most negative and destructive ever attributed to anyone in relation to sport. Winning in sport is neither everything nor the only thing. Winning with honour is everything. Is a victory honourable, I ask, is it of substance or sweet, if it is achieved by means other than decency, within the rules, by sheer honest endeavour and on a level playing field? Not to me. To me Lombardi was far from being the high priest of wisdom by which, thanks to that quote, he is being portrayed. To me he was a dangerous fool.

Those who disagree will label me a hopeless romantic and retort that Lombardi was a realist; that he was merely observing a dogma that reflected the reality. True, I am a romantic. But I am also a realist, because I believe romance is a core component of the empirical reality that is sport. Without romance there is no sport reality and if you excise romance out of sport you will surely kill it. Lombardi was wrong. What he said might be valid in war or business. But it is not valid for sport.

Within this context I am cautiously prepared to say that football is more likely than most sports to be able to preserve at least some of its sporting integrity. Football is a team game, probably the last of the team games in which – once the whistle goes – it is essentially the players who decide just about everything. Football has no time-outs; it has limited substitutions; and there is no electronic gadgetry by which a coach can manipulate a game while sitting on the bench. Football is still a players' game, where player ability counts for everything and usually decides the outcome. Coaches make their selections and draw their fancy geometrics on black-boards, playing the game of combat generals. But once a game starts, they are powerless to intervene. As much as they might scream and yell from the dugout, the players usually don't even hear them. This must not change.

Probably the biggest pressure football faces in the modern era is the move to introduce technology to scrutinise and overturn refereeing decisions. I am violently against this, for it flies in the face of the human spirit and the romance that characterises football. The pressure is exacerbated by the fact that other sports have introduced all sorts of gizmos, and third and fourth umpires, in order to project themselves as being totally correct and above reproach when it comes to fair outcomes. But sport is ultimately not about being totally correct and above reproach. Sport is about contests played out by humans: players, coaches, referees and others, all flesh and blood and fallible, each with a capacity and a right to make mistakes. What kind of a human contest would it be if everyone performed his task with perfection and slide rule accuracy? It would be boring: no one would win and no one would watch. A refereeing error, though distressing, is as much part of football as a striker duffing a shot or a goalkeeper dropping a clanger.

In the midst of these lofty debates, we in the public forefront of the game often forget where we came from. We forget that originally we were turned on as kids by the immense joy of playing the game. Every so often, I remind myself of the bald tennis ball in the backyard in Budakeszi, of the joy those frolics gave me and the role they played in fashioning my spirit as a man. Today, there are some 400 million souls around the world doing that stuff: gathering daily on a dusty street, in a park, on a farm or a beach, kicking a sphere of some sort – not always leather, and often without boots – and getting enormous pleasure out of doing it. This, not Manchester United, David Beckham, Milan or even the World Cup, is the essence of football. It is where the great players – Di Stefano, Puskás, Pelé, Best, Cruyff, Eusebio, Maradona, Zidane, Ronaldinho and the others – all came from. Football is not just about its elites. Football is about egalitarianism and opportunity, a readiness to accept all who come and want to play.

In the big chase for money, trophies and new markets, the players are not entirely blameless, of course. The gluttonous clubs have drawn them into their webs, fattened them up with obscene salaries and deadened their sense of sporting decency. They no longer think of such things as the shirt, team loyalty and the quest to win honourably, but of getting the best contract, of their images and their fleets of sports cars. The Bosman ruling of the mid-1990s freed up players from effective modern day slavery and gave them back their right to choose the club they wanted to play for. But as much as Jean-Marc Bosman, when he brought his case to Europe's highest court, was driven by the most natural of human rights, his victory led only to a revolution whose currency became not rights or ideals but avarice and greed. The professional footballers of Europe are richer than they have ever been. And what was Jean-Marc Bosman's reward? On his retirement he had enough to buy a modest house somewhere in the provinces of Belgium. It didn't occur to any one of the fat cat players that perhaps they should pass the hat around and reward the man for what his courage had brought them.

Is all hope lost? No, at least not yet. What quarantines the game and its virtues is national team football. Elite football players, as beings, remain just football players, no matter where their club-managers and slick image makers may lead them. And it is a thrill to see them revert back into real footballers every time they don the shirt of their countries. In this realm there are no Bosmans. In club football, players can always select their masters, depending on the size of the offer. But not so when it comes to playing for their country, where their shirt colour and their allegiance are chosen for them and they are stuck with it. At this point footballers become footballers again, shunted back to their roots, no longer playing for a bonus but for something resembling honour and glory. Yes, they get paid for playing for their country, and they do get a premium for winning. And yes, they do stand to score a good club contract if they shine in a national team shirt. But they will only benefit personally if they perform with honour and with pride for a team that has been chosen for them. It is sweet indeed to still hear players say their biggest ambition is to represent their country.

This is why the World Cup, and not any of the rich club tournaments, reigns as the pinnacle of the world game. FIFA, and all of the world's football governors, must protect the integrity of national team football at all costs if the game is not to die.

There have been a few very human football icons who epitomise what some might call my old-fashioned ideals. Not long before I wrote these words, George Best died. He was pretty close to being the embodiment of all that I grew up to admire about football. Sadly, he was no Pelé – but only because Pelé ended up stable, wealthy and sober. George was debonair and stylish, brilliant and sublime but he died drunk, his liver shot – like Garrincha's. There are great similarities between Best and Garrincha in all respects. Each was a winger, a number seven, with an equal capacity to mesmerise and dismantle defenders with a swerve of the torso and the drop of a hip. Both had a penchant for women and both were partial to drink. Then there was Maradona, another street kid from the poor side, all-conquering at play but with a dominant gene for self-destruction. What is it with these football geniuses, each bred by the unwashed – the tier in society that is the lifeblood of the game – yet each lacking the essential gift for making the best of their talents once they reach the doorstep of immense opportunity and universal envy? Why is it that they die young, or at least fade early, because they flunk the test of negotiating the cumbersome transition between being players and becoming men?

When in Brazil, on that trip I finally undertook soon after Johnny

Warren's death, I went to the home village of Garrincha, a sleepy rain-forest cul de sac called Pau Grande. It was here that the boy genius grew up, talking to the little birds after whom he was nicknamed, to become a colossus among football entertainers and winners before his other passion, booze, finally consumed him and he died bloated with alcohol at the age of 49. Garrincha was the man who embodied more than anyone – including Pelé – the true spirit of Brazilian football: the *jogo bonito* that conquered the world in his time and for much of the time since. Don't take that from me: ask any Brazilian. He was a street footballer as a kid in Pau Grande and right through his career, including when he won the World Cup for Brazil almost single-handedly in 1962. He always played for fun: not for money, not for trophies and never for glory. It is for this that he was so loved.

Yet you wouldn't think so if you visited Brazil. There are a few run-down mementoes honouring him in Pau Grande and at the top of the hillside cemetery where he is buried is a memorial stone engraved with the words: 'He was a sweet boy, he spoke with the birds'. But that is the extent of it.

After returning from Brazil I penned a column about my disillusionment at that experience, in which I wrote:

As a footballer Garrincha embodied, perhaps more than any other professional in history, the playful side of football, that which is the purest essence of the game, that which belongs to the children, that which attracted us to the game in the first place. He was forever the amateur spirit caught in the body of a pro who succumbed to the oppressive challenges of that conflict. He was the innocent face of football, a game whose elite level even in his day, not to say now, corroded the ideals of sport and tempted athletes to become willing victims of commerce and greed.

It is for those reasons that Garrincha was a champion, a unique man who, if not in life, certainly in death, deserves more than he got. Something should be done, or else his memory will die and so will the dribble with it.

Garrincha, not unlike George Best, charged into football history via the dribble: that skill of purity, that one sweet component of the game which brings smiles to the faces of children and which entertains millions. With the passing of George, and earlier the death of Garrincha, what is there left of this skill in our age if there are no mementoes to it or sacred reminders that football can be great? Best and Garrincha won many trophies during their lives but it is not for their trophies that they are remembered. It is for the way they played to get them.

I say these things because I am genuinely fearful that football, if its wealthy elites are allowed to dominate our thinking, may lose its spiritual essence.

Whatever the future of the game, I am grateful for the life of immense charm and joy it has given me. It has been a fine ride. Like billions, I became a fan when I was very small; but I am one of the privileged handful who has managed – through all sorts of luck – to turn my passion into my profession. The ride has taken me to all manner of heights: the big occasions, meeting the big people, going to the most beautiful places.

But what I value most in all of this is what football, as a centre-piece of my life, has taught me. In 1988 I interviewed Pelé for the first time. In a private hotel room in Adelaide, I spent 40 minutes, one on one, with the most recognised man in human history. His quiet humility, his warm smile and his readiness to connect with whoever faced him quite astounded me. I saw first hand on many later occasions how Pelé never refused a request for an autograph and how he treated every interview as his first. I learned then, from him, that fame – or any degree of recognisability – should only be repaid with humility and warmth. And that people lucky enough to be approached, harangued and harassed by members of the public are best advised to behave themselves.

When you are involved in football, a world game, this can happen to you anywhere. I once checked into a hotel in Newcastle in England under some duress: sweaty, frustrated, irritable and exhausted after a long flight. All I wanted was my room number and the key. But the man behind the counter wanted to make conversation and, in a barely discernable Geordie accent, said: 'You're that football bloke from Australia.' I said: 'Yes. And when did you live in Australia'? He said: 'Are you kidding? I have never been outside Newcastle in all of my life.' It appears he watched the SBS World Cup coverage on some kind of pirated signal beamed into Tyne-Tees and couldn't forget a face. How could I respond other than with retreat and laughter?

Later, in a quiet moment, I pondered on the incident and concluded that it couldn't have happened without the medium of football. I doubted if I could have forged this acquaintance – a connection between an Australian and a jolly Geordie – if I was a golf man, a travelling business executive or a politician. Football is a wonderful lubricant for breaking down barriers and forming links: a language spoken by all. I have found this everywhere on my travels: in China, in Japan, in the United States, in Canada, in Israel, in Morocco, in Argentina and in Vanuatu. There was nowhere in the world where I couldn't open a door or find a friend once I began to speak the language of football.

Albert Camus, the existentialist philosopher, was once a footballer – a goalkeeper no less – and described football as his greatest source of learning about the human spirit and life. His notion was that humanity was, or should be, like a football team: a team of individuals, all pulling together, looking after team-mates, in the interests of individual victory in struggle. I have seen enough in my life to suggest that he may have been right.

I have often been asked what I will do in retirement, not that I am doing much thinking about that just yet. But the answer is this: when the time comes, I will do what I have been missing most since I became blessed by this career. I will go back to being an ordinary fan. Like most football fans, and sports fans, I spent most of my early life high in the stands, a member of the unwashed public: yelling, screaming, crying, laughing, depending on how my team, or the referee, was doing at any time in a given game.

There are few things more pleasurable in life than having the freedom to call the referee – or the other team's coach – a wanker, out loud at the top of one's voice.

Since becoming a recognisable figure, I have not been able to do that. Everywhere I go I have to be cordial and upright: gentlemanly, unbiased and civilised. I miss the freedom to get emotional, to let fly with the most child-like of my instincts. Football, after all, is just a game, and we grown men are like little boys, spending our energy and time being preoccupied by it while others more mature and serious – our women, for example – stand back in amazement, wondering at our juvenile stupidity. But who cares? It's enormous fun, and those who have the most fun are the fans. Alas, I am one of the professionals, but I crave for the day when I can be an amateur again, one of the nameless, cueing up to buy a ticket, donning a scarf and being able to say to the guy next to me, 'We're gonna kick their arse today.' That is where I will go, back to my roots, when all this is over.

Other sacrifices have been more personal, more painful, touching me more deeply and leaving me uneasy about what has gone on and whether it has been right. In absolute truth, what drove my career in the first place was not my passion for football and the mission, but something more personal: my family and my family responsibilities. Men tend to do this. They pretend to labour, sacrifice and give for their careers. But what really drives them is a quest to impress those whose love they seek. I have two daughters, Tania and Natalie, each as beautiful as the other, both the most sweet of things, straight-laced and innocent as tweeting birds on a spring morning. How they turned out to be this way is a mystery to me. Maybe it was a gift from their mother, Eva, a colossus of motherhood, a model of generosity when it came to providing for the two little girls. Neither is a major sports fan although both get passionately caught up in the World Cup and argue: one supports Brazil, the other Italy. (Neither is silly enough to support the birthplace of their father.) Thankfully, that will go in the 2006 World Cup when Australia's presence will ensure unity between the sisters and there will be no more arguments.

They seem to think I was a good father to them although I know I could have been better. My career involved long hours and many trips away, as it still does. In one 10-year stretch I missed nine of Tania's birthdays, always being away at some event or on some shoot in the northern summer. When SBS covered the NSL, I was on location doing the match of the day every Sunday, year upon year. The family Sunday lunch was a rare thing in my household. In 1992, while on the Tour de France, I sent a 13th birthday message to Natalie on video via satellite, as I stood in front of a splendid chateau in the Loire Valley. It was played at her birthday party and helped alleviate my sense of guilt. But I guess they always knew I loved them: their enemy was not me, but my work. Aside from my work and the taxing demands it made on my time, all my dedication went to my family. The family, not my career, was my first priority. I have never been one to troop off to the pub for a beer with the boys after work; I don't go on golf days; and have never accepted invitations to that obnoxious and primitive ritual, the bucks night. Once I bundied off, however late that was, I raced home to be with the girls.

My life's training, the influence of my mother, the crazy decade of love, freedom and tolerance of the '60s and – above all – football, formed my values and it is those that I tried to impart to my children. Those values were about fair play, about playing the game of life on a level playing field. They were also about a sense of decency, an acceptance of and respect for everyone, no prejudice and no hate. Some of this must have rubbed off, for neither of my daughters has a sly, hostile or bitchy bone in her body.

Though women have surrounded me for much of my life – mother, wife, girlfriends, daughters – I have not been especially lucky in love. Tania, a gifted songwriter, even wrote a song about this. It is ironic, really, because I have always been partial to women and placed them high on a pedestal well above the other gender. Fact is: I love women. I love the way they look and dress, the way they hang their hair, the way they smell, the way they strut and sashay down the sidewalk and drop their eyelids in self-protective innocence every time a male, desirous or otherwise, confronts them. I love their company and their talk, and would sooner spend five minutes in conversation with a woman in a bar than three hours with a bunch of silly males, even if they were discussing football. I am not sure exactly why this is. But perhaps it is partly because I feel that women confront us, reminding us how much we try to remain boys, reluctant, unlike them, to grow up. Whatever the reasons, I find them a challenge, enlightening and a joy.

Sadly, most of my relationships with women have ended up petering out into a kind of nothing. There are probably a number of reasons for this, high on the list being the fact that, ultimately, football and my career took precedence over the needs of the relationship. The women were left wondering what it was that I was married to and what it was that drove my soul. I can't help believing that my affection for that round ball and its interests has tampered with my chances of forming lasting bonds. There were broken hearts for sure along the way, but at least I could always go back to my other love, football.

Finding a noble purpose in life, a need which first surfaced in my idealistic teenage spirit, was something that faded from my consciousness by the time I hit my 30s. By that stage, I was devoting all my energies to cashing in on my break to become Australia's first full-time football television man. I was chasing my career, intent on providing well for my family: everything else was shut out by the blinkers. But by the time I was nearing 40, and my career was sailing smoothly, the query surfaced again. I spent some days pondering these questions. What noble purpose can there possibly be in spending most of my life rabbiting on about a sport, a mere diversion, on a small television screen? Could I not have done more for my fellow man by working for the United Nations, being a country school teacher, or handing out bowls of soup to the starving in Africa? Eventually, it occurred to me that, with my work, I was bringing joy into people's lives. And not just a few people, but thousands, sometimes even millions of them. I was an agent of pleasure, I figured, on the one hand helping to bring sweet relief to those migrants who had been starved of their football, and on the other helping more people discover the beauties of the world at play in its favourite game. This was no small thing as a reward for one's work, and I calculated that I was probably giving more this way than I would have done working in a soup kitchen.

I have received many thousands of letters from viewers during the years that I have been doing this. But my favourite one came from an elderly lady after the SBS broadcast of the 1990 World Cup. In it, she wrote that neither she nor her husband had ever been soccer fans but had discovered something magic in the World Cup, notwithstanding the fact that the games were being broadcast between midnight and dawn. She mentioned that she and her husband had been domestically estranged for years, but that the World Cup had changed all this. Now, her husband would wake to the alarm at two in the morning to watch a game, she would bring him a nice warm cup of tea, and the two of them would snuggle up under the blanket and watch the football in quiet togetherness. The World Cup had brought them back together again and she wanted to thank me.

Given the length of my career in football and journalism, I am often asked what has been my favourite moment. It is impossible to pick only one, for I have been immensely lucky. I have attended most of the world's great sporting events: not just football, but many others besides. I have dined with Pelé, have met and rubbed shoulders with most of football's folk heroes, have seen Maradona and Ronaldinho in the flesh, and have been to so many places so many times that when I land in any of the world's great cities I no longer need a map. High on the list are the thrills of being embedded in Australia's repeated World Cup campaigns, the repeated failures and then, finally, the euphoria when Uruguay was overcome in November 2005.

These were all immensely treasured moments. But my most prized experiences, at least in my career, have been those where I shared in the joy of others. I don't have a favourite moment. I have many. My favourite moments have been those where someone somewhere – be it a taxi driver or some citizen in the street, someone nameless on the other end of the phone, the signatory of a letter or a card – said thank you. Thank you for bringing us all that great football and the virtues of the beautiful game. That is the real reward in this kind of life. And it is the fans of the game, who have empathised so much and – like me – kept believing that I have to thank most of all for what I have gained out of this career.

In our professional lives we all have a yearning to succeed. But that begs the question: what is success? It is, of course, different things to different people. Some measure it in money, others in power, in fame or glamour, in having a healthy family and creature comforts, or a combination of all these. In the case of the world's teeming poor, providing a daily loaf of bread or bowl of rice for one's family can be seen as success and a brilliant career. Still others measure it by what difference they have made to others. I fall into this category. I cannot be sure, of course, whether I have really made any difference to anyone. But I sleep sweetly each night for having tried.

This story began with the account of a questioning teenager in a dark time, deeply troubled by the challenges of adult life and what might become of him if he didn't rise to those challenges and find reason for his being. Then he got lucky and found a meaning, a vehicle and a purpose.

And many years on, he arrived at this, a point where a publisher said: 'Write us the story of your life.' It was not something for which I was really prepared. For a start, I feel that there is life in the old dog yet. And in any case, why? The journey from László Ürge, born in Pápa, to Les Murray and beyond has been colourful, full of all sorts of twists and drama that might tickle some curiosities.

But all lives have an element of this. All lives are fascinating dramas, rich in detail and punctuated with questions about meaning and purpose. This has been no different.

Index

Also from Random House Australia

Sheilas, Wogs and Poofters
Johnny Warren with Andy Harper and Josh Whittington

An incomplete biography of Johnny Warren and football in
Australia.

From a nine-year-old who was initially rejected by his local
under-12s team because he was 'too small and needed to go
home and eat more porridge' to leading the Socceroos from 1964
to 1974 through three World Cup campaigns as captain and vice
captain, Johnny Warren witnessed every stage of Australia's
football journey for over fifty years.

From the days you were called a 'sheila', 'wog' or 'poofter' if
you played football to today when players such as Harry Kewell
are celebrated as our brightest sporting stars and prized by
overseas clubs; from the curse placed on the Socceroos in 1969 by
an African witch doctor, through to more than thirty agonising
years of trying to qualify for football's Holy Grail, the World
Cup, the late, great Johnny Warren's story reveals the highs and
lows of Australian football's past, and how its future success can
be achieved.

This is not a goal-by-goal account of Australia's on-field soccer
performance. It's a fascinating and compelling insight by one of
our nation's most respected (and sorely missed) players, coaches
and commentators into why acceptance of the world game in
Australia has been such a long time coming.

Mr and Mrs Soccer
Andy Harper

Les: Our friendship evolved when Johnny decided that he wanted to be my friend, other than it being the other way around. People become friends for a host of different reasons but they stay friends out of choice.

Johnny: I think back on our time together a lot now. When you get to a certain age, reflections on life start to become more frequent. In thirty years of knowing each other we haven't really had a falling out, which in itself is remarkable. But for both of us, football was the reason and is the reason. It has forged a friendship that will endure.

Les Murray and the late Johnny Warren were Australia's pre-eminent football commentary team and well known to football fans as 'Mr and Mrs Soccer'. These intimate stories and confessions – from behind the commentary box, of women, wine and song through to fiery football politics – will preserve the memory of one of Australia's greatest friendships, and is a heartfelt tribute to one of Australia's greatest sporting legends, Johnny Warren.

'Funny and forthright' – *Herald Sun*

'Raise your glasses to Johnny and Les. A long overdue recognition of a perfect partnership! – Martin Tyler

Our Socceroos
Neil Montagnana Wallace, with a foreword by Craig Johnston

Since 1992, there have been more than 650 men who have had the honour of being called a Socceroo. Some have played once in a 'friendly', and an elite group of eleven has played over fifty 'A' class matches. Only a small group has experienced the elation of making it to the world's biggest stage while many have experienced the heartache of failed World Cup qualifying campaigns.

Once upon a time, Socceroos were paid a pittance. Now they can earn millions of dollars playing internationally. From the days of nailing their own studs into ankle-high boots and sweating in thick, woollen jumpers, to today's lightweight, multi-coloured boots and high-tech jerseys, one thing remains unchanged: these men have all worn their hearts on their sleeves and are united in the passion, sacrifice and commitment that it takes to earn the right to be called a Socceroo.

Twenty-six legendary Socceroos, from the 1940s through to the present day, share previously untold accounts of their lives and careers: Abonyi, Barrtz, Baumgartner, Bignell, Cole, Davidson, Durakovic, Farina, Grella, Henderson, Ivanovic, Krncevic, Lord, Marston, Neill, Okon, Postecoglou, Rooney, Schwarzer, Slater, Smith, Tansey, Tobin, Warren, Williams, and Yankos. Individually, their stories show what it takes to make it to the top. Collectively, they paint a picture of Australia's football history and its reflection of our multicultural nation.